An Enchanted Journey: The HILDEGARDEN

Gate entering The Abbey of St. Hildegard in Rüdesheim-Eibingen, Germany

Shanon Sterringer, Ph.D., D.Min

Copyright © 2016 Shanon Sterringer

All rights reserved.

ISBN-13: 9781535004336
ISBN-10: 1535004339

July 2016

Dear Bob,
Prayers for your journey – St. Francis is walking with you!
Sharon

This book is dedicated to my dad Jack Funnell (April 15, 1979). I know in my heart he has always been walking this journey with me. And to his brother, my uncle Dug Funnell, for having enough faith in me to "get into the wheel barrel."

This book is also dedicated to Linn Maxwell (June 18, 2016) who inspired me through her extraordinary talent to include a creative writing piece, *The Soliloquy of St. Hildegard*, in my dissertation.

Robert Francis Daniel Paladin

CONTENT

Foreword by Rev. Dr. Peter Mihalic	
Called to Ministry, Shanon Sterringer	1
Viriditas Who Was Hildegard of Bingen?	25
Ordinate Feminas	91
St. Hildegard *ora pro nobis*	118
HILDEGARDEN Honey Bee	139
Introduction to the Soliloquy	157
Soliloquy of St. Hildegard	170
Hildegard and the Hierarchy Today	212
Hildegard and Women Church Leaders	220
Post Script – Some Weird S*it	231
References	233

LIST OF FIGURES

All images included in this book were taken by Dr. Shanon Sterringer in Germany 2015 or Ohio 2015-2016. Full color copies are available matted or framed in The HILDEGARDEN gift store. Please indicate figure # when ordering.

#		Page
1	Church at Bermersheim	28
2	Church at Bermersheim	28
3	Statue of Hildegard in Bermersheim	28
4	Disibodenberg	30
5	Disibodenberg	30
6	Cell Window Disibodenberg	31
7	Map of Ruperstberg	38
8	Hildegard Abbey Church	45
9	Hildegarde Abbey Church	45
10	Reliquary of St. Hildegard	45
11	Hildegard Pharmacy	69
12	Natural Hildegard Herbal Products	69
13	Disibodenberg	78
14	Bingen Train Station	120
15	Bingen Ferry	121
16	Hildegard Abbey Vineyards	122
17	Abbey Sign	123
18	Land of Hildegard Tourist Center	124
19	Bermersheim Woods	125
20	Disibodenberg	127
21	Rupertsberg	128
22	Cellar at Rupertsberg	129
23	Parish Church Eibingen	130
24	Parish Church Eibingen Cornerstone	130
25	Church Window depicting Herbs	130
26	Church Window depicting Scivias	130
27	Trinity Mosaic & Reliquary Eibingen	131
28	St. Rochus Church Bingen	132
29	Hildegard Herbal Tonic	133
30	Sky in Eastlake	136
31	Second Sun Sky	136
32	Second Sun Sky	137
33	Abbey Church / The HILDEGARDEN	143
34	Healing Woman Hildegard Statue	153
35	HILDEGARDEN logo, by Patsy Gunn	155
36	Front of The HILDEGARDEN, Fairport Harbor, OH	156
37	Statue of Hildegard Abbey Gardens, Germany	219

FOREWORD

It has been my privilege and pleasure to have been on this "enchanted journey" with Dr. Sterringer for almost twenty years. I have witnessed close at hand the many ways she was called to ministry and the creative responses she has made to these divine and ecclesial invitations and demands. It takes courage and faith to get up and go when called, especially when the route and ultimate destination are unclear. In this book Dr. Sterringer clearly articulates everything that is involved when such a summons is given and answered. This book is a personal testimony to her faith in God, her love for the Church and the treasured respect she has for its Tradition.

G. K. Chesterton at the beginning of his book Orthodoxy, talks about a man who wished to sail off to the South Seas and there discover new territories for Britain. As he sails off he doesn't realize that the winds have turned his sails around and brought him back to England. When he disembarks and begins to explore this "new territory", he gradually realizes that he is back at home. Dr. Sterringer was repeatedly called to journey forth into unknown territories with the hope of discovering something new. But hers was, as Chesterton calls it, the most enviable experience of all: to venture forth into the unknown and there experience a homecoming.

Dr. Sterringer has found herself at home in her parish in Fairport Harbor, at the seminary, with ministry, with the Roman Catholic Church, with St. Hildegard of Bingen, and with many people like herself who are constantly seeking the presence of God in their lives. Her document celebrates the workings of grace and embraces the challenge to welcome newness ever grounded in the Tradition which offers the stability necessary to build and rebuild the structures that form God's people, the Church.

Rev. Dr. Peter Mihalic

INTRODUCTION

*Once in a while, right in the middle of ordinary life,
love gives us a fairytale. – anonymous*

I can remember the conversation as if it were yesterday. There I sat on the bench with my dad on Arrowhead Drive under a cherry tree that seemed far too big for my grandparent's side yard. My grandpa liked to climb that tree, even though his heart doctor warned him not to, in an effort to beat the birds to the cherries each summer. His heart was weak. In the fall of 1978 his heart gave out and he died suddenly. I was six years old. That same year my dad's condition worsened. Initially everyone had said he had a cold, but it had been over a year and his cold wasn't getting any better. He had been at Euclid Hospital for what seemed like forever and when he did get to come home it didn't even look like my dad. He was so thin and had lost his beautiful thick hair. As I got older I would hear my family talking about Agent Orange, though I had no idea what it was. Many of the men who had been drafted into the Vietnam War died or came home sick from it. My dad was one of them.

As we sat together on the bench this afternoon, everything was perfect. The sun was shining, temperature cool, and the birds chirping. Though our encounter only lasted a few minutes, I can still feel his presence when I close my eyes today. Sitting beside me he looked intently at me and said, "I have to go now. Be good and listen. Everything will be okay." And that was it. I wasn't able to ask him any questions and he never came back to the bench, though I prayed for it for many years. I woke up from this dream knowing my dad had really been there, though I can't explain how. I just felt him there.

I don't remember what day or even month I had this dream, but only a short amount of time had passed from that devastating Easter morning, April 15, 1979. My brother and I had stayed at my grandmother's house, my mom's mom, the night before. We had put out carrots for the Easter bunny before bed. When we got up early the next morning we went into the kitchen to see what the bunny had left for us. I could see out the window above the sink that overlooked the cherry tree. It was Easter morning and my mom was sitting at the kitchen table crying. I don't remember what was said, but I would never forget why she was crying. My dad had died.

It is not uncommon for people to have dreams of their deceased loved ones. There are many "rational" explanations for why and how these types of dreams manifest and in some cases it may be a plausible explanation. For me, however, I know in my heart it wasn't an emotional or psychological projection. My dad appeared to me in a way that was more real than anything I remember from when he was alive. Just as St. Paul's experience of the Risen Christ transformed him into the most significant missionary in the history of Christianity, the experience I had of my deceased dad transformed me in some way. While the fruits of my experience cannot be compared to St. Paul's, the experience was powerful enough to carry me through some very difficult years that were to follow. His words stayed with me. Granted, I wasn't always good, and I didn't always listen, but I did always trust that everything would be okay. This was the first of many "God-moments" that would guide me along my journey.

When we look back over our lives we can see key moments that were influential – good and bad – in the making of our story. The person I am today has been strongly influenced by having grown up without my dad. I loved being with him. One day he was with me being the perfect dad and the next day he was gone. For many years I prayed for a "fairytale" to bring him back, even if it was just in my dreams. I wanted so much to rewrite or recreate my story; to remove the pain and suffering and preserve only what was good. That is what I thought "happily ever after" looked like. I wanted to find that fairytale place that existed in my imagination. Instead I found myself on a journey; a long and wonderful journey.

We all have amazing stories to tell. I decided to share mine, not because I feel it is necessarily more amazing than anyone else's

An Enchanted Journey

(although I have had some very profound "God moments" along the way), but because I believe when a person opens up and shares her/his story it encourages others to do the same. I believe it is imperative that lay ecclesial ministers, especially female ministers, tell their stories. Lay female ministers are called and gifted for ministry. They are sharing their gifts in remarkable ways, yet they often are forgotten or dismissed in the conversation regarding vocations. My call is as real, and as needed in the Church as a man called to ordination. Our roles are different, but are equally necessary and valid. I am a Roman Catholic minister who happens to be female, and I have a story to share.

In taking time to reflect on and share our stories, we become much more aware of the ongoing presence of God every step of the way, even in those dark moments when God feels so far away. Recently, while making the rounds through a local antique store, I came across a sign that read, "fairytales are real" - I believe that. Not in the sense that I prayed for a fairytale as a child, but rather as a magical or enchanted journey full of good and evil. Regardless of how your story unfolds, no one ever stumbles into "happily ever after" – it is a daily choice that is only possible when one has successfully conquered darkness, over and over again. It is a life-long process. The decision to journey into the darkness; the woods, the sea, the desert, the inner city, the countryside, and into one's own soul, is a decision to integrate into a whole person. "Happily ever after" takes a lot of ongoing personal work. It is what Carl Jung describes as embracing one's shadow side in order to become whole again. This is what creates a story with a heroine/hero. Not perfection, but courage to walk the journey laid before each one of us – lined with both monsters and miracles.

We do not embark on our journey at any prescribed time. For some it happens early in life, for others it takes place in the second half of life. Most "mid-life crises" are actually misdiagnosed spiritual awakenings. We can become so distracted by daily life it blinds us to the reality right before us. When we begin to awaken we are either propelled into a new way of being (personal/spiritual transformation), or we grasp at something to keep us where we are at – a new car, a new job, a new spouse, a new anything - to keep us comfortable and asleep. The awakened journey is difficult. This is evident in the story of the greatest hero, Jesus of Nazareth, whose life was marked with the encounter of demons along the way. When Jesus asks the disciples, "Can you drink from the cup I must drink" (Matt 20:22) he is aware that the journey requires more than some are willing, or even able, to sacrifice. It can be scary. Nonetheless, we are all called to discover our own heroic self; to appreciate more fully the sacred substance from which have been created; to journey inward, into dark places where brilliant and beautiful light shines forth.

This is a motif repeated in most familiar fairytales - Little Red Riding Hood finds her strength when she encounters the wolf in the dark woods; Cinderella when she faces her abusive stepmother and stepsisters; Dorothy when she learns to appreciate that buried deep within is everything we need to be the people we are called to be; and Elsa when she learns how to use her unusual gifts and talents for others. These stories instill in the reader a sense of hope and faith in goodness and love, in the midst of a world marked by brokenness. It shines a bright light into an otherwise darkened world. For a woman, finding her inner heroine can create a place within the patriarchal system – a place previously unavailable to her - where her gifts and talents can shine forth.

Looking back I believe God called me when I was a child sitting on the bench with my dad, though I wouldn't recognize a formal call for another eighteen years. That initial dream experience opened up for me a relationship with God that would remain steadfast throughout my life. My relationship with the Church would be rocky at times, but my relationship with God never wavered. For many years I found myself on an unfamiliar and daunting path, however, through the grace of God I always found my way back on track. As an adult, nearing mid-life, I entered into a very dark place, one that almost pushed me permanently out of the Church. I needed something big to put me back on track and so God (probably together with my dad) brought me to a place where I would encounter the 12th century German Benedictine nun, Hildegard of Bingen. Having met her on the journey literally changed my life.

It's a risk to say my life has been a fairytale because it would assume there is only one way to define such a story. In his book, *The Irresistible Fairy Tale*, Zipes (2012) describes five elements that characterize a fairytale, particularly in the experience of a heroine. These elements are:

1) Something erupts in a girl's life which causes her to separate from family/home as she knew it.
2) She seeks seclusion for a time in an idyllic setting (such as a church).
3) A traumatic event, a violation of some kind (physical or psychological) drives the girl from the idyllic setting.
4) There is a period of wandering or discernment – a dark night if you will.
5) An accomplishment of a set of tasks leading to a "happily ever after" experience.

While my journey has been made up of all of the above, I think it would be more appropriate to say that I have been on *an enchanted journey*, one that has spanned my entire life. It has been a life-long experience of ordinary people and places engaged in a series of extraordinary (and at times unexplainable) events. I believe my story fits into a long line of stories where ordinary people, even sinners, were called by God through extraordinary means: for Moses it was a bush that burned but wasn't consumed; for Jacob a dream which left him marked with a perpetual limp; Mary Magdalene it was the unconventional friendship of Jesus; for Paul it was a blinding light so powerful that it changed his very being; Joan of Arc it was the voice of Catherine of Alexandria calling her to go where no woman had gone before; Oscar Romero it was the collective voice of the people of San Salvador crying out for justice; and for me it was first my dad and then many years later, a

German medieval nun, Hildegard of Bingen. You may be thinking it is audacious to put myself on the same level with these holy women and men listed above, but by the very nature of our baptism we are each called in this way. To be holy is not to be without fault – to be holy is to possess a willingness to say yes to one's call without really knowing where it is leading. Holiness is being willing to completely surrender one's self.

The Call

May you find heaps of sunshine in your heart today.
- unknown

Olim (*Once Upon a Time*) something inside of me called me to follow. So, I dropped everything and followed. The end.

****

This is the way most of us imagine our call will come: simple and clear. In the Christian tradition it is assumed when Jesus calls we will answer "Yes Lord" and all will make sense. This is the way we often interpret the call of the disciples in the Gospel of Matthew chapter 4: Jesus called to Peter and Andrew to drop their nets (their very livelihood) to follow him. He promised to make them fishers of people and they dropped their nets and followed, as though they were zombies or robots never doubting or questioning. In reality, the Scriptures preserve a much more complicated picture that unfolded over their lifetime. Peter never fully understood his call. At one point (Matt 16:23) Jesus asks him, "Who do you say that I am?" and Peter's response provokes Jesus to say, "Get behind me Satan!" After Jesus is arrested Peter denies that he even knows Jesus. It wasn't until the Holy Spirit infused the minds and hearts of the disciples at the Feast of Pentecost that Peter's call became clearer giving him the strength he needed to be an authentic witness. But still, he continued to struggle with Paul and some of the other leaders to understand what was really necessary to bring others to the faith.

It was not only the male disciples who didn't fully understand, but even Mary, Jesus' mother, who had experienced the incarnation of God within her womb. Mary had to discern in an ongoing way God's will for her. She said yes to God, and stayed faithful to her call, but it wasn't always clear how God was acting in her life. For example, in Mark's Gospel (3:21) we read that Jesus' family (including Mary) were outside of a house that Jesus was preaching in and they thought he had "gone mad" because they didn't understand yet his ministry. As Mary stood at the foot of the cross watching her son innocently suffer and die it is most certain she did not fully understand why God would call her to such a role, to be *Theotokos* (*Mother of God*), and then allow her son, God's Son, to suffer such a violent and terrible death. She had been warned that a "sword would pierce her heart" (Luke 2:35) and it did.

Each one of us is called. Our calls are specific and our journeys unique. The funny thing about responding to our call is that it will necessarily pull us into a dark place, almost always a place we don't want to go. It will require us to let go of the things in our life that are no longer necessary. This is what it means to "die to oneself." This sacrifice, however, is not in vain. There is grace to be found in our sufferings. In the Book of Job it is written, "For He wounds, but He binds up. He strikes, but his hands give healing" (5:18). God promises resurrection, as witnessed by Jesus, when we are willing to let go of our own desires and agendas in order to make room for God's. I had to learn this lesson repeatedly over the next nineteen years.

Fairport Harbor, 1998
God creates each one of us out of love, uniquely, before we are even conceived: "Before I formed you in the womb I knew you" (Jer 1:5).[1] Yet it often takes many years, and for some a lifetime,

---

[1] It is often argued that the Catholic Church's steadfast position opposing a woman's right to choose to keep or abort a pregnancy is exclusively the result of a patriarchal power structure desiring to control women's bodies. While there may be some truth to the fact that a patriarchal institutional does

to come to understand God's call. Others may never hear the call or may misinterpret it as some sort of life crisis. This is not because God waits until a certain point in our life to reach out, or fails to reach out to some. It is because we need to be able to hear/see the presence of God in our midst and our ability to hear/see is formed by our life experiences and our disposition.

My call to a relationship with something bigger than myself came as a child when I encountered my dad under the cherry tree. My call to formal ministry, however, came on a beautiful weekday summer morning in Fairport Harbor in 1998. I had been married now for 8 years (Rick and I were married right out of high school in 1990 when I was 17 and he was 19). My family was living on 2nd street, just a few houses down from the historic Fairport Harbor Lighthouse, on the first floor of a two unit house which was much too small for our growing family. My mom and stepdad lived on the 2nd floor. Due to the tight space our bedroom was on the front porch. Though a bit unusual, it was comfortable with its white walls, antique windows, and stained glass accent. For weeks I had been waking up at the same time each night feeling as if something was waking me. One morning I woke up early to an overwhelming dose of sunlight shining through the many windows. The room was brilliant. Something inside of me was calling me to get up and go to church. Trisha and Angel were still sleeping (Maria was not born yet), and it felt like a good day to go to Mass.

I hadn't been going much over the last few years. I was angry with the Church. History preserves a story of the Church marked by corruption, greed, and scandal. I couldn't understand how an institution claiming to be guided by the Holy Spirit could be

---

exercise an enormous amount of decision making power over women, and at times unjustly, it is sincerely the belief of the Church that every single life is sacred because it has been created by God. This passage from Jeremiah stating that even before conception God knows each one of us intimately is foundational to the Church's desire to protect the dignity of human life. While there are many issues involved in this debate, fundamentally all life, human and otherwise, comes from and belongs to God – from womb to tomb.

responsible for so many sins. Not only historically, but the terrible situation of countless sex abuse scandals were hitting the news around the same time and it was infuriating. If all of that wasn't enough, the non-admittance of women to ordained ministry was becoming a significant concern of mine as well, especially as I became more aware of the active roles of women in the early Church. I was at a point in my faith journey where all I could see in the Church was greed, power, sexism, and corruption. I felt I had been lied to all those years in Catholic grade school and I was angry. I did not want to be connected with an institution I felt was run by a "good old boys club" who cared very little for women or children. Without ever losing my faith in God, I was quickly losing my faith in the Church.

One day, a few years earlier, when Trisha was about two years old, I asked my stepdad to remove the Mary statue and grotto from our front yard and get rid of it – I told him to put it on the curb. I didn't want to be Catholic anymore. I was hurting. Being the good altar boy that he was (although he hadn't been to church in decades), he looked at me like I was crazy. "I will not put Mary on the curb!" he said. But, he did take her out of the yard for me and tucked her in the garage where she stayed for a couple of years.

I grew up in an Italian-Catholic household with a family member who was a religious sister. I wanted so much to go back to the place of faith I had known as a child. The place where I believed holiness and goodness resided in the Church. I wanted to go back to that place. It took years, and lots of focused prayer, to work through the anger and doubt. In the midst of it I did have my daughter Trisha baptized soon after she was born because there was still something deep down that felt she should be. There was the nagging feeling that in the midst of so much pain, God was present. My conscience (maybe it was Catholic guilt) would not allow me to deny her the sacrament of Baptism, to take something so sacred from her, because of my feelings. And so Trisha was baptized. My experience with the associate priest at that parish was not pastoral, in fact, it was hurtful and insulting. It did not offer any opportunity for healing or reconciliation. Given that experience, what later transpired is all the more remarkable. That should have been the last straw for me, but deep down I wanted very much to find my way back to the Church. What I needed was something or someone in the Church to believe in again and I found that at St. Anthony's Church in Fairport Harbor.

I knew the morning I was called, as the sun shined into the porch windows, something was different. My mind and heart were filled with a feeling of love radiating from the sunlight that was saturating the bedroom porch. While I couldn't explain it, I knew a higher power was calling me. Something was pulling me to Mass. It was a feeling that cannot be put into words. I decided to get the girls up and dressed, we pulled out the stroller, and we walked to St. Anthony's for morning Mass. This was something we came to do regularly for many years to come.

As I began this new journey I had no idea where it was headed. All I knew for sure was that whatever God had in mind for me involved St. Anthony's Church and Fairport Harbor. It would take 18 years of parish experience, a BA in religious studies, 2 MAs in theology and ministry, Diocesan Master Catechist and Pastoral Ministry Certification, a D.Min (Doctor of Ministry) from the seminary and a Ph.D. in ethical and creative leadership before I would truly begin to understand the task that God had been calling me to embrace. God had a plan for me, as God has a plan for each one of us; I could feel it, but could not see it. Looking back it is clear that God had sent in a "big gun" this time - a German *Magistra*, St. Hildegard – to whip me into shape. One of the first things I did was pull Mary out of the garage. I cleaned her up, gave her a paint job, and to this day she continues to be a part of our yard.

The years that followed my initial call were confusing, emotionally painful, and at times felt like a nightmare. For many years I could not figure out where I fit into the parish, the seminary, and the Church in general. Trying to juggle being a mom and wife, a student, a parishioner, and a developing minister in a community so small was challenging. Everyone was in my business and it made the discernment process difficult. Women like me do not fit into a traditional vocation and so my constant presence at the Church was misinterpreted by some, including myself. I did not understand exactly what was happening or how to respond. It was a challenging experience on a number of levels. In the process I came to know one of the auxiliary bishops well as he was assigned to address the incoming mail downtown from those who decided writing to the bishop was the best way to address their questions, or air their complaints regarding my sudden presence and new role in the parish. The first time I came home and saw on my phone that I had missed a call from the Bishop's office I was ready to "shake the dust from my feet" and move on. I kept thinking, "I don't know what I signed up for but I didn't sign up for this!"

As it turned out, the auxiliary bishop (coincidentally a Benedictine like St. Hildegard) who called that day ended up being a constant source of support for me throughout my journey. I saved every letter and card I have received from him over the years because I drew strength from believing that there is a lot of good within a less than perfect institution. I came to experience that in an institution responsible for some very serious sin, there are some holy and dedicated clergy and laity trying very hard to do things differently. In his first letter to me, the one he sent in response to the initial wave of letters downtown, he wrote:

> *The ordinary bishop has asked me to address this pastoral concern that has been brought to the Diocese... It is the right and responsibility of a pastor to hire a well-formed, educated team of staff that share in his vision of ministry... You are to be commended for your investment in ongoing education and formation for ministry... We understand how difficult it can be, but keep up the good work...*

I must have read his letter a hundred times until the storm passed looking for a source of strength. I still look forward to checking in with him on occasion to let him know what's happening. The day I was certified as a diocesan lay ecclesial minister he came and found me after Mass to tell me how he remembered the "early days" and how proud he was. When there is an effort made to bridge the wide and impersonal gap between the clergy and the laity, especially lay ministers, authentic relationships form.

I have also been graced with the friendship of another dear bishop from India. While we come from different worlds, and at times have a different lens through which we view theology and even ecclesiology, his friendship has had a tremendous effect on my formation. Though our roles in the Church are different, he has always treated me with the dignity and respect of a colleague. If more bishops and priests treated lay leaders in this way, our Church would be a much healthier, happier, and vibrant place.

My pastor and our parish deacon, both of whom I love dearly, have prayed with me and supported me every step of the way. God sends people to walk with us on our journey. I had struggled for so long with my relationship to the institution, I needed a positive pastoral experience. I am not sure I would have found my way back to without the friendships I have formed in the institution over the years. The love and support I have experienced in individuals has made a very real difference in my ministry, as I'm sure it has in others. The way in which clergy are formed to work with women (or not) is going to have a significant impact on the leadership model that emerges in the Church in the future.

Something needs to be said regarding clericalism (which is misogynistic and self-serving) because, as Pope Francis has stated, it has had a very negative effect on the Church. In my journey I have met many infected with the disease of clericalism and the consequences have at times been serious. You could say on my journey I have encountered my share of "monsters" on the way and they have been the source of overwhelming pain. The Church has historically so tightly defined vocation as either priest (male) or sister/nun (female) that when someone, like myself, is called to full-time ministry outside of those two roles, it could be confusing to people, and it was. It still is. Officially the Church recognizes the importance of lay ecclesial ministry in the everyday mission of the Church. In 2005 the USCCB (United States Conference of Catholic Bishops) published a document, "Co-Workers in the Vineyard of the Lord" discussing the fundamental relationship between ordained and lay leaders in the Church. The bishops described the call of lay ecclesial leaders as authentic, not as simply "helpers to the priest" but as ministers in their own right. It is safe to say many bishops and priests in this country have either not read the document (or even heard of it) and if they have, many simply don't care or are carrying into their ministry misogynistic and sexist ideas, which inevitably get passed on to the people in the pews. Pope Francis has made numerous statements regarding the indispensable role of women leaders in the Church, but again, if the clergy do not appreciate the call of lay leadership, particularly of women, they will continue to treat us as though our role is ancillary (helpmates) to theirs as opposed to complementary and essential. Women are called to formal ministry in the Church.

Looking back at my journey I realize we were making the path as we walked it. There were many days (even months) when I felt I lacked the courage or strength necessary to keep going. My cross was so heavy. There are a couple of priests that come to mind who treated me terribly, and still do on the rare occasion when I encounter them. Over the years I grew tired, sick, and even a bit depressed. Yet, something much bigger than my fear, sadness, and anger kept me motivated to continue growing in wholeness and holiness within this community. The love and support of my family and friends encouraged me to keep going. Every difficult experience was simultaneously grace-filled. I drew strength from the well of love with which I had been graced and that carried me through those challenging years. I continued on my journey praying, studying, and trying to discern the will of God in my life. I knew someone was walking the path with me, probably many people, because it was lined with an extraordinary number of

"God-moments" providing me with what I needed to keep my faith as I forged ahead.

When I finally realized I was being called to some type of formal ministry in the Church I decided to change my college major from accounting to religious studies. Sitting at the table with my grandfather (who was Episcopalian) I announced my decision. He looked at me grumpily, and said (as only he could), "What the hell do you want to be? A priest? You aren't going to make any money!" To make a very long story short, I switched my major and graduated from Cleveland State University with a BA in Religious Studies in December 2003. Upon graduation I was immediately hired at St. Anthony's as the Director of Religious Education (though I wasn't quite ready yet to assume the role – I had to quickly learn the position). On one hand there was excitement in beginning a new role and I was happy to be a college graduate, yet something was missing. Something inside told me my academic career was not concluding, but had just begun.

My pastor and dear friend, Fr. Pete Mihalic, encouraged me right away to enroll in the seminary graduate school where he was a professor of Church History and Patristics. Shocked, I asked, "Since when does the seminary program admit women?" As it turns out, there are many opportunities for women's leadership development in the seminary program. Taking advantage of them I was able to complete a MA in Theology in 2007 and subsequently a "M.Div. equivalent" in 2008. Those years were very formative for me in good ways and bad. Certainly the education I received was high-quality and I am grateful for that privilege. At the same time, the environment is not always the most fertile for female ministers. Actually, it can be oppressive. The seminary's first goal is "to form men for the priesthood" and that is to be expected. However, it is considered the CPL (Center for Pastoral Leadership) housing all three diocesan formation programs (priest, deacon, lay ecclesial minister). The atmosphere communicates (though not always consciously) to an "outside student" or non-seminarian, that s/he is secondary. This as not necessarily the attitude of the faculty, but certainly it is the attitude among the students. This took an emotional and spiritual toll on me. Nonetheless, I forged on.

After having spent several years full-time in the seminary academic programs, I was admitted to the doctoral program at the seminary. I couldn't believe it - I was officially a D.Min student! My first semester, however, something didn't feel right. There was that voice inside nudging me in a direction I was sensing I really did not want to go. Life was good right now. I didn't want to mess things up. In my heart I felt I should write my D.Min dissertation on women and leadership in the Roman Catholic Church. But, out of fear that it would not be well received in that context I chose another topic, a "safer" topic. As the second semester started I found myself quickly slipping, plummeting actually, into a "dark night" experience. The last straw came for me when I had a humiliating experience with a priest in another part of the diocese (which I will not put into writing). I came back to St. Anthony's in tears. It wasn't the first, or the last, time a clergy member hurt me with his words or attitude. But at that moment I had decided that was it. No more. I had had my fill of misogyny and sexism. I knew I had hit bottom the day I just sat in my office chair not wanting to do anything but cry and polish off the bag of Valentine candy hearts I was holding. How could clergy, men called to function *in persona Christi,* be so mean? Christ wasn't mean or self-absorbed or clerical. It felt as if I was back where I had started.

At this point, however, I had so much going for me - I did not want to lose what I had worked so hard for. I wanted to be at the seminary studying and fitting in, pretending all was well. Ignoring the comments and discriminatory attitudes. Yet I couldn't bring myself to go back. I felt the need to withdraw from everything and go back to a place that was simple. So I tried doing exactly that. Although a very wise Notre Dame sister told me, "you can't put the toothpaste back into the tube." There was no going back. Nonetheless I withdrew from the seminary programs. I was entering into what some would call a "feminist awakening" and I couldn't stop crying.

The dean at the seminary was shocked when I withdrew from the D.Min program. He reminded me of how hard I had worked to get into the program and how I would most certainly succeed if I stuck with it. He also reminded me that it was the desire of my pastor that I stay in and finish the program. It was not an issue of me succeeding, and it had nothing to do with my pastor at that point. It was me. All of the issues I had been struggling with in regards to the Church as a young adult had resurfaced and I could feel myself getting angry again. How could I carry myself with integrity when I had not done my own personal work? For over a decade I had pushed these issues under the rug rather than addressing them. I had pretended it was okay for me to feel subordinate or "less called" simply because I was a woman. How could I raise my three beautiful and very intelligent daughters, to believe that they have a dignity equal to men, if I myself was sending a different message? God was calling me to go to a place I did not want to go – into the world of women and leadership in the Church – a place where there were some very difficult questions that needed to be asked and injustices that needed to be addressed. Deep down I knew my call, but my fear of the consequences was preventing me from embracing that call.

During this time in 2010 I never formally left the Church, and I kept my struggle hidden from pretty much everyone except those with ecclesial authority over me (I can only imagine what is in my personal file...) During this time I tried to function as normal as possible while I sifted through the avalanche of feelings under which I felt buried. In my mind I kept seeing all of the people I have ministered to over the years and what their response might be if I "jumped ship" to another denomination. It was largely a sense of personal responsibility to the community that kept me from making any rash decisions. I spent many hours totally immersed in prayer. In the end I recognized that I needed to go into that dark place in order to find, once again, my light. It was a grace-filled experience. Without death there is no resurrection. That's what I kept telling myself.

Anyone who knows me will attest to the fact that when I set my mind to something it gets done quickly. All I needed to venture down into the depths of despair and rise again in victory was one semester. As I started to regain my focus and my motivation I found myself back in the seminary programs full tilt. While I was still unsure of my particular call, things started to come into clearer focus for me in 2011 when I met, in my D.Min research, the most extraordinary woman, Hildegard of Bingen. Her message of healing, reconciliation, and wholeness saved me. Looking back to that day I felt called to get up and go to daily Mass, I am convinced it was Hildegard who had awakened me and invited me (actually knowing Hildegard the way I do now, she kicked me into motion) to walk with her on this spiritual journey. With a renewed sense of purpose I finished my D.Min in December 2011 and was certified as a diocesan lay ecclesial minister the same year. I was so happy to have accomplished what had seemed only a short time before to be impossible. At the colloquium one of the board members jokingly asked, "So, now you are going for a Ph.D.?" The seed was planted.

In St. Hildegard I found an example to emulate. Having heard the call to ministry and having obtained the credentials needed to validate that call, it would seem reasonable to be content with where the journey had taken me. I had accomplished so much, and was so well respected and loved by the community, but something still didn't feel right. It felt more like a beautiful rest-stop on the side of the road, not quite my destination. One day I just stood in my office sobbing as I looked at my wall of degrees and certifications. I wanted to feel accomplished – I wanted to be done with school. Yet, I had an overwhelming feeling that my professor was intuitive – I felt a Ph.D. program calling. I knew what that meant. Three more years of writing and researching and tuition. I was so tired. Yet, something was pushing me forward. I knew I needed to formally study Hildegard of Bingen, but why? When I finished sobbing I acknowledged my task. On May 22, 2013 (my birthday) I was interviewed and accepted into a Ph.D. program. Having had the faith to go down this road has led me to the beautiful, enchanted place I am at on my journey today. The seed for the HILDEGARDEN has sprouted from this Ph.D. and for the first time in almost twenty years I feel like my path is coming into clear focus. I believe I am in the place I was created for and I need to say - it is truly an amazing place – a happily ever after.

My story is in many ways extraordinary, to the point where the "God-moments" have almost been overwhelming. They alone would fill pages. This journey has in every way been extraordinary; however, I personally am not extraordinary. It is God alone who is extraordinary. After my dad died our family life was difficult. It was often lonely. My loneliness was both a blessing and a curse. I have spent my whole life struggling to overcome an unhealthy relationship with food, which I believe emerged from my inability to understand who I was and the path I had been chosen to walk. As a result I am a steadfast believer in the power of whole, living, healthy foods. But, I'm still in many ways damaged. I have sincerely come to understand what it means to say "I am simply a vessel, cracked and misshapen, struggling to get it right." I do not have any supernatural gifts, outside of a family and community who loves me dearly, and a guardian angel (or angels) that won't give up on me.

For most of the last twenty years I have been trudging along not really knowing what was happening or why. I would often share with my pastor that as much as I love my ministry and my place within the community, something has been missing. He would tell me, "Stay focused, have faith, take it a day at a time and you will know." I believe when we have the faith to truly open ourselves up in steadfast faith to the will of God – a day at a time - to be vessels of God's light, without fear of the possible consequences, the result is extraordinary.

This book is a glimpse into my journey. You too are on a journey. God calls each one of us. The journey will be difficult, there will be persecutions, doubt, weakness, but through perseverance we can become a beacon of light for others. That has certainly been my experience. A beautiful example of this radiates from the life story of St. Hildegard of Bingen, which will be discussed in some detail throughout this book.

The entrance to the path might be dark (as depicted in the picture on the cover of the book), but God does not send us into the dark alone. God endows us with many gifts to sustain us on our way. Next to my family and friends, I have found my greatest treasures to be contained in books, which is where of course I met Hildegard. As I thought about the various approaches I could take with this book, two books that have nothing directly to do with Hildegard came to mind.

The first is a book written by a priest Fr. Edward Hays who on his own journey had been profoundly influenced by a community of Benedictine monks (coincidentally Hildegard was a Benedictine Sister). Hays was a brilliant storyteller and spiritual writer and his book, *The Ethiopian Tattoo Shop*, truly transformed me as I read it. The second book that has inspired me is written by a Lutheran pastor in Colorado, Rev. Nadia Bolz-Weber. Her book entitled, *Pastrix: the Cranky, Beautiful Faith of a Sinner & Saint* has had a profound effect on the way I understand ministry and leadership. Bolz-Weber is a popular pastor, a renowned national speaker, a well-loved author, and to the surprise of many she is covered in tattoos! You may notice a theme developing between these two authors. The approach I am going to take in sharing with you some of what I have learned about St. Hildegard, parish ministry, and faith is going to come from the lessons I learned from these two books regarding leadership, community, spirituality, honesty, and the transforming power of tattoos.

If you know anything of St. Hildegard of Bingen you probably know that she was a visionary. She experienced repeated encounters with the *Living Light* from the time she was a child. The *Living Light* revealed to her an innate source of wisdom and knowledge. Through her visions she saw the world with an "inner eye" revealing much of what is otherwise hidden. When we grow in wisdom and understanding and knowledge we too develop an ability to see a deeper reality than what we once thought existed. When we become "light-filled" we become more transparent to others. With that in mind, this book not only provides some background information on St. Hildegard of Bingen, but it is a personal testimony of my own journey and an opportunity to bring to light some of that which has been hidden. It is an honest, transparent, testimony of my journey.

Throughout the many years I have been engaged in theological studies and parish ministry, I have faced prejudice and gossip in many forms because I am a woman immersed in what has traditionally been a man's world. This is not to say that I am without fault or that I did not do or say things that may have fed misunderstanding, gossip, or discrimination. We learn from our mistakes and I certainly have made my fair share of them. In response to some of the pastoral situations I have encountered, I developed an exaggerated need to conform to the expectations of the institution as well as the community. I have always tried to be sure my "t's were crossed and i's were dotted" so that I did not do anything to draw unnecessary negative attention. I have at times sacrificed my own creativity and ideas in an effort to dismiss misunderstanding so that I might fit into an already established context. The problem always being – you can't put a round peg into a square hole just as you should not put new wine into old wineskins (Mark 2:22). The result can be disastrous. In an effort to conform there have been times along the way when I began to forget who I am and what I was being called to be. There were times when I started to become who everyone else – including the institution – told me I need to be. Of all the mistakes I have made, sacrificing the person God created me to be in order to please an institution or an ideology was certainly the most serious.

An Enchanted Journey

Celebrating and developing one's unique gifts and talents is not an easy thing to do in an institution that has so strongly favored obedience and uniformity. And while that has changed considerable over the years, "free-thinking" is still discouraged. It can be a dangerous path and venturing down it takes courage and faith, not only in God, but in one's own self. Each time I had an experience that led to a personal awakening, I marked my journey with an indelible mark that would remind me of who I am and what it is God is calling me to be.

What is an indelible mark? We use that term to describe the change that takes place within each person when s/he is baptized. The Catholic Christian community believes that when a person is baptized s/he receives an indelible mark indicating that s/he now belongs to the Body of Christ. Certainly every human being is marked with an image of God by nature of her/his humanity and shares in a sacred dignity. But baptism is viewed as a permanent mark, like a tattoo, indicating that a person now belongs to Christ.

So, what is my big secret? You may have guessed that I have a tattoo. You may be thinking, "That's it? That's your big secret?" Actually I have four tattoos ☺ Most people would not expect a parish minister to have any tattoos. Some may even feel tattoos are unholy. Given the fact that I have been misunderstood in the past, I have hesitated to share this personal part of me. Most people have not seen my tattoos because, in an effort to be pastorally sensitive I keep them hidden. The life of a parish minister is often lived in a "fishbowl" meaning everything you do (or even don't do but are thought to have done) is visible to the community. Ministers are sometimes formed with a sense that the institution tightly controls one's ideas and behaviors. The reality of both the "fishbowl" and the "ever watching eye of the institution" can create an oppressive context for someone in ministry. Some deal with it well, others do not. I do not. It was starting to feel as if I was on constant "lock down" and I had become so fearful that I would say or do something that would be considered unorthodox. It took me a long time to realize that neither of the situations mentioned above are as serious as what I had made them in my mind to be.

In a leadership class with Bishop Anthony Pilla he stated, "The Church does not have a mold we are pouring you into. God called you with your own unique personalities and gifts – don't lose those in the formation process. Be yourself." I'm not sure he had four tattoos in mind when he said that, but I believed his words were sincere and they stuck with me. Building up the courage to be unique in this context meant undoing much of what I had been taught. I had to "do some more of my own work" and heal some of the misconceptions I held regarding my Catholic faith. I needed to spend some time getting to know myself and accepting that I don't have to become this "cookie-cutter" minister that I imagined I needed to be. God does not plant mono-crops because mono-cropping is destructive to the environment; it's unstainable, it breeds disease and super-pests, and it fails to recognize God's grandeur. God is an exceptional farmer who plants a diverse garden filled with a variety of fruits, vegetables, and even exotic wild flowering plants. All of which come together in a beautiful, sustainable harmony. Each unique in function and form.

I have accepted that I do not fit into any prefabricated mold of what a pastoral minister should look or think like. We are all created uniquely with our own characteristics and idiosyncrasies. I love my tattoos. They are an expression of me, my faith and my long and difficult journey. They are "indelible" marks of where I've been and where I am called to go. They are signs that I have been marked, anointed if you will, and for a particular purpose. They serve for me as visible signs of an invisible reality that has been both sacred and transforming. They are simultaneously "war wounds" and images of hope. I am going to use my tattoos throughout this book as a means of not only marking milestones along my path, but also as a way of introducing the extraordinary genius of St. Hildegard of Bingen.

At this point you, if you are not too busy judging me because I have tattoos, you are probably wondering what kind of tattoos they are and where they are hidden! I will discuss each of them within the context of a chapter. To begin, I would like to share an excerpt from the first book I mentioned by Fr. Edward Hays. Throughout Hays' book the reader is taken on a spiritual journey which transforms not only the body, but more importantly the mind and the heart. The scene begins as he enters a dusty old tattoo shop in Ethiopia. He is a pilgrim in search of the sacred. He musters the courage to open the door and is greeted by an older black Ethiopian tattoo artist:

> *"You have come for a tattoo?" he asked as he moved from the dark shadows into the faded, yellow twilight of the late afternoon. "I was only curious," I replied. "I thought I would merely stop in to inquire about the cost… I was… I thought…" My words trailed off as I searched for what to say. The eyes of the Ethiopian were of particular interest, especially his left eye which seemed to be watching a part of myself that even I had not seen. "Are you a pilgrim or merely a tourist?" he asked as he came closer. "I am a pilgrim," I answered. I was seeking the holy but had come to realize, now halfway around the world, that its dwelling was everywhere! "Do you want a tattoo? I have many designs, ancient, sacred, and magical," he continued without a trace of a smile. "The tattoo you know is more than some decoration. It holds the power to heal to protect, to drive away evil spirits. It is your passport; you are a pilgrim, are you not?" As the Ethiopian tattooist sat down, he reached up and turned on the single light that wore the funneled shade. A swaying circle of white light floated around the table. He was seated directly across from me, and that unique left eye welcomed me, caressing me, as if I were a friend unseen for years. As the slowly swaying circle of light washed over me, I knew that some great adventure was about to begin.* (pp.9-11)

The second author that has captured my attention is a popular Lutheran pastor in Colorado, Rev. Nadia Bolz-Weber. She is referred to as the "tattooed pastor" because, as you probably assumed, she is covered in tattoos. Bolz-Weber is a recovered drug addict who through the grace of God found salvation. She was "bitten by the Lutheran vampire" as she describes her experience and became an ordained minister and pastor. Her tattoos include St. Mary Magdalene and a liturgical calendar. She uses her tattoos as a sign that we are simultaneously saint and sinner called by the grace of God to be holy, even in our brokenness. She wrote a beautiful description regarding the nature of grace:

> *Grace is when God is a source of wholeness, which makes up for my failings. My failings hurt me and others and even the planet, and God's grace to me is that my brokenness is not the final word. My selfishness is not the end-all... instead, it's that God makes beautiful things out of my crap... It's God saying, "I love the world too much to let your sin define you and be the final word. I am God who makes all things new." (p.50)*

I love that statement - "God loves the world too much" to let us remain in sin. What a different world we would live in if we really embraced God's enormous gift of love. God loves sinners – throughout the Scriptures Jesus is found lovingly caring for those who have been labeled, gossiped about, and marginalized by society. He states that he has come to call the sick – the sinner – not the righteous (Mark 2:17). St. Patrick, one of my most beloved saints (next to Hildegard of course) began his writing, *Confession*, with the line, "I Patrick am a sinner. The worst among men." God calls us in our brokenness, in our ignorance, and even in our selfishness, to embrace the divine light that sparked us into being and continues to burn within us.

This book is not really a memoir, though it does include many personal stories that testify to the love and grace I have experienced in my call to formal ministry in the Church. The grace that I believe called me to fall in love with St. Hildegard of Bingen. It is a story of an enchanted journey, which has taken me to a place that I never could have imagined existed.

VIRIDITAS

Your chosenness is for the sake of letting others know they are chosen too. – Richard Rohr

My first tattoo experience is one that I will naturally never forget. As Hays describes in his text, I too was apprehensive to open the door, and even more scared to go in. Once inside it was an environment unfamiliar to me, especially as I looked around at so many images that I did not understand people wanting tattooed on them – skulls, demons, and other "scary" images. These are the images which line the walls of most American tattoo shops. I had spent the last decade pretty sheltered between the parish and the seminary. Upon entering this tattoo shop it felt as though I had stumbled upon something unholy, far outside of my comfort zone. Without saying a word, my mind was racing with so many questions. Would the tattoo artist be kind? Would it be painful? Most importantly, would I sorely regret my decision? The young tattoo artist must have picked up on my vibes. He was very kind and assured me that they offer "tattoo removal" if I changed my mind in the future. My fears aside I decided to take a chance and get the tattoo. In preparation for the experience, I had consumed a large glass of green juice before I left the house hoping that the physical essence of *viriditas* would sustain me if it was painful. He asked me what kind of tattoo I was looking for – he probably assumed I was the butterfly type. As I pretended to flip through some of the images in the book on the counter I really wasn't looking for anything in it. "What I would like," I said, "is a Latin phrase - *viriditas* in green ink across my right forearm with ivy and foliage." He quickly drew up a sample. I was thinking about keeping it small to test my tolerance for the pain, however, as he sketched it out it became something much larger and beautiful.

It was at this point in my spiritual journey that I had not only completely fallen in love with Hildegard of Bingen, but I was marking a new chapter. I wanted to be filled with the spirit of *viriditas*, to grow in greenness, the sacred life-force. I saw the act of getting this tattoo as an indelible mark of my personal transformation – my movement from spiritual death to new life. It was also an expression of my individuality as I was beginning to feel a loss as I grew in my role as a leader in an institution that tends to discourage individuality.

As he began his work it was painful, though I did not flinch or indicate to him I was in pain. Instead I consciously chose to use the experience as a prayer. As he drew lines and wrote text it felt as though he was using a knife to cut my previously undefiled skin. I offered up my pain for the millions of women who have suffered physical torture over the centuries at the hands of religious men – Christian and Muslim – in the name of God. I told myself the pain I was feeling was minimal compared to the pain inflicted on so many women unjustly condemned as witches throughout the Middle Ages for promoting the spirit of *viriditas* in much the same way as Hildegard had done; or the women suffering from "honor killings" or other forms of torture simply for expressing a desire to be individuals. My prayer was a way of standing in solidarity with these women who held much the same faith that I do, the same faith that Hildegard held, regarding the sacred presence of God in every aspect of the created world. In some cases they suffered merely for being a woman. The experience of being tattooed not only left me physically transformed, but emotionally and spiritually as well. When he finished my tattoo he washed it off, stepped back and asked me what I thought. I took a long look at it and told him honestly, "It is beautiful."

You may be asking yourself, "What is this concept of *viriditas* that she would be willing to permanently tattoo on her right forearm?" Or you may simply be thinking, "She is crazy!" I probably am a bit crazy, however, the concept of *viriditas* is not. It is not a concept Hildegard defined or developed overnight. It took her a lifetime to unpack it. One cannot understand Hildegard without understanding *viriditas*. Before delving into the theological concept of *viriditas* - which translated literally means "greening power" - one must first know something about Hildegard herself and her theology.

Who was Hildegard of Bingen?

From what is known of Hildegard of Bingen she was not born in a remarkable way. Aside from her somewhat noble birth, she came into the world much the same as any other child of her day. She was born in 1098 AD to Hildebert and Mecthilde in Bermersheim, Germany. Not much is known of her parents, including the extent of their nobility. Her biographical information is presented in this book through the use of a critical translation of the *Vita S. Hildegardis* by Silvas (1998). The origin of her biographical information is not clear. It is presumed that while still alive Hildegard and her secretary Volmar began recording her biographical information. Following Volmar's death in 1173 AD, his successor Godfrey picked up the task before his death in 1176 AD. He was replaced by Guibert of Gembloux who continued the work of recording the life of both Hildegard and her predecessor Jutta von Sponheim. Guibert was called away from Rupertsberg after Hildegard's death in 1179 AD and was unable to complete the *Vita*; however, he took the compiled notes with him leaving them to Theodoric of Echternach in the diocese of Trier, who finally brought the work to completion in the late twelfth century.

According to this early biography, Hildegard's family was noble and from the town of Bermersheim. There are no historical records of where her family lived, but it is assumed that they may have resided on the property where a small church still stands today (figures 1 & 2 are pictures from the Church in Bermersheim, Germany taken in May 2015). The Church in Bermersheim has a statue of St. Hildegard outside claiming it is the place of her birth and baptism (figure 3). Whether or not the historical claim of the Church is factual is undetermined, nonetheless it adds a rich element to her story.

Figure 1

Figure 2

Figure 3

Hildegard's *Vita* claims that her family was connected to the well-respected Sponheim Family which would end up having a profound influence on her life journey from a very young age. Having been born the tenth child to devout Christian parents, it was expected she would be tithed to the Church, as directed in the Scriptures (Lev 27: 30-33; Deut 26:12-13), and so she was. Her *Vita* states that her parents, while focused on worldly desires, "were not ungrateful for the gifts of the Creator, and set aside their daughter for the service of God" (Silvas, 1998, p. 138). However, some suspected the event of her tithing was much more complicated than simply following divine law. Her family may have tithed her to the Church as a result of her chronic physical sufferings and extraordinary spiritual gifts.

From the time Hildegard was three years old she experienced visions from what she described as the *Living Light*. There is a story told of her, at the age of three, having predicted unusual markings on an unborn calf and when the calf was born, it was marked in exactly the way she had predicted. Hildegard herself does not mention this event, but it is preserved in a later redaction of her *Vita* referred to as *Acta Inquistionis*[2] written by a monk named Bruno (Silvas, 1998, p.267). According to this story, Hildegard's nurse "marveled" at what had happened and immediately shared it with her mother alerting her to Hildegard's unique spiritual gift. It is interesting that this story is told in a laudatory fashion since historically women with this type of vision were often assumed to be witches,[3] not saints. Nonetheless, this story has found its way into almost every contemporary biography, though it may be little more than historical embellishment. There is nothing in the original manuscripts to support this tale, outside of the account preserved in the *Acta*. However, in a translation by Dronke (1984) Hildegard does state in her *Vita* that she had extraordinary visionary experiences as a child:

---

[2] The *Acta* was prepared around 1233 AD to support her cause for canonization. Attempts at her canonization failed several times until 2012 AD when Pope Benedict XVI declared it official.
[3] See Summers (1971) translation of *The Malleus Maleficarium*.

In the third year of my life I saw so great a brightness that my soul trembled; yet because of my infant condition I could express nothing of it. But in my eighth year I was offered to God, given over to a spiritual way of life, and till my fifteenth year I saw many things, speaking of a number of them in a simple way, so that those who heard me wondered from where they might have come or from whom they might be. Then I too grew amazed at myself, that whenever I saw these things deep in my soul I still retained outer sight, and that I heard this said of no other human being. (p. 145)

The nature of her childhood experiences, however, is left to the imagination of the hagiographer.

According to her *Vita,* at the age of eight years old Hildegard was tithed (together with another young girl) as an anchorite to the Benedictine Monastery at Disibodenberg under the care of Jutta of Sponheim, a recluse also born of nobility (figures 4 & 5 are pictures of the ruins of Disibodenberg taken in May 2015).

Figure 4   Figure 5

When a woman embraced the role of anchorite, she was essentially declared "dead" to the outside world. It was common for a funeral rite to be celebrated at her entering the anchorage to emphasize her death to the world as well as to provide the necessary sacraments in the event she actually died in seclusion (Maddocks, 2001, pp. 27-30). Hildegard's secretary and confessor at her death, Guibert, declared in his *Letter to Bovo*, that the funeral rites customary for an anchorite had in fact taken place; "And so with psalms and spiritual canticles the three of them were enclosed in the name of the most high Trinity... Except for a rather small window [similar to the one in figure 6], all access was blocked off, not with wood but with stones solidly cemented in" (Silvas, 1998, p. 108). There would most likely be a window[4] attached looking into the church for the anchorite to observe Mass and also on the outside for pilgrims to come and seek spiritual guidance, but it was assumed they would stay in seclusion indefinitely. Women often embraced this role willingly in order to avoid an arranged marriage. Ironically, in this isolated state, many women found liberation otherwise unattainable at the time.

Figure 6

---

[4] This window in Figure 6 at the ruins of Disibodenberg is often discussed in popular literature as "the very room Hildegard was enclosed in" creating a legendary tale. It may have been her cell, or it may have been the cell of one of the many male monks at the monastery. There is not enough historical evidence to confirm with any certainty that Hildegard stayed in this room, but it most likely is a valid representation of her cell.

It is uncertain if Hildegard was enclosed as an anchorite at age eight when she was tithed or when she took her vows as a young teenager. The literature suggests that Hildegard and Jutta enjoyed more freedom than normally ascribed to an anchorite (King-Lenzmeir, 2001, p. 5).

Sutherland (2010) wrote an article examining the actual age of Hildegard's entry in Disibodenberg, questioning the commonly held assumption that at the event of her tithing at age eight, she went directly into the anchorage, as suggested in Guibert's *Letter to Bovo* (Silvas, 1998, pp.107-108). Jutta's *Vita* indicates that she may have gone on a pilgrimage around the year 1110 AD (when Hildegard was about twelve years old), indicating that possibly Jutta and Hildegard lived together, but not as anchorites. Some scholars conclude the biographical data suggests they were enclosed when Hildegard "took the veil", which would have been several years after she was tithed (Sutherland, 2010, p.58). In addition to the discrepancies in the *Vita* of both Jutta and Hildegard, other historical documents suggest Disibodenberg was not built up enough in 1106AD to have received women anchorites (Sutherland, 2010, p. 64). It is reasonable to assume that the monks at Disibodenberg not only needed time to prepare for hosting cloistered women, but the women's facility may have been made possible as a result of the dowries being offered, particularly by the Sponheim family. Regardless of what age Hildegard actually entered into the anchorite, it is clear that from the young age of 8 years old, she had been betrothed to the Church in service to God.

What was this abbey like that was blessed to have received such a precious gift? The Abbey at Disibodenberg was formed in the tradition of the Benedictine Order and followed the Benedictine Rule[5] including the call to embrace *ora et labora* (prayer and

---

[5] It is believed that Benedict of Nursia ca. 480-ca. 547 wrote his Rule to organize his monks. There are some scholars who question the actual existence of Benedict of Nursia, some feel he was little more than a legend.

work). The Benedictine Rule required one to pray several times a day in addition to living simply and working hard. Jutta was an extreme ascetic, embracing the Rule of St. Benedict to such an extreme that it may have been the cause for her early death.[6] Hildegard's disdain for corporal forms of penance and her great love for the sacredness of the human body may have stemmed from her having grown up witnessing Jutta's abuse of her own body.

Around the year 1115 AD, at the age of about sixteen, Hildegard "took the veil" from Bishop Otto of Bamberg and became a vowed religious. The literature suggests this is when the liturgical rite for seclusion as an anchoress took place. However, during these years the extraordinary reputation of the holiness of both Jutta and Hildegard began to spread and other women, mostly born in noble families, came to Disibodenberg seeking admittance to this growing community of religious women. The male monks at Disibodenberg gladly expanded the cloister as it meant an influx of dowries and noble connections. This created a monastic environment for the women less secluded compared to a traditional anchorage. While both lifestyles were rigid and preserved the nun

---

Regardless the Rule of Benedict became very much a part of medieval monastic culture. Over the years the Rule has been embraced by women and men, lay and ordained, as a way to live in cloistered community. While Hildegard does not talk much about the Rule in her other writings, she did live as a Benedictine religious from the time she was tithed at just 8 years old. In response to a request from another monastery, the Convent of Hunniensis, Hildegard wrote a work entitled, *Explanation of the Rule of Benedict* possibly in the late 1150's or early 1160's (Feiss, 2205, p. 8). The translation by Feiss (2005) recounts her opening words, "And I, a poor little female in form, unlearned by human teaching, looked toward the true light and to the memory of blessed Benedict as you requested, in order that the matters in the teaching of the Rule which are more difficult and obscure to human understanding might be revealed to me through the grace of God" (p. 48).

[6] According to Jutta's *Vita*, following her death Hildegard and two other nuns prepared her body for burial. When uncovering the body they discovered, "innumerable marks of her passion and a chain (cilice) which she had worn on her flesh" (Silvas, 1998, p. 80).

from contact with the outside world, Hildegard seems to have enjoyed a bit more freedom than what would have been expected.

During her younger years at Disibodenberg Hildegard learned Latin and music. The music that she produced is often categorized as Gregorian Chant; however its ethereal nature is distinct from traditional Gregorian style. Barbara Newman (1988) describes it in the following way; "Hildegard's poetic world is like Sibyl's cave, difficult to access, reverberating with cryptic echoes" (p. 32). In addition to music she studied the Scriptures, philosophy, and the art of natural medicine including the use of herbs and gems. She learned to preach and came to master the art of administering a monastery, which would later expand to two monasteries. For most of her life the monastery of Disibodenberg was under construction. As a result of having observed many building projects, she also came understand what was involved with building a monastery, which may have inspired her to take on the task of building Rupertsberg. Hildegard's talent as a leader was exemplified as she grew in wisdom and understanding on a number of levels.

In 1136 AD Jutta died and Hildegard was named the new *magistra*[7] of her community. For many years Hildegard had kept hidden her extraordinary visions out of fear that she might be accused of heresy. In 1141 AD, however, Hildegard claims she experienced a vision commanding her to put into writing what her internal voice – the *Living Light* – revealed to her. The experience she had of the *Living Light* reflected the visions she had experienced from the time she was three years old. The difference with this vision is that she was commanded to share her visions publically. These types of experiences were not uncommon in the

---

[7] The role of *magistra* was similar to abbess but without the canonical authority of an abbess. The nuance in title may seem insignificant, but its implications are profound because an abbess was endowed with a significant amount of autonomous authority, as opposed to a *magistra* who remained under the authority of the male abbot. The limiting of her canonical power may have been intentional.

Middle Ages, especially among vowed religious. However, there was always the question of the source of the visions and this was a time when religious imagination saw the Devil everywhere. Before she could freely write what she "saw and heard" the hierarchy had to verify that the source of her visions were divine. This would require an examination of her works by a tribunal consisting of male clergy (many of whom did not view women warmly). A negative reaction from the clergy could have resulted in her having been accused of heresy or possession for which the "remedy" or consequence was often violent.[8]

Hildegard's relationship with the abbot was rocky and so she confided in her priest friend and confessor, Volmar, who became her advocate to the abbot. In 1146 AD she courageously sought permission by contacting the well-respected and powerful Bernard of Clairvaux (who had a reputation for not liking women) to continue writing. Without permission (and blessing) from the magisterium, Hildegard could easily be accused of heresy and condemned for her writing. She needed magisterial approval. Her initial writings were well received by the hierarchy and in 1148 AD Pope Eugenius III publicly read excerpts from her first work (which was still in progress) the *Scivias* at the Synod of Trier. It was determined that her writings were in fact coming from a divine source and she was given permission to write down all that the

---

[8] Hildegard lived centuries before the serious witch-hunts in Germany began, nonetheless, there had always been groups within Germany who hunted those accused (predominately outspoken, "uncontrollable" women) of heresy and witchcraft. Cawthorne (2003) stated, "Germany took its witchcraft seriously. At least a hundred thousand people were executed, with burning alive the prescribed punishment and torture the tool to extract a confession" (p. 108). The origin of the fanatical craze began with a German clergyman Heinrich Kramer, and his document (1480AD) *Malleus Maleficarum*. Aside from her political connections, possibly what might have protected Hildegard (or at least kept her off of the "heresy radar") was that most attention was being directed towards the heretical sect known as the Cathars, which she openly preached against. Had she lived a few hundred years later, she most likely would have been subject to the witch-hunt craze and may not have lived to have made the valuable contributions that she did.

Living Light revealed to her. In the introduction to *The Classics of Western Spirituality* (1990) Newman (1990) wrote:

> *The importance of this papal seal of approval cannot be overestimated. Not only did it increase Hildegard's confidence and security in the face of continuing self-doubt, but it also authenticated her publicly and protected her from the censure she was bound to attract for violating deutero-Pauline strictures on female silence and submission* (p. 13)

With the help of Volmar and one of her dearly beloved nuns, Richardis, she completed her first theological book, *Scivias* which was completed and published a decade later in 1151 AD.

As Hildegard's reputation grew so did the number of women (wealthy and well-educated) seeking entry into her religious community. The influx of newly vowed religious created a need for larger quarters. Soon after the Synod granted Hildegard permission to write theology, she received a vision instructing her to move her sisters out of Disibodenberg to their own monastery where they would be free, to some extent, from the direction of the abbot and the male hierarchy. She would not possess autonomous authority, but some freedom would result from the move. Her request was unacceptable to the abbot Kuno (in charge of Disibodenberg[9]) and he initially refused to grant permission, in part because of the implication it might have for the nuns' dowries and future pilgrims. In her *Vita* Hildegard states:

---

[9] Kuno is often depicted in film and popular writings on Hildegard as having been the abbot in charge when Hildegard was tithed, However, from the time Hildegard was promised to Disibodenberg until the time she was named *magistra* there were actually three abbots. Adilhun and Fulcard would have been in charge for the years prior to Hildegard's having been named *magistra*. Kuno was named abbot in 1136AD, the same year Jutta died and Hildegard was named *magistra* (Feiss, 2010, p.10). The literature suggests there was an ongoing tension regarding authority between Kuno and Hildegard from the time of their appointments.

> *Now when my Abbot and the brother, and the people of that district realized the nature of the proposed change, that we were wanting to go from a lushness of fields and vineyards and from the beauty of that place to an arid place with no conveniences, they were shocked and conspired among themselves to block us so that it should not come about. They were even saying that I was deceived by some kind of vain imagination... There was a certain noble marchioness we knew approached the Archbishop of Mainz and put the whole story before him and other wise people... [They replied] that it seemed reasonable for this proposal to go forward. Thus, with the Archbishop's permission and in reverence for God we came to that place with a great escort of our neighbors and other visitors.* (Silvas, 1998, pp.163-164)

With some difficulty (and courageous effort) she sought, and received permission from the Abbot and the Archbishop of Mainz to move her sisters to their own monastery. Hildegard took about twenty of her sisters to a piece of land endowed to them by the Margravine of Stade (the mother of Richardis of Stade, one of Hildegard's most precious nuns). The tension that resulted between Hildegard and the monks at Disibodenberg over her request never fully subsided. The abbot Kuno and his successor Helengerus wrote a letter to Hildegard, to which she responded critically. She concludes a letter to Helengerus in 1170AD with the warning, "When you work your own will to the exclusion of all else, as if you were not to look to God, then harm will befall you, and you will fall into those misfortunes which I have heretofore proclaimed" (Baird & Ehrman, 1994, p.171). The tone of this late letter (written almost twenty years after she moved her convent to Rupertsberg) suggests the event created a wound between her and the monks at Disibodenberg that never fully healed.

Hildegard, however, believed the vision to move her sisters out of Disibodenberg to Rupertsberg on the Nahe and Rhine Rivers, was divinely ordered. It was a sacred place. This is where the remains of St. Rupert were buried. With some effort (and the financial support of the Margravine of Stade) they successfully built their own monastery (figure 7 depicts a historical reconstruction of what Rupertsberg most likely looked like in its day).[10] The convent chapel at Rupertsberg was blessed by Heinrich, Archbishop of Mainz, in 1152AD.

Figure 7

Why was the location of Rupertsberg so important to Hildegard? It was believed that St. Rupert, a beloved saint of Hildegard, had lived and was buried on that land (thus giving it the name Rupertsberg before it was likely destroyed by Vikings in the ninth century) and so he, together with St. Disibod (an Irish bishop who had founded the monastery at Disibodenberg in the seventh century), held a very special place in Hildegard's heart (Flanagan, 1989). While she wrote most of her music in honor of St. Ursula and the Virgin Mary, she wrote several hymns in honor of St. Rupert and St. Disibod as well.

---

[10] Unlike Disibodenberg, most of the ruins of Rupertsberg no longer exists. A business building has been built over the remains. All that remains are a few underground cellars which were reconstructed in the sixteen century and discovered in the last century when the land was being excavated to build the railroad system.

From the time she was a child Hildegard was frequently ill, leaving her bedridden for long periods of time. As she grew older these periods of illness often occurred following a vision, or when difficult situations with the hierarchy emerged. For example, this onset of illness is described in her *Vita* at the time when the abbot Kuno refused to let her move out of Disibodenberg. Hildegard describes her illness at the time as being so severe, even the *light* was gone from her:

> *I could not see any light because of clouding over my eyes, and I was so pressed down by the weight of my body that I could not raise myself. So I lay there, overwhelmed by intense pains. Why I suffered like this was because I did not make known the vision in which it was shown to me that I must move with my young women from the place where I had been offered to God, to another place. So I endured these pains continually until I named the place where I am now.* (Silvas, 1998, p. 163)

Hildegard's *Vita* states that once he gave permission for her to move from Disibodenberg, she began to recover. The coincidental onset of illness at times when situations are not going in Hildegard's direction are often highlighted, and even embellished, in films and fictional writings on her life.

In 1151 AD, Hildegard moved her nuns to Rupertsberg and completed the first of her theological works *Scivias*. Both of these accomplishments were certainly among the greatest experiences of Hildegard's life. However, at the same time, she also experienced one of the most tragic events of her life; one from which she would never recover. The Margravine of Stade, her long-time supporter and financial patron, demanded a favor in return for having endowed Hildegard with so many gifts. She requested her daughter Richardis (and also Adelheid, the Margravine's granddaughter) be granted permission to leave Hildegard's monastery to become abbesses of their own. This was a move which would strengthen the political position of Richardis' family (her brother Hartwig who was already serving as the archbishop in Bremen had arranged this position for his sister). Richardis was Hildegard's dearest friend next to Volmar. She loved Richardis more than she should have, according to the Rule of Benedict (which called its adherents to moderation in all things, including personal relationships). The thought of losing Richardis was more than Hildegard could handle. She refused to oblige.

Hildegard was so overcome by her personal feelings for Richardis and her devastation at the loss of her beloved nun that she responded by pleading with anyone she felt might be able to help her cause. A number of letters have been preserved between Hildegard, the Margravine, the Bishops of Mainz, Pope Eugenius III and Hartwig demonstrating her refusal to grant the Margravine this favor. Hildegard pulled every political and religious string she possessed, yet the decision had been made. For what was probably the first time in her career, she failed in her effort. In 1151AD Heinrich, Archbishop of Mainz (Hildegard's friend and support) wrote to her (letter 18) commanding her to free Richardis from her authority; "If you [do not accede to these requests] we will issue the same command to you again in even stronger terms, and we will not leave off until you fulfill our commands in this matter (Baird & Ehrman, 1994, p. 70). Hildegard appealed to the Pope, and after receiving a negative response from him, she reluctantly submitted. Richardis (and Adelheid) left the monastery at Ruperstberg to go on to lead in their own monasteries. This event left Hildegard devastated. It would be the last time Hildegard ever saw Richardis.

Some contemporary scholars have suggested Hildegard may have experienced homosexual love (Rush, 2013, p.132) for Richardis, whether or not she ever physically acted on it. This suggests a relationship much more profound than Hildegard indicated. It is always the case that when someone in a position of religious authority displays emotional feelings for another person, people begin to question her/his motives. However, there is no reliable evidence to support that Hildegard and Richardis were involved in a questionable relationship. Hildegard herself described it as having had her own daughter ripped from her, and her reaction, she claims, is that of a mother's love. In a letter (16) to Richardis, recognizing that she had no power or control over what was happening, she wrote, "Woe is me... Now, let all who have grief like mine, mourn with me, all who in the love of God, have had such great love in their hearts and minds for a person – as I had for you – but who was snatched away from them in an instant, as you were from me... Be mindful of your poor desolate mother, Hildegard, so that your happiness may not fade" (Baird, 2006, pp.47-48). Shortly after her appointment at Bassum, Richardis decided to return to Hildegard at Ruperstberg; however, she died suddenly and never made it back.

In the midst of her grief Hildegard continued writing. Throughout the course of her life she would write two additional theological texts following *Scivias*: *Liber Divinorum Operum* (*Book of Divine Works*) and *Liber Vitae Meritorum* (*Book of Life's Merits*). In addition she wrote two texts on medicine/natural healing (*Physica, Causae et Curae*); seventy-three hymns collected in her *Symphonia* (mostly liturgical settings and songs for feast days); the first known morality play *Ordo Virtutum* (*Order of the Virtues*); hundreds of letters corresponding with popes, kings, bishops and abbesses; a collection of homilies (from four Church sanctioned preaching tours); two hagiographies (St. Disibod and St. Rupert); and a new alphabet /language entitled *Ignota Lingua* (*Unknown Language*) and also a few random texts including an *Explanation of the Rule of Benedict, Solutions to Thirty-Eight Questions* and two texts not normally included in Hildegard's corpus *Visio de Sancto Martino* (Vision of St. Martin) and *Visio ad Guibertum Missa* (Vision sent to Guibert).

In addition, in 1158 AD the Bishop Arnold of Mainz (the diocese within which both Disibodenberg and Rupertsberg are located) gave Hildegard permission to go on a series of four preaching tours, which was unheard of for a woman at that time. Kienzle (2011) published a translated copy of her collection of homilies. In the introduction she writes, "Hildegard of Bingen composed a book of fifty-eight homilies… They [the homilies] establish Hildegard as the only known female exegete of the Middle Ages" (p. 2). She preached in the great cathedrals of Mainz and Cologne. Her homilies were collected and preserved and serve as an example that women preachers existed long before the feminist movement of the twentieth century. In fact, her collection of homilies suggests she had more authority to preach in the twelfth-century than women in the Catholic Church today.

Throughout her life Hildegard corresponded with high ranking men, civil and religious. One of the most profound political relationships she engaged in was with the Emperor Barbarossa. Her relationship with him began at a meeting in Ingelheim years before he was named Holy Roman Emperor. She predicted his appointment as emperor but warned him not to allow his own agenda to get in the way of God's will for him and the empire. He later wrote to Hildegard (letter 314) informing her that everything she had predicted at that meeting in Ingelheim had come to fruition (Baird & Ehrman, 2004, p. 113). In several subsequent letters Hildegard harshly criticizes Barbarossa for his actions, including having appointed several anti-popes. She warned him (letter 313) of the consequence of failing to live up to his divinely appointed role; "Beware, therefore, that the almighty King does not lay you low because of the blindness of your eyes, which fail to see correctly how to hold the rod of proper governance in your hand" (Baird & Ehrman, 2004, p. 113). In spite of harsh criticism, her relationship with Barbarossa (and his protection of her and her convent) remained intact.

In 1165 AD Hildegard founded a second monastery at Eibingen across the Rhine River from Rupertsberg. Schipperges (1998) stated that the monastery in Eibingen had already existed as an Augustinian cloister but had been deserted at the time Hildegard discovered and revived it. The Eibingen monastery became home to thirty Benedictine nuns, many of which were not born of noble decent. She traveled back and forth across the Rhine River twice a week to fulfil her duties as the leader of this new abbey in Eibingen[11].

In 1173 AD, while Hildegard was in the process of writing *Liber Divinorum Operum* (Book of Divine Works) her priest, friend, secretary, and confessor of sixty years, Volmar, died. Many contemporary films and writings present the relationship between Volmar and Hildegard in ways that suggest they may have been closer than friends. The translation of Hildegard's *Vita* records their friendship as "loving" in the same way it describes her relationship with Richardis. "There is no reason to doubt that Hildegard and Volmar enjoyed an affectionate, yet deeply religious and chaste *amicitia*/friendship lasting for decades, from the time they were young until Volmar's death in 1173" (Silvas, 1998, p. 133). Following Volmar's death the abbey at Disibodenberg (to whom Hildegard's nuns were still answerable) sent three subsequent monks in an attempt to replace Volmar including Godfrey and Guibert, both of whom contributed to the writing of her *Vita*.

Near the end of her life Hildegard faced a very difficult challenge with the hierarchy. She had been accused of burying a heretic in her monastery grounds. She was ordered to remove the body from consecrated ground, to which she refused. Some accounts state that she took her staff and disrupted any markings of where the grave was so that the clergy would not be able to locate it (Schipperges, 1998, p. 62). She claimed the soldier had repented, had been absolved, and therefore was reconciled to the Church and had every right to be buried in consecrated ground. She held fast to her position that to exhume him would be a sin against God bringing upon her far graver consequences than offending the bishops. She and her sisters were placed under an interdict for six months (which forbade them to celebrate Mass or sing the liturgy

---

[11] Over the years the monastery suffered several fires and was subsequently destroyed in 1802 AD. It was rebuilt in 1935 AD and continues to serve as a parish church.

of the hours). Liturgy (singing/reception of Eucharist) is the heart and soul of Benedictine spirituality. To take that away from Hildegard and her sisters was to cut them off from the very core of their spiritual practice.

Hildegard wrote a scathing letter to the bishops and warned them that it is the Devil that deprives humans of celestial harmony. She warned the bishops (letter 23) of the eternal consequence if they continue to forbid her convent the divine right to sing, praise, and receive sacraments:

> *And I heard a voice saying thus: Who created heaven? God. Who opens heaven to the faithful? God. Who is like him? No one. And so, o men of faith, let none of you resist Him or oppose Him, lest He fall on you in His might and you have no helper to protect you from His judgment. This time is a womanish time, because the dispensation of God's justice is weak. But the strength of God's justice is exerting itself, a female warrior battling against injustice, so that it might fall defeated.* (Baird & Ehrman, 1994, p.79)

In her fury she traveled at the age of eighty years old to Mainz on foot (about a day's walk) to contest her case, which initially was not granted in her favor. Through the grace of God (and the influence of a few men in high places) the interdict was eventually lifted and she died a few months later in 1179 AD at the age of eighty-one years old at Rupertsberg. Coincidentally, while Hildegard never really considered Eibingen her home, when Rupertsberg was destroyed in 1636 AD by the Swede's in the Thirty Years' War, it was the restored monastery at Eibingen that offered a safe place to preserve Hildegard's relics. Her works are preserved today at the Abbey of St. Hildegard Abbey, Rudesheim-Eibingen (Figures 8 & 9).

Figure 8

Figure 9

Her few remains, tongue and her heart (Higley, 2007, p.3), are preserved in a reliquary at the parish church in Eibingen (figure 10 below), down the hill from the Abbey Church.

Figure 10

Outside of certain areas in Germany, Hildegard has been virtually unknown for almost eight hundred years.[12] Her works were rediscovered in the mid-twentieth century, and since it has taken scholars, and the Church, decades to not only digest the "summa" that had been preserved, but has taken time to translate the texts from the Latin. The depth of her work is still being explored and studied by scholars, theologians, artists, musicians, feminists and ecologists. From a Roman Catholic perspective, her contribution rivals the male "greats", such as the Summa compiled by Thomas Aquinas. In 2012 Pope Benedict XVI canonized Hildegard of Bingen a Saint and named her a Doctor of the Church. She is only the fourth woman in the history of the Church to be named a Doctor,[13] putting her on the same level with the male doctors. She was a strong female leader and has much to offer the Church today. Like a rare diamond, Hildegard's gift to twentieth-century leadership is multi-faceted offering so many possibilities for growth and change. Her works, however, are vast and complex.

Many are asking the questions, "Where has she been?" and "Why the sudden interest in her today?" Some scholars have attempted to answer that question by presenting aspects of her teaching and applying it to contemporary issues, such as ecology, natural alternative medicine, and even music therapy. All of which are beneficial and good. However, from the perspective of a Roman Catholic female leader, there is more. She offers an example of a non-ordained woman who, by nature of her prophetic call, spoke

---

[12] Dr. Barbara Newman, professor at Northwestern University, was a pioneer in American Hildegard studies. She wrote her dissertation, *O FEMINAE FORMA: GOD AND WOMAN IN THE WORKS OF ST. HILDEGARD* in 1981 at Yale. In a personal interview on April 22, 2016 Newman stated that at that time the topic was so obscure she was surprised her advisor allowed her to write on it. She chose the topic, not because she felt a particular "call" to Hildegard, but "was a doctoral student hungry for a topic that had more primary sources than secondary sources." She said she never imagined Hildegard's popularity would become what it is today.

[13] 1970 Pope Paul VI named Teresa of Avila and Catherine of Siena doctors; 1997 Pope John Paul II named Therese of Lisieux a doctor and in 2012 Pope Benedict XVI named Hildegard of Bingen the fourth female doctor.

with the authority equal in dignity to the clergy. Her authority came directly from a divine source, the Living Light. She was (by today's definition) a lay ecclesial minister who stepped up and provided preaching, catechesis and pastoral care, in spite of a clerical culture that normally assigned the role to ordained men. In addition to her having something to offer today in regards to ecology, feminist studies, and holistic health, her recent popularity also provides a renewed interest in traditional theology, ecclesiology, and Christology, all of which many Catholics are hungering for today.

Hildegard's model of leadership is very much in tune (and style) with the magisterium, offering an example of strong, female voice, carrying canonical authority, yet her lay (non-ordained) status offers an example of a new paradigm for ecclesial leadership in the Catholic Church today. Hildegard carried a crosier (staff carried by a bishop) and she spoke with divine authority, often offering theological advice and admonitions to the bishops themselves! And she was respected for it. This is an important to note because the Catholic Church is not discussing the possibility of ordaining women at this time,[14] yet Pope Francis, and the bishops, have stated that an increase in the authentic leadership roles of women is

---

[14] Pope John Paul II, in his 1994 document, *Ordinatio Sacerdotalis,* forbade the conversation. While the "Catholics in the pews" can certainly go against a pastoral directive, anyone in a position of authority or in a teaching office (clergy, lay leaders and teachers), are expected to uphold the teaching of the Church. To go against a directive will necessarily result in loss of job, ministry, and in extreme cases, excommunication. A good example can be found in Fr. Roy Bourgeois, a Maryknoll priest for forty-years. In 2008 Bourgeois preached the homily at a schismatic Mass for the ordination of several women to the Catholic priesthood. Over the course of the next several years, Rome demanded he recant and publically profess the Church's teaching for the non-admittance of women to the priesthood. Bourgeois eloquently refused stating that he could not in good conscious affirm his call was valid, while telling a woman's hers was not. After several "warnings" and opportunities to recant, Bourgeois was removed from the clerical state and excommunicated in November 2012, incidentally just a month following Hildegard having been named a Doctor of the Church.

needed in the Church. She offers an avenue for creating a paradigm today which might endow a woman with legitimate power and authority, even without the sacrament of ordination.

Hildegard emphatically insisted on the importance of relationships in creating balance and harmony. The leadership in the Roman Catholic Church, especially over the last several centuries, has not engaged the female voice or experience, creating imbalance and disharmony. In the early Church, and even through the Middle Ages, there has been a long tradition of *Mothers of the Church*, and their role was respected and celebrated by the hierarchy. The Church today is in need of spiritual mothers. Centuries of exclusively male leaders, referred to as "fathers", without a strong presence of "mothers",[15] has created an imbalance of male and female, which has led to a "drying up" of *viriditas*. Hildegard is a "Saint for our Times" as Fox (2012) calls her, but not necessarily for the reasons outlined in his book, or necessarily for reasons Pope Benedict XVI stated when he canonized her.

She is a saint – and Doctor of the Church – for Catholics of our time because the Catholic Church is in need of a female voice, one that not only preaches with the voice of a prophet, but speaks with the authority of a bishop on morals, doctrine, and spirituality, while also being concerned with how all of that fosters and nurtures one's relationship with God, with others, and with the whole of creation. A voice concerned with the healthy growth and development of the human person. This is true particularly today following decades of scandals and abuse at the hands of an all-male hierarchy. Baird (2006), in his introduction to her

---

[15] The elevated role of Mary among many of the clergy, particularly in the pontificate of John Paul II, indicates the innate need for a feminine presence. While the image of Mary presented by patriarchal religion is at times grossly distorted in relation to the real experience of women, it still demonstrates the need for balance and harmony with the feminine, even in contexts where it is denied.

abbreviated correspondence stated that in Hildegard the reader will find:

> *A saint, to be sure, but a saint with all her personal foibles and idiosyncrasies, a woman who sorrows and hurts, who is compassionate and tender, yet unshakable on principle; who is vulnerable as a poor little form of a woman and absolutely unyielding as the voice of the Living Light. Hildegard was, clearly, the most remarkable woman – one is tempted to say person – of the Middle Ages, and, in a large sense, she too was not for an age but for all time.* (p.14)

The Roman Catholic Church today needs a woman, a holy *magistra*, to help get it back on track, to renew the greening moisture of *viriditas,* and if anyone could accomplish that task today, it is Hildegard of Bingen.

There are many within the Catholic Church that long to hear the message of Hildegard of Bingen on a level that they can comprehend. She appeals to the Catholic imagination in such a way that draws in followers. Her visions and theology, however, are complicated and can be difficult to not only read, but even more so to make practical applications. The intent of this entire work is to bring Hildegard into everyday life, to make her personable and knowable. To present her in such a way that the work is faithful to who she was (attention to historical context), while at the same time gleaning from her wisdom, inspiration, and even humor to inspire growth, *viriditas*, in the Catholic Church today. She has an enchanting story that needs to be told, and this project, The HILDEGARDEN, is a context in which to tell it.

Timeline of Key Events in Hildegard's Life

- 1098 AD Hildegard born the tenth (the youngest "tithed") child
- 1106 AD Hildegard joins Jutta von Sponheim at Disibodenberg
- 1115 AD Hildegard "takes the veil" from Bishop Otto of Bamberg
- 1136 AD Jutta dies at the age of 44 years / Hildegard named *Magistra*
- 1141 AD Hildegard receives a VISION calling her to write down "all that she sees and hears".
- 1146-1147 AD Hildegard writes to Bernard of Clairvaux seeking permission to write *Scivias*
- 1147-1148 AD Excerpts from *Scivias* is read at the Synod of Trier by Pope Eugenius III
- 1148 AD Hildegard receives a VISION to move her sisters out of Disibodenberg
- 1150 AD Hildegard moves twenty of her sisters to Rupertsberg and builds a monastery
- 1151 AD Hildegard's beloved nun Richardis is removed from Rupertsberg to Bassam
- 1151-1158 AD Hildegard writes *Physica* and *Causae et curae*
- 1152 AD Richardis dies
- 1151-1159 AD At some point Hildegard meets with the Emperor Barbarossa in Ingelheim
- 1158 AD Bishop Arnold of Mainz assigned to protect Rupertsberg and Disibodenberg
- 1158-1161 AD First Preaching Tour to Bamberg
- 1158-1163 AD Hildegard writes *Liber Vitae Meritorum*
- 1160 AD Second Preaching Tour to Trier
- 1161 AD Third Preaching Tour to Cologne
- 1163 AD Emperor Barbarossa grants imperial protection to Rupertsberg
- 1163 AD Hildegard writes *Liber Divinorum Operum*
- 1165 AD Hildegard establishes Eibingen monastery across the Rhine
- 1170 AD Fourth Preaching Tour to Swabia
- 1170 AD Hildegard writes *Life of St. Disibod*
- 1173 AD Volmar, Hildegard's beloved priest /friend of sixty years dies
- 1178 AD Interdict is placed on Hildegard's convent
- 1179 AD Interdict lifted. Hildegard dies on September 17
- 2012 AD Pope Benedict XVI names her a Saint and Doctor of the Church
- 2016 The building of The HILDEGARDEN ☺

Hildegard's Theology

Hildegard of Bingen's theology is normally described as *mystical* theology. In a way that description is appropriate, but she was not a mystic in the traditional sense. The essence of her mystical nature is not always properly understood because, like everything else she did, it was unique. She did not experience an encounter with God while in a state of ecstasy or hysteria, or even while immersed in deep meditation, which are all characteristic of mystical experiences. Rather she describes her encounters as *illumination* which distinguishes her from other mystics (Maddocks, 2003, p.58). Newman (1987) points out that she also did not write mystical prayer or contribute to the mystical tradition (p. xx). To understand her mystical gift, it is important to understand the culture and world in which she was formed. In his book, *German Mysticism*, Weeks (1993) described the characteristics of visionary mystics in medieval Germany:

> *Visionary mysticism was frequently, though not always, combined with illness or physical suffering... The manifestations varied from visionary dreams to reported stigmatizations... Not only the world of God, Paradise, and the angels was seen. Hell, Purgatory, Satan, and the Apocalypse appeared to medieval visionaries... A nun or monk who knew God sometimes visibly and sometimes inwardly did not alternate between being a visionary and being a mystic.* (p.40)

Hildegard's visions often coincided with illness, sometimes leaving her bedridden for months at a time. She also described in detail, visions of both heaven and hell. However, she claimed she was always awake (never dreaming) when experiencing a vision.

Hildegard's innate understanding of the cosmos and the omniscience of God are evident in her writings, music, artwork, holistic healing, and her letters. A renewal of this awareness in organized religion is very much needed in the world today. For a variety of reasons, institutional religion has separated its understanding of God from a relationship with the natural world. There is a need today for a holistic, cosmic approach to spirituality, and this has led some to misunderstand, and even over romanticize[16] Hildegard's theological thought reshaping her from what she was, to what some would like her to be. This has resulted in part because contemporary scholars have honed in exclusively on her eco-spirituality while failing to take into account her theological writings, which are virtually unread outside of academic circles. To present her in this way does a disservice to her complex genius and her authenticity.

Hildegard brought a fresh perspective to traditional theology which tended to focus heavily on sin and the ever present need for repentance. While her visions are grounded in the theme of atonement, adhering to the accepted theology of her day, they also radiate hope. She lived her entire life within a monastic setting providing ample opportunity for theological reflection. Hildegard radiated an innate understanding of "Wisdom, a way of knowing that goes beyond one's mind, one's rational understanding, and embraces the whole of a person: mind, heart, and body" (Bourgeault, 2003, p.27). Hildegard embodied both systematic and holistic theology.

Having lived the life of a twelfth-century German nun for seventy-three years, she was steeped in medieval Catholic theology. The German Church was rigidly ordered. Her conservative views on Christology, complementarity (divinely ordered roles for men and women), and judgment/salvation permeated her writings and visions. Mysticism is often described as an experience that, "transcends doctrine, confession, and the particularities of culture and historical period", but German mystics tended to "express the conditions of their cultures, periods, and confessions" and are heavily Christocentric (Weeks, 1994, p. 10). This is accurate of

---

[16] Newman (1992) wrote a critical article examining the approach of Matthew Fox and medieval "creation mystics" in which she states, "Fox's theology in fact bears little resemblance to any historic form of Christianity" (*Touchstone: A Journal of Mere Christianity*. Summer 1992).

Hildegard's visions and theological writings. Her mystical experiences were deeply Christocentric and were steeped in systematic theology. At the same time, her deep respect for creation and the sacred feminine was unique. She saw in the incarnation the union of the physical and spiritual. Humanity is the place where the sacred and secular intersect.

There is a theological struggle taking place today between the "left and right" regarding Hildegard's theology and worldview. It has been said that Hildegard has been "hijacked" by the New Age movement to promote a radical theological agenda.[17] There are elements to her writings and visions that can nourish an open, inclusive theology. However, her corpus of writings reflects a systematic theology strongly rooted in medieval Catholic thought and not much of her theology is either open or inclusive, though it is holistic.

Harmony and balance are foundational to Hildegard's understanding of the universe. Many of her visions are revealed through mandalas which she sees as an image of wholeness. It reflects an integration of opposite, which has drawn the attention of Jungian analysts. For Hildegard everything had an opposite – virtue/vice; light/dark; hot/cold; male/female – though she was not dualistic in her thinking. She presented a theology that was able to integrate opposites into a newly formed whole.

In an analysis of Hildegard's morality play, *Ordo* Virtutum, Allen (1985) stated, "Hildegard developed sex complementarity in connection with her theory of virtue… The complementarity of male and female, represented as a relationship of root and branches, as shadow and light, is carried forth throughout the play" (p.310). Hildegard understood the complementary role of male and female as a part of divine order. This theological notion of Hildegard has become very popular within Roman Catholic theology today, having been developed further by Pope John Paul

---

[17] http://legacy.fordham.edu/halsall/med/hildegarde.asp

II in his popular teaching on *Theology of the Body*,[18] as well as Pope Benedict XVI and most recently Pope Francis in their program *Humanum*.[19] In his official declaration of Hildegard as a Doctor of the Church, Pope Benedict XVI stated, "The human being exists in both the male and female form. Hildegard recognized that a relationship of reciprocity and a substantial equality between man and woman is rooted in this ontological structure of the human condition" (2012). This theology is considered conservative (some prefer to call it "orthodox") and has been a point of heated debate within Catholic academic circles.[20] This is important to understanding her theology because in this regard she falls far to the "right" in her thinking, yet she is hailed in many circles as being a voice for the "left". Theologians have a responsibility to engage in faithful historical scholarship, even if it does not fit a contemporary, popular worldview.

To some degree, all of Hildegard's writings were theological texts, including her letters and medical texts. However, she wrote three texts specifically expressing her theological and philosophical thought. A systematic presentation of her theology is preserved in

---

[18] http://www.theologyofthebody.net/ The doctrine of *Theology of the Body* is not the result of a single document or declaration, but was delivered by Pope John Paul II over a series of Wednesday addresses that spanned years.

[19] *Humanum* does not exist at this point as a comprehensive work, but is a collection of writings, videos, homilies, and an ideology supported by the magisterial teaching of the Church. http://brandonvogt.com/humanum-videos-extraordinary-display-marriage-family/

[20] Two well-respected Catholic female theologians, both religious sisters, Elizabeth Johnson and Sarah Butler have debated this for many years. In a book, *The Church women want: a Catholic woman in dialogue, (2002),* Butler affirms the position of the magisterium on the teaching of complementarity. Johnson, while affirming it reflects progress from the traditional notion of women as temptresses not fully in the image of God, she warns of the implications of assigning gender specific roles. "The proposed division of labor inevitably privileges men in terms of social, political, and economic power. In the church this model justifies the practice of excluding women from positions of ritual leadership and public governance" (p.53). In addition, it does not leave any room for dialogue regarding same-sex relationships and other socially conditioned gender issues.

her three major theological texts, *Scivias, Know the Ways* (1151 AD), *Liber Vitae Meritorum, Book of Life's Merits* (1163 AD), and *Liber Divinorum Operum, Book of Divine Works* (1173/1174 AD). These works are based on the writing down of the visions she received from her encounters with the *Living Light*. Her theology clearly develops from its early stage until her last work. The task of exploring, to any real depth, these three texts extends far beyond the scope of this project. Her theology and art will be presented here in very broad strokes offering a brief introduction to the writings and a presentation of a handful of her visual pieces of art in an attempt to provide a glimpse into the complexity of Hildegard's visions and theological thought.

Theology of her Visions
Hildegard had a gift for listening to her inner voice, which she described as the *Living Light*, and having been able to transcribe that voice in such a way that people were drawn into its message (Schipperges, 1998). Over the course of approximately four decades Hildegard completed the three major theological works reflecting forty-two visions she received through her encounters with the *Living Light*. Her visions reveal the reality of humanity's relationship with God and one another and the implications / consequences of those relationships. Her first work, *Scivias*, contains twenty-six visions broken down into three sections (six, seven, and thirteen visions); *Liber Vitae Meritorum* contains six visions focused on the virtues and vices; and *Liber Divinorum Operum* contains ten visions divided again into three parts (four, one, and five visions).

Scivias was the first, and lengthiest, of her major works. The oldest manuscript of *Scivias* is kept today in the Abbey of St. Hildegard in Rüdesheim-Eibingen. The illuminated copy *Schovias-Kodex* is a faithful copy of the original *Ruperstberg-Codex* believed to have been penned (or at least dictated) by Hildegard herself. The translation used in this dissertation is from Hart & Bishop (1990), which not only contains the written text, but is accompanied with the art image. In the *Scivias* Hildegard claims in her opening statement that she had been receiving theological visions from the *Living Light* throughout most of her life. She had kept the visions to herself out of fear that she would be ridiculed or that it would be assumed her visions came not from God, but from an evil source. According to her introduction in the Scivias, when she was forty-three years old the *Living Light* commanded her to write down all that was revealed to her. She initially resisted the command of the *Living Light* to share her visions, until she became seriously ill, "having lain in a wasting illness for a long time" (Silvas,1998, p.141), which she assumed was because she had not followed the will of God. She shared her visions with Volmar, who in turn shared them with Kuno who took them to the Archbishop Henry of Mainz.

To secure the approval of the hierarchy, Hildegard went beyond Kuno and wrote her first letter (at least it is the first letter extant). She wrote it in 1146-1147 AD to the well-respected, and feared, Bernard of Clairvaux, one of the most powerful clergy of the day (a crusader), seeking permission to write down her visions:

> *O, venerable father Bernard, I lay my claim before you… Father, I am greatly disturbed by a vision seen not with my fleshly eyes but only my spirit…When I hear from your pious wisdom, I will be comforted. For with the single exception of a certain monk [Volmar] in whose exemplary life I have the utmost confidence, I have not dared to tell these things to anyone, since there are many heresies abound in the land, as I have heard.* (Baird & Ehrman, 1994, pp. 27-28)

Bernard responded positively to her request, allowing her to complete in 1151 AD her first theological text, *Scivias*. She had begun her writing in 1141AD (five or six years before she contacted Bernard). This indicates she was not so concerned to obtain permission before writing, but rather needed hierarchical approval before making the text available to the wider public.

Scivias is divided into three parts (again following a divine order which is Trinitarian in nature). It preserved the visions she received of the Creator (God the Father) in Book One; the Redeemer (God the Son) in Book Two; and the History of Salvation / the Church (God the Holy Spirit) in Book Three. The visions recorded in this text are considered "prophetic" as Hildegard speaks on behalf of God for the good of humanity. Each book contains a vision followed by an explanation or commentary on what that vision means. She claims no divine knowledge of her own, but sees herself (as she wrote in letter 40r to Odo of Paris) as a vessel, a "feather on the breath of God,"[21] lacking formal education and strength, yet blowing about as God wills (Baird & Ehrman, 1994, p.111).

Book One of *Scivias* records the revelation of God as the source of Creation and the human response of sin and what is referred to in Catholic theology as the *Fall*. She describes the shape of the universe in Book One using the feminine symbol of an egg (see figure 2:3) as it "faithfully shows Omnipotent God, incomprehensible in His majesty and inestimable in His mysteries and the hope of the faithful" (Hart & Bishop, 1990, p. 94). Hildegard also described in Book One the journey of humanity (humanity in the Christian West which to Hildegard was the entire world) through the Old Testament period concluding with a celestial vision of the *Choir of Angels*.

Book Two of *Scivias* presents her theology of the incarnation of Jesus and the Trinitarian nature of God. In her image of the Trinity she depicts the incarnated human person of Christ in the center of what appears to be two labyrinthine circles. She describes her vision in these words; "and the bright light and the glowing fire poured over the whole human figure, so that the three were one light in one power of potential" (Hart & Bishop, 1990, p. 161). Throughout the remaining visions recorded in Book Two, Hildegard describes the gifts God gives humanity (grace and

---

[21] Hildegard in a letter to Odo (40r) (Baird & Ehrman, 1994, p.111).

wisdom), particularly in the sacrifice of Christ celebrated in the sacramental life of the Church and the power it has to protect one against the temptations of evil. Near the end of Book Two Hildegard wrote:

> *But when humanity was lying in great darkness of infidelity and could not raise itself, I sent My Son for its salvation, miraculously incarnate of the Virgin, true God and true man...He conquered death and mercifully delivered humanity therefrom... God calls His faithful people to the glory of the celestial inheritance... But the ancient deceiver [Devil] lurks to ambush and tries to hinder them... But he is conquered by them.* (Hart & Bishop, 1990, pp.288-289, 294)

Hildegard's Christology reflects medieval thought[22] and for that reason she received high praises from the hierarchy when excerpts were read aloud by Pope Eugenius III, at the Synod of Trier in 1148 AD.

Book Three of *Scivias* is focused on the Church, where the Holy Spirit abides. The visions in this section describe the breaking in of the Kingdom of God in this fallen realm. Vision Twelve contains a detailed image of the Last Judgment iin which Hildegard describes the Son of Man:

> *And suddenly from the East a great brilliance shone forth; and there, in a cloud, I saw the Son of Man, with the same appearance He had had in the world and with His wounds still open, coming with the angelic choirs. He sat upon a throne of*

---

[22] One contemporary issue that arises with Hildegard's theology is the attempt to understand her Christology through the lens of "Cosmic Christology" which tends to put a much more positive spin on the incarnation than does traditional theology of atonement, which permeates Hildegard's visions. See Fox (1983), *The Coming of the Cosmic Christ* and Craine (2013), *Hildegard, Prophet of the Cosmic Christ*. This is not a judgement on the validity of creation theology. But, it can be argued that the creation theology lens has created a distortion of the actual writings and theology of Hildegard.

flame, glowing but not burning, which floated on the great tempest which was purifying the world. (Hart & Bishop, 1990, p.515)

Hildegard used language and imagery similar to that found in the Book of Revelation to describe the unfolding of the final judgment scene. Her vision, simply put - the righteous are given the gift of eternal life and the wicked are condemned to hell.

The fear of hell and the danger of being tricked by the "antichrist" are dominant themes in Hildegard's writings. In Vision Eleven she wrote, "Almighty God, have mercy on us! Let us return! Let us return; let us hasten to the covenant of Christ's Gospel; for ah, ah ah! We have been bitterly deceived!" (Hart & Bishop, 1990, p.494). The "fire and brimstone" tenor of Hildegard's theological thought is prominent in her writings and preaching and therefore are fundamental to understanding her theology, which is not always in tune with a an overly positive notion of "Original Blessing" as some contemporary scholars, including Fox (2000) have imposed on her. Hildegard's theology is in many ways quite conservative (including her notion of gender complementarity) which is a reason why she was granted the honor of being named not only a saint, but a Doctor of the Church in 2012 by the traditionalist Pope Benedict XVI. This is important to note because there is tension today regarding the nature of her theological thought.

The last vision of this Book, Vision Thirteen, is not really a vision, but is described by some scholars (Harp & Bishop) as a "concert" praising Mary, the angels, the saints, and the virtues, particularly the most important virtue, humility. It records the beginning lines of her great liturgical composition, *Ordo Virtutum (Order of the Virtues)*, which she later completes and is thought to have been performed for special feast days and/or at times when women were preparing to take their religious vows. Again, in this vision there is a battle between good and evil. The soul struggled to embrace goodness (virtues) while resisting the temptation of the Devil, personified by the only male, non-singing part. In the end the soul is saved through the help of the virtues, the queen virtue being *humility*. This morality play is entirely unique in its composition.

Liber Vitae Meritorum

This text is preserved in three manuscripts (in Brabant, Berlin, and Trier) dating from around 1170 AD, at the time they were written. The translation of the text used for this dissertation is Hozeski (1994). This work presents the relationship between thirty-five vices and their corresponding virtues. Her visions begin with a description of a man; "I saw a person who was so tall that he reached from the summit of the clouds of heaven right down to the abyss" (Hozeski, 1994, p. 10). Throughout the six visions the man looks over the entire earth, each vision in another direction, assessing its current state of human weakness and sin. Some have suggested that this is a pastoral text, directed towards her nuns who may have forgotten their vow to embrace a lifestyle void of excessive comforts and worldly desires. Maddocks (2001) states:

> *Hildegard may have drawn as much from the Heavenly Light in its visionary incarnation as on experience inside her own cloister at that time, of which she writes feelingly, and with frank self-awareness, in the Vita… In her own words she saw that some of her noble-born daughters had become caught in a net with an array of vain thoughts.* (pp.214-215)

Hildegard emphatically stated in this work that pride is the source of all other evil and appeals to the reader to embrace humility, the antidote to pride. The intended audience may have been her sisters, of whom she would have known well their sins (vices). For example, she recorded an image she saw of disobedience (possibly a message to her nuns) followed by the *Living Light's* response, affirming the divine command to be obedient, as even the *Living Light* must be:

> *From a storm cloud I heard a voice responding to this image: "I, who obey God, have a certain bondage…*

> *However, when the first angel came to life, he thereupon opposed God. I then said that the works of that one did not have life since he wanted to be something he was not... I [the Living Light] am the root of all God's works, just as the soul is to the body. Just as a man's will accomplishes what he desires, so also I do God's will by doing all the things that he commands. I consulted with God a long time ago and he ordered all the things he wanted to do through me. I sound like a lyre at the command of his world because I obey all his commands... You, however, O transgressor of the command of the Creator, in your presumptuousness you say that you are God and, therefore, do not search for the true God. Whatever you wish, you do. Where, therefore, are the heaven and earth you created?"* (Hozeski, 1994, p.130)

If this book is a pastoral text, it is possible that Hildegard's nuns may not have been as obedient to her authority as she felt that they should have been. It is also likely, though she did not enjoy the official title of abbess, that she heard her nuns' confessions, which was the common practice of the day (Macy, 2008, p. 82).

Liber Divinorum Operum (De Operatione Dei)
The last of her theological texts is preserved in the Biblioteca Statale, Lucca. This work, unlike *Liber Vitae Meritorum*, is more similar in style and layout to *Scivias*. The scholarly translation of the text used for this dissertation is Campbell (forthcoming) and the poetic translation Fox (1987). This text has been described as a "deep and healing medicine for what may well be [Western civilization] its number one disease in the past few centuries: *anthropocentrism* (Fox, 1987, p.11). In her foreword, Hildegard states that when she was fifty-six years old she had a vision that was so intense she trembled and became ill. This vision became her final theological work. She spent the next seven years recording the vision and its corresponding miniatures.

The translation of this work by Fox (1987) was the only available translation for several decades. It is not a critical translation, it is abridged (missing large sections of text), and it is highly influenced by Fox's own theological worldview. There is a critical, scholarly translation being published in 2018 by Nathaniel Campbell which is far more faithful to the original text and much more appropriate for historical research. An example of the difference can be found in the fact that Campbell's work contains the entire section of Vision Five, Book Two, on the creation of the world. This vision is a commentary on the Genesis story that is totally omitted from Fox's translation. This is significant in that it was most likely omitted by Fox because it does not correspond or support Fox's image of Hildegard or her theology. A brief example can be found in Fox's claim that Hildegard encouraged the faithful to look beyond the clergy, to even discard hierarchal order (2012, p.23), yet this omitted passage claimed something quite the opposite:

> *And God said, 'Let there be lights in the firmament of heaven, to divide the day and the night; and let them be for signs, and for seasons, and for days and years, to shine in the firmament of heaven and to illuminate the earth.' And it was so." This should be considered thus: God spoke through the Holy Spirit in the hearts of his disciples, "Let there be priests and teachers in my Son, to illuminate the Church that was built upon the solid rock that is Christ—from that stone the justice of right faith flowed forth. Let these priests be sent into every church, illuminating it to discern for the people by their words the day—the salvation of faith—and announce the felicity that they will obtain through that faith if they keep it. Let them also suggest to the people the night—the eternal torments that belong to infidelity. And this let those teachers demonstrate this to them with various signs, to announce what they must keep—the feasts to be celebrated, the seasons of fasting that are binding, and the days that can be dispensed in God's law—so that they observe the year with its established precepts. And may these precepts shine through faith in heaven—in my Son—for they follow the angels' praise; and*

may they also illuminate the Church, the land of the living, with God's praise. (Campbell, forthcoming, p.342)

Both translations were used, but given the pastoral nature of this project, Fox's translation is used more frequently due to its poetic style. Fox has made Hildegard accessible to many who would not otherwise have discovered her. However, the lack of attention to Hildegard's historical or theological context in Fox's interpretation needs to be noted. Hildegard began her work having again described God's role in having created the world and everything in it. She also emphasizes that humanity has been created in God's own image and likeness. She saw a shape similar to the egg captured in the book of *Scivias*, but described it in the shape of a wheel and protruding from this image was a man, she describes as the *Godhead*, enclosing everything within itself and exceeding everything (Fox, 1987, p. 26). It is incarnational.

In another vision Hildegard saw an image of a great wheel encompassing humanity within it, describing in detail the relationship between the physical, emotional, and spiritual nature of the human body: "The soul itself experiences the organic functions of the entire body" (Fox, 1987, p, 95). Hildegard discussed the four humors in the body in relation to the four elements of the earth. Throughout her writings (particularly in *Physica* and *Causae et Curae*) she emphasized relationship between the humors, indicating when any of the four are sick or out of harmony with the others, illness of the mind, body, or spirit results in the whole. A Jungian scholar named Clendenen (2009) stated, "The Essence of Hildegardian insight is that the physical problems are a sign of deeper imbalances within the soul" (p. 101). In Vision Three: 6 Hildegard summarized holistic health in the following way:

And again I saw that, when any of the winds of all the aforementioned qualities is stirred up in some region of the world—whether by the changing course of the sun or moon or by God's judgment, as indicated above—so that in that place

> *it emits its own blast after the air has been mutually stirred and tempered by it, that same air blows throughout the world and preserves the things that are in the world by tempering them; and according to that breeze, it grants to humankind a bit of its mutability in their humors. For when a person whose natural quality coincides with that breeze, inhales and exhales that transformed air, it is transformed within them so that they take it up into their spirit and transmit it to the inner parts of their body. So the humors that are in them are also transformed and often introduce into them either infirmity or health, as shown above.* (Campbell, forthcoming, p.117)

Hildegard used the images of air (wind) and smell (sometimes stench) to describe the condition of the humors and the overall health of the body (human or earthly). If the image smelled fragrant, it represented health (virtue); if it stunk, it represented illness (vice). In much the same way, if it was green and verdant, it represented life (virtue); if it was brown and dry, it represented death (vice).

Hildegard's Theology in a Nutshell
The core message of her visions – God created the world in light, beginning with the angels followed by the material world. God bestowed the greatest dignity and light on the angel Lucifer (translated from Latin means "light bearer"), but Lucifer did not use the gifts to serve God, but to serve himself (pride) and chose to turn from God becoming the fallen one, otherwise known as the Devil or Satan. Subsequently Lucifer's fall has negatively affected all of creation[23] necessitating the incarnation and salvific work of Christ which can only be transmitted or communicated (according to her visions) through the sacramental life of *Ecclesia, Mother Church*. Because the power of evil is so strong in the world, many souls have been conquered. However, through the *Living Light*, the soul can come to know the virtues, especially the virtue of humility (antithesis of pride) and can be redeemed. The human soul is created with the spark of *Living Light* and must continue in

---
[23] In Catholic theology this concept is called *Original Sin*.

its struggle to embrace virtue so that it may be green (*viriditas*) and fragrant.

Art - Illuminations
Thirty-five of Hildegard's forty-two theological visions are enhanced by artistic images. The illuminated images of *Scivias* are kept today in the Abbey of St. Hildegard in Rüdesheim-Eibingen. The images from *Liber Divinorum Operum* (also referred to as *Liber Operatione Dei*) are kept at the *Biblioteca Statale* in Lucca Italy.[24] There is scholarly debate regarding Hildegard's role in producing the thirty-five images (referred to as miniatures) that accompany the visions. Some scholars "distance Hildegard from the production of the miniatures" while others, such as Madeline Caviness, "have made a persuasive case for Hildegard being the ultimate source and designer of the miniatures, suggesting that during her visions she sketched designs on wax tablets" (Emmerson, 2002, p. 95). Regardless of her direct involvement, the images that accompany her visions seek to provide a visual presentation of the complex images revealed to her.

Hildegard's visions recently became the subject of analysis by Jungian psychologists due to their rich symbolism which incorporated both light and darkness of the human condition, as well as her use of mandalas which represent wholeness. Carl Jung notes that mandalas were prevalent in her visions, though she had no awareness of their existence in other faith traditions (Clendenen, 2009, p.186). Jung attributes this to her ability to descend inward (through meditation and/or her religious experience of the *Living Light*) into the world of archetypes. Hildegard acknowledged that evil exists in the world and that the

---

[24] Many of Hildegard's images are preserved at the *Abbey of St Hildegard, Rüdesheim-Eibingen*. These images are part of the *Schovias-Kodex*, also known as the "former Rupertsberg Codex" in some publications. A full list of the images preserved in this codex can be found on the Abbey of St. Hildegard website. The images from the *Liber Divinorum Operum* are held by *Biblioteca Statale, Lucca/Italy*.

individual needs to be aware of not only its existence, but the soul's tendency towards it. She did not shy away from its reality, but she embraced it. Through her experience of being formed in the Benedictine Rule (*ora et labora* and moderation in all things), she offered a number of antidotes (physical, spiritual, and psychological) to it, including prayer, music, meditative work (gardening, cooking), and regular participation in the sacramental life of the Church.

In a collection of essays edited by Newman (1998), Caviness describes her art, including the images depicting figures such as Christ, the Church, and Holy Wisdom as, "strange composites – part abstract, part figural, and even part beast" (p. 110). She suggests that the "idiosyncratic" style of art present in the thirty-five miniatures preserved reflect a style of art that would support the claim that Hildegard may have suffered from debilitating migraines before, during, and following a vision of the *Living Light*. Like her writings and her music, the manner in which Hildegard's art was created was from a divine source. The virtue of humility was the highest good to be sought after in medieval monastic life (not only in Hildegard's thought), and so suggesting her works, including her art, were the result of genius would not have been acceptable in her day, however, many are making that claim today.

One of the most well-known images of Hildegard is her self-portrait in the beginning of *Scivias* depicting the *Living Light* descending upon her[25] as she dictates her visions to her dear friend, and priest Volmar. Hildegard acknowledges her lack of formal education resulting in poor, unpolished Latin. Volmar, and her beloved nun Richardis, assisted in copying down her visions and correcting her Latin grammar. This image depicts Hildegard's staunch insistence that every bit of knowledge was endowed on her

---

[25] This is important regarding the conversation of Hildegard as a mystic. Traditionally a mystical experience was the result of focused meditation to discover the presence of the divine within. For Hildegard, this presence seems to be coming from outside of herself.

directly through a divine source. The extent of her actual education as she grew is undetermined, other than the presumption that she had access to the Benedictine library at Disibodenberg in addition to the tutoring provided by Jutta and Volmar.

Natural Medicine / Remedies
Hildegard wrote two major theological texts, *Physica* and *Causae et Curae*, on natural medicine and holistic healing remedies. For Hildegard, everything in the world is properly ordered through the lens of Catholic-Christian tradition, which was essentially the only lens she ever used. This is so important, and has been repeated, because without this lens her writings cannot reflect fully her intended message. Healing and health for her were a combination of a proper diet and proper prayer life; both were necessary.

She took seriously the story of Genesis which describes how God placed humanity in the midst of the created world giving to human beings all that they need. Viewing her scientific texts through a religious lens does not negate the use of her natural remedies outside of a religious context, because today they certainly are being used in a number of secular ways. But for Hildegard, they were intended to be used in conjunction with one's relationship with the God through the life of the Church – as part of a holistic lifestyle nourishing one physically and spirituality. Spiritual health, as she perceived it, resulted when one was living in right relationship, following the path of virtue.

Hildegard preached strongly in her homilies and some of her letters against the twelfth-century heresy of the Cathars. This was such a sensitive issue for her, and relevant to the theme of holistic health, because the Cathars taught that the material world, including human nature, was evil. Aside from the issues that it caused with Christology, it violated the very core of her understanding of what it means to be human. She believed the soul infused every part of the human body:

Then, as God wills and as he decreed it to happen, the breath of life comes and, without the mother knowing it, touches that form [the embryo] like a strong, warm wind, like a wind blowing against a wall with a roar. Thus all the differentiated limbs of this form separate sweetly from one another as a flower unfolds toward the glow of the sun... The spirit passes through the entire form, filling it completely and strengthening it in marrow and blood vessels, so that it grows...The soul itself strengthens the physical figure, vivifies and illuminates it. (Berger, 1999, pp.45-46)

As the sun is the light of the day, so too the soul is the light of the waking body. And as the moon is the light of the night, so too the soul is the light of the sleeping body. (Berger, 1999, p.67)

The saturation of the physical body with the spirit (divine light, *viriditas*), resulted in a human person created in the image and likeness of God. To deny the sanctity of the material world was incomprehensible to her. It also justified her insistence on a holistic approach to one's physical health.

The translations of her science texts that will be used for this study are Throop (1998), *Physica* and for *Causae et Curae*, Bergers (2009), *Hildegard of Bingen on Natural Philosophy and Medicine,* and Pawlik and Madigan (1994) *Holistic Health. Physica* is composed of nine sections describing various groupings within the created world, the most developed sections being plants, trees, and stones. *Causae et Curae* is roughly divided into five parts (by a later redactor) and it was composed of an explanation for the causes and remedies of human illness and disease. These two texts will be examined using the contemporary lens of Strehlow & Hertzka (1988), German medical doctors who have taken the works of Hildegard on natural nutrition and holistic health and have applied them for use in modern medicine. In their book, *Hildegard of Bingen's Medicine,* Strehlow & Hertzka (1988), Dr. Strehlow wrote:

This book is meant to be an important contribution towards bringing Hildegard medicine to the modern world. It is the result of decades of medical experience, and of scientific research and development in the field of Hildegard medicine. Over 500 remedies and methods of treatment have been tested by Dr. Hertzka and myself over the past forty years, and have proved to be successful for thousands of patients. (p.xviii)

Hildegard's natural (herbal) medicine is relatively well-known in Germany, while it remains "alternative" medicine. Many of the drug-stores and health-food stores carry Hildegard health products. The photos below are of a *Hildegardis Apotheke* (figure 11) and a line of herbal Hildegard products (figure 12) in Bingen, Germany in May 2015.

Figure 11   Figure 12

Hildegard mastered the use of natural substances; foods, herbs, and gems/precious stones. There are some scholars that suggest Hildegard was so well versed in the natural world that she used mind-altering substances to assist with her visions and her creative process (Rush, 2013, p. 92). The visions Hildegard experienced, whether induced or not, endowed her with understanding of nature and the human body beyond what she claims she learned through human experience.

Hildegard was a gifted healer and she believed that the healing power of *viriditas* was at work when a person was in union with God (resulting in a total integration of mind, body, and spirit). In her writing, *Physica,* Hildegard stated, "In all creation, trees, plants, animals, and gem stones, there are hidden secret powers which no person can know of unless they are revealed by God" (Strehlow & Hertzka, 1988, xviii). It is remarkable that Hildegard used natural elements – plants, gems, and lunar cycles – to heal in the name of Christ. So many other women (and a few men) during her time, and certainly in centuries to follow, were tortured and/or burned at the stake for doing likewise. When she was named a Doctor of the Church in 2012, the Vatican affirmed "no doctrinal error" in her writings. This certainly begs the questions, "Had she lived a few centuries later, would Hildegard have been accused of witchcraft, and most likely tortured and killed, as so many others like her were? Would her political allies have been enough to protect her?" Barstow (1994) stated:

> *Much of women's power lay in their being perceived as being able to manipulate magical forces... Denied the role of clergy or the newly emerging one of doctor*[26] *women drew on their own networks of information and skills inherited from their mothers*[27] *to serve as counselors and practitioners... In addition to empirical methods, these women depended also on rituals based on magic. Incantation, the wearing of amulets, and the repeating of charms were universal practices. In order for herbs to be efficacious, as one gathered them one must say five Lord's Prayers, five Hail Mary's and the Creed.*
> (pp.109, 114)

---

[26] This passage is referring to a time period a bit later than Hildegard.
[27] In Hildegard's case, Jutta was her spiritual mother and most likely taught her the natural healing skills she possessed.

Hildegard did not hesitate to share her faith in the power of the earth to heal, and she was respected for it. She wrote down her scientific knowledge, shared it with her sisters in the monastery, and they used it in the infirmary at Rupertsberg. This becomes all the more interesting in light of the declaration in 1130AD at the Council of Clermont prohibiting religious from engaging in the practice of medicine (Pawlick & Madigan, 1994, xv).

In the last couple of decades there has been a renewed interest in natural alternative health, creating a new interest in Hildegard's writings. She was limited by the science of her day, yet many of her observations and recommendations are surprisingly relevant and still practiced today. Hildegard used foods, plants, and gems to heal those who came to her infirmary with physical or mental illness. She did this in conjunction with prayer and music.

Her medicine was structured in accord with the commonly practiced medicine of her day which used the bodily system of humors to explain illness and disease. This system, in a nutshell, taught that nature (fire, water, wind, earth), and the elements (hot, cold, wet, dry) significantly impacted the humors (yellow bile, blood, phlegm, black bile) in the body creating one's temperament (chloric, sanguine, phlegmatic, melancholic). For Hildegard, certain foods, herbs, and gems could help to balance (or subsequently throw off balance) homeostasis in this system. She used similar techniques to what is found in Ayurvedic and homeopathic medicine today.

Music
When someone hears the name Hildegard of Bingen one of the most familiar of her talents that comes to mind is her music. Due to the work of medievalists in the last thirty years, her music became one of the earliest of her works to be translated and published. Contemporary groups including *Sequentia, Vox Anima,* and *Anonymous 4* have made her music popular and available in a number of digital formats. In 1983, an album entitled, *A Feather on the Breath of God*, won a "coveted

Gramophone award" (Maddocks, 2001, p. 189). Her music was written, composed, and sung in Latin and it is often enjoyed by listeners today unaware (due to the language barrier) that she is singing praises to God and the saints, often in the form of liturgical settings. Her music was known during her own day, and was even sung outside of Ruperstberg and Disibodenberg, possibly in Trier and in Brabant (Newman, 1988, p. 12-13). While the words that accompany Hildegard's music are exquisitely composed, her music itself cannot be described in print. It must be experienced. Unfortunately, the full experience of her music cannot be transmitted to this written text. The music of Hildegard can be organized in two major categories: the *Symphonia* (collection of hymns) the *Ordo Virtutum* (morality play).

One of the most powerful discourses of Hildegard on the divine nature of music, and her understanding of its relationship to salvation history, comes from a seething letter she wrote (23) within a few months of her death to the clergy at Mainz when an interdict of silence was imposed on her monastery:

> *Consider too, that just as the body of Jesus Christ was born of the purity of the Virgin Mary through the operation of the Holy Spirit so, too, the canticle of praise, reflecting celestial harmony, is rooted in the Church through the Holy Spirit. The body is the vestment of the spirit, which has a living voice, and so it is proper for the body, in harmony with the soul, to use its voice to sing praises to God. Whence, in metaphor, the prophetic spirit commands us to praise God with clashing symbols and cymbals of jubilation (Ps 150:5), as well as other musical instruments which men of wisdom and zeal have invented, because all arts pertaining to things useful and necessary for mankind have been created by the breath that God sent into man's body. For this reason it is proper that God be praised in all things... [we are urged] in the Psalm (ps. 32:2; 91:4) to confess the Lord with the harp and to sing a psalm to Him with the ten-stringed psaltery... Therefore, those who, without just cause, impose silence on a church and*

> *prohibit the singing of God's praises and those who have on earth unjustly despoiled God of His honor and glory will lose their place among the chorus of angel*s. (Baird & Ehrman, 1994, p. 79)

Hildegard believed music and song connected human beings to the celestial realm, to the choirs of angels, and thus to God. In addition to writing three major theological works over the course of about four decades, Hildegard wrote over seventy-three hymns[28] (sixty-nine with music and four without), mostly Mass settings and chants for the Liturgy of the Hours. The actual dates of these compositions are assumed to have been over the course of her lifetime. It has been noted that no other composer from the Middle-Ages left a corpus of music as large as Hildegard's: "She is quite simply the most prolific composer of monophonic chants known to us" (Fassler in Newman, 1998, p. 150). Hildegard titled her collection of music, *Symphonia*. This title not only referred to her understanding of musical harmony, but for Hildegard, when a person was living in "right relationship" with God, others, and the whole of creation, s/he was living in *symphonia* or harmony. It denotes total and complete harmony. A critical translation of the *Symphonia* was published by Newman (1988/1998) presenting both a literal and poetic translation of the original Latin text. Newman stated (2016)[29] that she desired to produce a freer translation in an attempt to capture the poetic style of Hildegard, however, she was cautious to stay faithful to the text and included the literal translation together with it.[30]

---

[28] There are varying opinions as to whether or not there were seventy-three or seventy-seven hymns. For the purpose of this study the text from Newman (1988) was used and she lists seventy-three.

[29] Personal conversation, April 22, 2016 in Evanston, IL.

[30] Ibid., Newman stated that recently there has been a significant increase in the amount of requests for permission to use pieces of her *Symphonia* translation in audio, video, and even literary productions. Her concern is that the requests are for the poetic translation without acknowledgment of the literal translation, giving some the impression that Newman's poetic translation is a literal translation of Hildegard's Latin text.

Of the seventy-three songs, thirteen were dedicated in honor of St. Ursula (the only other saint to have more songs dedicated in her honor by Hildegard was the Blessed Virgin Mary). It was believed (until later excavation confirmed otherwise) that the relics of St. Ursula (in part) were buried at Disibodenberg. The legendary story of this saint played a pivotal role in Hildegard's formation as a child and her understanding of the call to vowed religious life.

What was it about Ursula that inspired so much of Hildegard's music and even her visions (in her vision of Mother Church *Scivias* Book Two, Vision Five, Ursula is standing in the most revered place)? The legend of St. Ursula is of a beautiful British princess betrothed to a pagan prince. She desired to remain a "virgin for Christ" and so to delay the marriage she requested to go on a pilgrimage (with eleven-thousand virgin maidens) to Rome where it is said the pope himself joined them on their return voyage. On their return they stopped in Cologne where they were viciously attacked by Attila the Hun. Ursula, as the story goes, refused to be taken as his concubine and so she, and the eleven-thousand virgins, were martyred in Cologne. Hildegard describes Ursula's courage having come to her in a vision which she received from the *Living Light*. In Sequence 64 for St. Ursula, Hildegard wrote:

> *Ursula fell in love with God's Son in a vision: her faith was true. She rejected her man and all the world and gazed straight into the sun, crying out to her beloved, fairest of the sons of men... When Ursula had spoken all people heard her and answered: how naïve she is! The girl has no notion of what she means! And they began to mock her in harmony – until the burden of flame fell upon her... and they discovered the fragrance of incense and myrrh.* (Newman, 1988, p.241)

As often happens in Catholic practice, whether or not there is any historical evidence to support the existence of a particular saint, once a cult (the term is being used here in a positive way) has been established, it becomes very difficult to uproot it.[31] A legend quickly becomes, in the mind of many, historical fact. This may have been the case with Ursula, however, her example and courage (whether real or fictional) served as inspiration to Hildegard and inspired some beautiful hymns.

When studying the codex containing the order of hymns presumed to have been organized by Hildegard herself, Mary is placed at such an elevated role in her music. Newman (1988) stated, "By setting Mary mid-way between God the Father and the Holy Spirit, in the place where one would expect to find Christ, Hildegard was making a pointed theological statement" (p.59). The statement, according to Neman, is that Mary is not simply one of the saints, but unique as the Mother of Christ. Christ is not excluded from the hymns, rather his praises are sung together with the seven hymns to the Father, sixteen hymns to Mary, and five to the Holy Spirit. She also notes that Disibod is given a place among the ancient apostles, though he did not live until the eighth century, attesting to a strong devotion to one of her beloved patron saints; "O happy soul [Disibod], a pilgrim in this world... your crown is the mind of God which made you its mirror" (Newman, 1988, p.185).

As can be seen in her visions and art, the focus of her music is unity and harmony. Her music is written in accord with the sacred voice of Wisdom praising all of her works. In an antiphon to the Holy Spirit, Hildegard proclaims:

> *The Spirit of God is a life that bestows life,*
> *root of the world-tree and wind in its boughs.*
> *Scrubbing our sins, she rubs oil into wounds,*

---

[31] In 1964, after Vatican Council II concluded in the Catholic Church, the Catholic bishops attempted to address this issue. They removed from the official calendar of saints any individuals, for which there was no historical basis, including beloved saints Christopher and Philomena. However, Catholics were not willing to give up their saints, just as Hildegard would not be willing to give up Ursula, and so Christopher and Philomena are very much alive in the minds and hearts of most Catholics.

> *She is glistening life alluring all praise,*
> *all-awakening, all-resurrecting.* (Newman, 1988, p. 141)

This image of the Spirit of God pervading every part of the created world is drawn directly from her visions. Boyce-Tillman (2000) describes music as "a metaphor for a symphonic view of the universe in which we are surrounded and upheld by divine Love" (p. 136). For Hildegard, it was much more than a metaphor, it was the energy force that connected heaven with earth.

Viriditas (holistic greening power)

Viriditas is a concept that is simultaneously simple and steeped in mystery. It is as much about her theology as it is diet and relationship to the environment. It encompasses every aspect of our human nature – physical, spiritual, emotional. In an interview (1989) with Dr. Barbara Newman, Professor at Northwestern University and leading Hildegard scholar, she was asked about Hildegard and *viriditas*. Giggling a bit she responded:

> *Some people think she just liked the color green having grown up in the lush Rhineland valley – and she may have – but it was also a theological concept. For her it was an association between the fertility of nature and the bounty of God the Father and the Holy Spirit. If one is filled with the Holy Spirit then she is filled with viriditas.* [32]

The theme of *viriditas* (translated "greenness" or "greening power") permeates Hildegard's writings. As Newman points out, the meaning of this phrase extends far deeper than a color or even a social concept, e.g. contemporary eco-based movements. These are effects of an appreciation of *viriditas,* but they do not capture fully the essence of Hildegard's understanding of *greenness.* It is not simply something we share in; it is constitutive.

---

[32] *A Source of Inspiration* (1989) A dramatized BBC Omnibus biographical documentary. West Long Beach, NJ: Kultur

Hildegard is credited with having coined the term *viriditas*, however, she did not create it. It was present in earlier writers, including Pope Gregory the Great (540AD-604AD) who wrote; "The life of plants is called *viriditas*. They live, I say not through *anima,* but through *viriditas* (Sweet, 2006, p.125). His understanding of the nature of *viriditas* was limited to the ecological world. Hildegard took this definition and redefined it and applied it to human beings; "With earth the human being was created" (Thropp, 1998, p.9).

Hildegard understood *viriditas* in the human body in two ways – physical and spiritual. In the physical sense she believed *viriditas* was taken into the body through one's relationship with the earth (including the foods one ate). In her theological work, *Scivas,* she wrote, "And so pouring heat on him by means of *viriditas,* the earth is the carnal material of man, feeding him with her juice, just like a mother nurses her child" (Sweet, 2006, p.152). In her *Liber Divinorum Operum* she suggests *viriditas* enters the body through the food one eats, particularly the green foods (Sweet, 2006, p.152).

In her book, *Hildegard of Bingen: An Integrated Vision,* King-Lenzmeier (2001) quotes a passage from the introduction of the translation of her letters by Baird and Ehrman (1994 & 1998) which so perfectly sums up Hildegard's theology of *viriditas*:

> *Perhaps the most notable example of [her creative use of Latin] is her use of viriditas, a word never far from Hildegard's reach. This viriditas, the despairs of translators, this "greenness" enters into the very fabric of the universe in Hildegard's cosmic scheme of things. In Hildegard's usage it is profound, immense, dynamically energized term. The world in the height of the spring season is filled with viriditas, God breathed the breath of viriditas into the inhabitants of the Garden of Eden, even the smallest twig on the most insignificant tree is animated with viriditas, the sun brings the life of viriditas into the world; and (in the spiritual realm) the*

> *prelate who is filled with [weariness] lacks viriditas, the neophyte [newly baptized] must strive for viriditas, and the holy Virgin [Mary] is the viridissima virga [most green twig]. Hildegard can even speak with aplomb of a saint as the viriditas digiti Dei, "the viriditas of the finger of God," as she does of St. Disibod.* (p. 7)

Hildegard was formed in the lush greenness of Disibodenberg. This experience certainly must have had an effect on her worldview. She uses nature metaphors throughout her writings, letters, songs, and art.

Figure 13

The image above (figure 13) was taken in May 2015 from an existing wall around the ruins of Disibodenberg. While the black and white image of this view does not do it justice, the vibrant greenness that flourishes in the Rhine Valley is breathtaking. It is plausible to assume her profound sense of nature and creation may have in part been due to her having lived her life in the lush green valley of the Rhine. However, her profound respect for creation, and her theology of wholeness, extended far beyond a love for nature. She saw the created world as being the vehicle through which God interacted with humanity, not only in the event of the incarnation, but through the physical and spiritual healing that resulted from the use of plants (especially herbs), gems, water and natural cycles (e.g. the lunar cycle).

The development of Hildegard's understanding of the powerful life force present in all of the creation undoubtedly was nourished by her many years in a cloistered context. If she was an anchorite, as her *Vita* claims, she would have spent many hours in theological reflection, at times with little more to reflect upon than the world around her. The great psychologist Carl Jung (1875-1961) recorded a series of dreams that he had, one which he called, "The Anchorite." In this dream he experienced the following:

> *The life of a solitary would be cold were it not for the immense sun, which makes the air and rocks glow. The sun and its eternal splendor replace for the solitary his own life warmth...His eyes rests on the garden, and his ears listen to the source, and his hand touches velvet leaves and fruit, and his breath draws in sweet perfumes from blossom rich trees. He cannot tell you, since the splendor of his garden is so abundant... And you yourself want to be that solitary who strolls with the sun in his garden, his gaze resting on pendant flowers and his hand brushing a hundredfold of grain and his breath drinking the perfume from a thousand roses... When you grow, then you see everything living again...You also see yourself in the totality.* (Shamdasani, 2009, p. 249)

Hildegard grew up a solitary in the Benedictine Monastery of Disibodenberg. She was surrounded by the lush Rhineland with all of its vegetation and animals where she embraced the Benedictine motto, *ora et labora* (prayer and work). She would have been nourished multiple times throughout the day with music, prayer, and Scriptures, and in her context would have had very little "worldly" distractions. All of this together contributed to Hildegard's profound understanding of the constitutive nature of *viriditas* and the presence of the *Living Light.*

Viriditas and Scripture

In addition to waking up each day to green hills of the Rhine Valley, Hildegard's daily routine was deeply rooted in the Sacred Scriptures. The Benedictine Rule required prayer of the Liturgy of the Hours seven times a day. The sisters did not have "prayer books" as we have today (the printing press had not yet been invented) and so it is assumed that the Scriptures were memorized. They fully integrated the prayers into their very being. *Viriditas*, as it permeates her writings, captures the image of Jesus depicted in the Gospel of John as the one true vine:

> *I am the vine, you are the branches. Those who live in me and I in them will bear abundant fruit. Those who don't live in me are like withered, rejected branches to be picked up and thrown on the fire and burned.* (John 15:5-6a)

In her understanding, *viriditas* is the spiritual source by which all life emerges. She uses gardening and farming images throughout her writings as a metaphor to describe the role of a minister to care for the community.

In *Liber Divinorum Operum,* Vision Ten: 19, she quotes from the Gospel of Luke describing Christ, "For if men use the green wood like this, what will happen when it's dry?" (Luke 23:31) For Hildegard, the degree to which we are connected to this source is reflected in the fruit that we bear. When a person becomes ill (in mind, body, or spirit) she believed it was because s/he had become disconnected in some way from the vital source, *viriditas*. There is a fundamental need, in her writings, to stay connected deeply to the *Vine*.

This theme of God's green life (the breath of God) is prevalent throughout the Hebrew Scriptures, which would have been read each day during the Liturgy of the Hours. Beginning with the Creation accounts in the Book of Genesis through the psalms, which sing of God's glory (e.g. Psalm 19) and the need of God's ever-present breath to sustain life (e.g. Psalm 104). The continued call to "wake-up" and recognize the presence of God in every part of creation is a theme that permeates the Sacred Scriptures.[33] When the fig tree fails to produce, due to its lack of *viriditas*, Jesus curses it.

Viriditas and the Incarnation

In Roman Catholic theology sin (often rooted in pride or selfish desire) is the cause of division between the Creator and creation. It is a break in wholeness. Creation, in its original state, before Lucifer fell and brought humanity down with him, was full of *viriditas*. Sin severs one's relationship with God and others which causes a disharmony and a drying up of *viriditas*. Hildegard imparted this belief in the closing lines of her morality play, *Ordo Virtutum*. "In the beginning all creation was verdant, flowers blossomed in the midst of it; later, greenness *(viriditas)* sank away..." (Dronke, 1981,1997).[34]

Roman Catholic Theology developed out of Platonic philosophy, largely as a result of the significant impact the thought of St. Augustine had on the developing Church. From a Platonic perspective there is a clear distinction between the mind, body, and spirit (soul). For centuries the Church focused on the importance of the soul with little or no regard for the sacredness of the body (including the mind). The body was viewed as evil, especially in regards to sexuality, and to some degree nature itself became associated with evil. Hildegard's theology was quite different. She believed that every aspect of the created person was sacred and reflected something of the nature of God. The sacredness of human nature was redeemed through revelation of the incarnation of Christ. She wrote, "Hidden within in [Hebrew Scriptures] it all

---

[33] Historically there was a tendency to interpret the Scriptures in such a way that ecology was ignored or even intentionally suppressed in response to the fear within the Church of paganism or pantheism. The results of this distortion of Scripture have been environmentally and personally damaging. In recent years the Catholic Church has tried to undo that damage and reinterpret these texts through a holistic, "green" lens.

[34] http://www.oxfordgirlschoir.co.uk/hildegard/ordovirtutumtext.pdf

the green freshness of life, when the New Testament, which is like the summer, causes every kind of seed and bud to reach maturity" (Fox, 1987, p. 243). The salvation Christ brought to the created world was not intended exclusively for human beings, but for all creation. Newman (1998) stated, "Hildegard is more interested in the relationship of God to creation than in the doctrine of the Trinity as such" (p. 58).

Hildegard saw Christ as the incarnation of greenness itself. This is not to say she was preaching pantheism[35] or panentheism[36] because Roman Catholic theology, to which Hildegard strongly subscribed, would not agree with either of the above. She was steeped in medieval dogmatic teaching. But, she did preach that God is the Creator of everything, therefore God's fingerprint is in everything, which makes everything in the created world sacred. In *Liber Divinorum Operum*, she wrote:

> *Jesus himself was the green wood because he caused all the greening power of the virtues... The Antichrist, however, is the dry wood because he destroys all the living freshness of justice and causes things that should be green in their integrity to wither away... In addition, the green wood consists of the days when human beings were aware that they were healed from their suffering... For heaven and earth will be stirred up in the judgement that is to come, as was foretold by the green wood.* (Fox, 1987, p. 244)

Jung also saw the incarnation of Christ as the revelation of *viriditas*. Upon waking from a dream he recorded:

> *One night I awoke and saw, bathed in a bright light at the foot of my bed the figure of Christ on the Cross. It was not quite life-like, but extremely distinct; and I saw that his body was made of greenish gold... the green gold is the living quality*

---

[35] This is the pagan notion that God IS everything – e.g. God is a tree or a fish.
[36] This is a contemporary notion held by creation-spirituality that God is IN everything – e.g. while God is not a tree, God is in the a tree.

> *which the alchemists saw not only in man but also in inorganic nature. It is an expression of the life-spirit... The Anthropos who animates the whole cosmos... the Spirit has poured himself into everything, even into inorganic matter; he is present in metal and stone. My vision was thus a union of the Christ-image with his analogue in matter, the filius macrocosmi.* (Dunne, p.153)

This image of the "green cosmic Christ" that has emerged over the last several decades has led some contemporary thinkers to interpret Hildegard in a way that has digressed significantly from her actual understanding of Christology. As a result, Hildegard has become well-loved among many contemporary spiritual movements, primarily because of a selective presentation of her theology and holistic worldview. I say this not because I am necessarily discounting any of the contemporary movements, but as a scholar I think it is important to at least recognize historical fact and some popular interpretations do not.

On its own, *viriditas* sufficiently supports creation-based spirituality. In the book entitled, *Hildegard: Prophet of the Cosmic Christ,* Craine (2013) highlights that Hildegard saw humanity (in its wholeness – mind, body, spirit) as a microcosm of the entire universe, which is evident in Hildegard's writings. In Craine's words:

> *If each of us opens the depths of our heart to the mystery of God in the concrete events of life and then – in freedom – decides for the good, then fecundity [greenness] of cosmos and nature will proceed from this very personal act... Each personal decision affects all of us. It can contribute either to the healing of the planet or to a further shriveling up in separation, hopelessness, fear, and pollution. We are responsible not only to God and to each other but also to the elements... The term viriditas, fecundity in all of its forms, can ground the faith and hope of fellow-God seekers in a common*

> *cosmos of meaning and a lived experience of Christic-viriditas.* (pp. 75-76)

This statement by Craine reflects an aspect of Hildegard's theology, one that is healing and nurturing and inclusive. It is a beautiful statement and certainly one that captures the richness of the symbol. However, what is also evident in Hildegard's writings, and often missing from many contemporary interpretations of her holistic theology, is her conservative theology of sin/redemption and her understanding that *viriditas* is restored through the sacramental life of the Church. This is not to say communion with the Church is necessary for one to be rooted in the spirit of *viriditas*. Today the Roman Catholic Church teaches that the Spirit, (*viriditas*), animates every part of the created world and is present in every human being, not only Catholics... But, this was not the understanding of the medieval German Church, neither was it Hildegard's understanding.

For Hildegard, the fear of being excommunicated (or condemned of heresy) was equivalent to having been physically cut down from one's life source, as a plant is cut from its roots. This point is made because it is important, particularly in the academic realm, to be cautious not to reshape a historical figure, or her writings, to fit a contemporary idea.[37] While there may be a lot of value to contemporary "creation-based spirituality" movements, many have adopted Hildegard as their "poster-girl" and much of the theology is not compatible with what she herself wrote and understood in her context.

Hildegard balanced tradition (mind), nature (body), and faith (spirit) within her writings and her lifestyle. She had a unique ability to integrate wholeness into her understanding of Roman Catholicism in a way that offers leadership today a new paradigm that involves collaboration between women and men, laity and

---

[37] Hildegard is sometimes presented as an "eco-feminist" when in fact she cannot properly be described as a feminist. In some of her writings, her understanding of the nature of women would be offensive to feminists today.

ordained. Hildegard understood the unique relationship between human beings and the entire created world. She saw the presence of God, *viriditas* not only in the sacraments of the Church and in the words of Sacred Scripture, but in every drop of water, leaf, vegetable, animal and human person.

Viriditas and the Eco-Spirituality

A renewed appreciation for *viriditas* is very much needed. The natural world is suffering. Pope Benedict XVI (2007) wrote, "Creation is groaning - we can sense it, we can almost hear it…" and Pope Francis (2015) wrote a ground breaking encyclical *Laudato Si*, calling the entire world to take an honest look at the many ways the earth, and it's inhabitants, are suffering. When nature is exploited, polluted, and destroyed, the results are not only a loss of the Creator's own mode of self-revelation, but the consequences for human beings, particularly the poor, are potentially devastating. Clendenen (2009) wrote:

> *If you accept that the masses of people on earth and the earth itself is in crisis, then any sincere, intelligent, studied approach to diagnosis might just lead to a treatment plan that results in the restoration of viriditas to address and redress the drying and dying out around and within us.* (p.167)

An awareness of the fundamental need for *viriditas* offers humanity, and the whole of creation, renewal. This awareness emerges in part from contemporary eco-social movements (reduce, reuse, recycle is certainly important), but it is much more than that. It is a total commitment to living in right relationship with God, with each other, and with the entire web of creation. In Vision Two: 19 of *Liber Divinorum Operum*, Hildegard wrote:

> *If we allow ourselves to become spiritual through our awe of God, we shall also begin to revere our God by ourselves. We shall go through life in wisdom and accomplish good and just works… If meanwhile we give up the green vitality of these virtues and surrender to the drought of our indolence, so that*

we do not have the sap of life and the greening power of good deeds, then the power of our very soul will begin to fade up and dry. (Fox, 1987, p. 38)

Hildegard believed paradise, as it was when the world was first created, still exists as a physical reality. This place, in her description, is "blooming with the freshness (*viriditas*) of flowers and grass and the charms of spices, full of fine odors" (Engen in Newman, 1998, p. 56). Today's eco-movement provides an opportunity for human beings to make right the wrongs that we have inflicted on Mother Earth in order to restore proper order. This is the charge of Pope Francis' encyclical, *Laudato Si*.

Viriditas and the Integration of the Whole

The twentieth century psychologist Carl Jung and others in the Jungian school of thought have been drawn to the writings and artwork produced by Hildegard. In regards to the concept of *viriditas,* Jung wrote, "This spirit, coming from God, is also the cause of the "greenness," the *benedicta viriditas*" (Clendenen, 2009, p. 164). Jung studied Hildegard's use of the concept of *viriditas* and Jungian analysts today continue to study her writings and artwork.

One could speculate that Jung relished the discovery of *viriditas* in Hildegard's theology and cosmology because it fit so well with his convictions on the interpenetration of the psyche, nature, and spirit and human potentiality to become whole" (Clendenen, 2009, p. 164). Carl Jung's psychology was deeply rooted in the integration of opposites – *anima* and *animus,* light and dark, good and evil. He recorded a series of dreams, one of which he descends into hell in order to ascend into wholeness. Hildegard used lots of images in her writings depicting the Devil and the dark side of human experience and Jung's interpretation helps to put her visions into perspective.

In his *Redbook*, Jung wrote; "To journey to Hell means to become Hell oneself. It is all frightfully muddled and interwoven"

(Shamdasani, 2009, p. 156). In her visions Hildegard journeys to Hell on a number of occasions. She describes these experiences as lacking in viridity, or moisture. For Jung, and Hildegard, "Taking the devil seriously does not mean going over to his side, or else one becomes the devil. Rather it means coming to an understanding" (Shamdasani, 2009, p. 218). The mystic is painfully aware that it is only through this difficult journey that *viriditas* sprouts like a "green seed from dark earth" (Shamdasani, 2009, p. 133) and one becomes whole.

Carl Jung, like Hildegard, used gardening metaphors to describe the spiritual journey. Regarding creativity, Jung (1875-1961) wrote:

> *I also had to detach myself from my thoughts through turning my desire away from them. And at once, I noticed that myself became a desert, where only the sun of unquiet desire burned. I was overwhelmed by the infertility of this desert...If your creative force now turns to the place of the soul, you will see how your soul becomes green and how its field bears wonderful fruit.* (Shamdasani, 2009, p. 142).

In her text, *The Creative Spirit: Harmonious Living with Hildegard of Bingen,* Boyce-Tillman (2000), wrote, "God is continually becoming incarnate in the process of renewal... We can participate in this by collaborating creatively. When we undertake a creative act we become *green*" (p. 175). Wholeness produces health (mind, body, spirit) which in turn brings forth fruit, "By their fruits you will know them" (Matthew 7:16).

Viriditas and Fertility

Hildegard used the theological term *viriditas* in reference to human reproduction. Hildegard saw the reproductive system as intrinsically sacred. This is profound for a time in the Church's history when women's bodies, especially women's reproductive systems were considered unclean - and to some degree this is still the case! She did not see the menstrual cycle as a source of shame, but a source of life. In her text *Causes et Curae* she wrote:

> *The menstrual flow of a woman is her greening viriditas, her flowering, because just like a tree by its viriditas produces flowers and leaves and fruits, so a woman by the viriditas of menstruation brings forth flowers and leaves as the fruit of her womb... Just as a tree does not bear if it lacks viriditas, so an old woman who does not have the viriditas of her flowering can no longer bear children.* (Sweet, 2006, p. 150)

Menstruation or other aspects of the female reproductive system had not been embraced by religious systems as sacred for centuries. Hildegard's presentation was unique, not only for her time, but for the periods preceding and following.

Another example of how Hildegard took the concept of *viriditas* and applied it to human nature is in her understanding of its relationship to human sexuality. She is often very blunt in her description of the human body and how the reproductive system is effected by *viriditas* (or lack of it), however, in some instances she uses gardening metaphors which reflect an idea of *viriditas* to get her point across (not only in regards to sexuality, but throughout her writings and letters on many different topics). In a commentary on *Causes et Curae,* Berger (1999) wrote:

> *The description of the male sex organs is explicit, but relies on metaphor. In place of the standard medical term virga "penis", Hildegard uses stirps "stem". Both expressions share the semantic link between vegetation and human reproduction. The reason for not using virga in the established medical sense may be that virga "rod, twig, bow", together with associated images of greenness, blossom, and growth is central to Hildegard's lyrics (e.g. O viridissima virga*[38]*).* (p. 141)

Viriditas, for Hildegard, is a much more than the color green; it is the ongoing incarnation of life itself. Whether she uses the word

---

[38] The title in this hymn refers to the Virgin Mary.

itself or a metaphor which captures its essence, her writings are, in every sense, green.

Viriditas and Eco-Feminism

For Hildegard, the concept of *viriditas* calls us to fully identify as one with God through our relationship to the created world. The source of every aspect of creation – nature, human sexuality, creativity – is green. It is the *viriditas* of God that not only brings us into this world but sustains us. How can we grow in our appreciation for nature, and for the sacredness of *viriditas*? Catholic scholar, Johnson (1993) stated:

> *Our intelligence needs to be converted to the earth, as does our heart, and this involves several turnings at once. We must change from an anthropocentric, androcentric view of the world to a biocentric, life-centered one. We must leave a dualistic model for a kinship one, seeing every creature linked to each other and to God in the dance of the universe. We must transform a culture that is spreading death to one that cherishes life. Simply put, all of us, women and men alike, need to fall in love with the earth as an inherently valuable, living community in which we participate, and be creatively faithful to it.* (p.62).

In regards to ecclesial leadership, the imbalance of male / female has led to a "drying and dying out" of *viriditas*. There is an increased awareness of the need to integrate women, and women's spirituality, into the male hierarchy. Her newly appointed status as a Saint and Doctor has opened up the door to new ideas regarding leadership in the Church. Rev. Mathew Fox (an ex-Roman Catholic priest and avid opponent of Pope Benedict XVI) wrote:

> *When Hildegard enters the well-guarded and thick patriarchal gates of the Vatican as Saint and Doctor of the Church, she brings many surprises with her just like the Trojan Horse of old… Hildegard is sure to lead the charge…on behalf of the return of the proper balance of the Divine Feminine and a*

> *healthy and Sacred Masculine... She is a herald of a new spiritual consciousness who will not be ignored, just as she wasn't silenced in her day..."* (Fox, 2012, pp.128-130)

Hildegard most certainly has penetrated the thick walls of patriarchy, as a flower occasionally finds a way to sprout beneath the concrete. Her understanding of the concept of *viriditas,* has the potential to heal for it is the greening power, the eternal life source. This interconnectedness between spirituality and the created world was prominent in Hildegard's theology and is evident throughout her works.

Ordinate Feminas

The most reverend and divinely favored deaconess Olympias,[39] I John, Bishop, send greetings in the Lord. – St. John Chrysostom

Write down what you see and hear. – St. Hildegard, Scivias

The journey of faith is a difficult one. We often find ourselves striving to walk in the footsteps of Christ not really knowing where we are going or why we are headed in a given direction. We walk by faith, yet inevitably we will stumble along the way. From the outside looking in it often seems as though the spiritual person, especially if s/he is a respected leader in the community, can see clearly the path God is calling her/him to walk. Most often, however, it is quite the opposite. There is a story told of Mother Theresa that captures the complex nature of discipleship. The world saw her as a holy woman, which she was, who seemed to know exactly what task God was calling her to embrace. She stood strong in her conviction to care of the poor and minister to the outcasts, the untouchables in the poorest areas of India. She seemed to know intimately the love of God and she shared God's love with others. From the outside looking in, she had it all together. Sure her call was difficult, but she must have felt the ongoing presence of God in her midst. Otherwise, how could she have persevered for so long? Following her death Mother Theresa's journal revealed something that had been hidden from most of the world. For almost fifty years of her life, throughout much of her ministry, she stated she could not feel the presence of God. She continued to walk the journey, following in the footsteps of Christ, without really knowing if God was even with her. What a profound testament of faith.

---

[39] Olympias the Deaconess was the recipient of seventeen of St. John Chrysostom's letters. She is referred to as his most "imminent female friend" and the theological content of his letters to her, at times seeking her insights, reflect a level of respect equal to a member of the clergy.
http://www.newadvent.org/fathers/1916.htm

Mother Theresa's feeling are not unique, we have all had moments in our life when we have felt God must have forgotten about us. Situations when we are trying to respond to what we perceive as our call, without really knowing if we are on the right path. Every spiritual person has at some point questioned God's will in her/his life. That is the reason formation, spiritual direction, and the discernment process are necessary. When the "dark nights" surface, there is always a temptation to walk away from the journey. Even Jesus experienced it when he resigned himself to the desert for forty days to discern the task God was calling him to embrace. The temptations brought before him – power, riches, comfort – were in fact very real temptations. Jesus knew what the consequences of his life would be if he chose the path of justice. Even at the moment of his Passion, as he prayed in the garden, Jesus asks for the cup he has been given to be taken from him. He doesn't feel at that moment that he has the strength to walk the road to Calvary. And of course as he hung on the cross he cries out in despair feeling as though God had in fact abandoned him. Jesus, however, at every stage continued on his journey, trusting that God had not, would not, have abandoned him.

For me, my darkest night came during the second semester of my D.Min studies and about half-way through the pastoral ministry certification process, which I mentioned previously. I had been plugging along successfully for a while, having had completed a BA in religious studies and then a MA in theology at the seminary while successfully enduring a number of storms within the parish and community. The road that had led up to this point in my journey was difficult, but I had always I felt confident that with the grace of God I could handle it, and I had. I believed that love could conquer all else and I truly had fallen in love with the community of St. Anthony's and Fairport Harbor and so that is where I placed my faith and drew my strength. I honestly thought my most difficult days were past.

Several incidents culminated in the late part of 2009/early part of 2010 that had pushed me into what would certainly become a pivotal moment in my journey. For a while I could not see any direction to where I was going. In the words of Hildegard, "even the light had gone." I felt, for the first time in a long time, absolutely lost. I tried to recapture the feeling I had felt that sunny morning on my front porch in 1998, but it was gone. I felt angry, lost, confused and seriously questioned the path I had chosen. It was a culmination of some very negative experiences I had over the years with some of the seminarians and a few priests, the realization that I was quickly running into a "glass ceiling" regarding my leadership opportunities in the parish, and my frustration with the fact that women could not be admitted to ordained ministry within the Roman Catholic Church. The feelings I had struggled with a decade earlier had resurfaced. I had made a concentrated effort to accept things as they were, including my subordinate role. Through many seminary classes I understood well the reasons why the Church was holding tight to its teaching on the non-admittance of women to the priesthood, and I respected the official mandate prohibiting Catholic ministers and teachers from discussing it. However, I had spent years studying Scripture and the writings of the early Church Fathers and I came to learn, without a doubt, that there were women deacons in the early Church – and they preached.

In his letter to the Romans St. Paul introduces Phoebe as a deacon and St. John Chrysostom often wrote to his dear friend Olympias, whom he addressed as a deaconess. These are only two women in a very long line of female deacons within the Catholic tradition. St. Mary Magdalene, remembered falsely for over a century as a prostitute, as a result of the poor Scripture scholarship of Pope Gregory the Great in the 6th century. Prior to the 6th century she was referred to by the Church Fathers as the *Apostola Apostolorum – The Apostle to the Apostles*. After Vatican Council II the Church Fathers affirmed that there is no historical evidence to support Mary Magdalene had been a prostitute. She was, as Pope Benedict XVI described her in a Wednesday address (February 14, 2007), the *Apostola Apostolorum*. Her description in the Roman Calendar of Saints was changed from "penitent" to "disciple" and just this past year Pope Francis elevated her Feast on July 22nd from a Memorial to a Liturgical Feast Day. She was one of Jesus' closest friends and his most faithful disciple. Her story, however, was severely distorted as it was preserved by a patriarchal institution, to the extent that most Catholics immediately think of a reformed prostitute when her name is mentioned. I once gave a presentation to a large group of adults on Mary Magdalene and explained to them why we need to remember her as a faithful disciple, and not as a penitent sexual sinner. The consequences of having distorted her image have been detrimental to female ministers. At the conclusion of my presentation a young priest stood up and told the group, "But, if you want to remember Mary Magdalene as a prostitute that's okay too." It most certainly is not okay to distort her historical character for a patriarchal agenda. We don't remember Peter as a perpetual sinner – though he denied the Lord three times. We remember Peter as a Rock. He has been exonerated. She deserves the same. While we are all in need of God's mercy and forgiveness, preserving her memory as that of a prostitute, without any historical evidence to support it, diminishes her role as a leader.

Mary Magdalene was one of the few disciples who stood by Jesus at the foot of the cross and at the tomb. She demonstrated enormous courage, unlike the male disciples who fled and hid in fear. Though women are prohibited from preaching under normal circumstances at Eucharistic celebrations today, Mary Magdalene preached the first Easter homily. She was the first witness to the empty tomb and the person Jesus commissioned to preach the resurrection to the male disciples. In 2007 even the Eastern Orthodox Church reinstated the female diaconate because of the overwhelming evidence that there were female deacons in the early Church. As I thought more deeply about it I became very angry with the way women are prohibited from functioning in any level of ordained ministry, including the diaconate, today. And so I pulled out of the pastoral ministry formation program and the D.Min program in order to take some time to discern if I was being called to a denomination where I might be called to serve as an ordained minister. The ground beneath me was becoming shaky.

When one looks through the Scriptures at the various people God has called to a task, women and men, saints and sinners, a common theme emerges with all of them. God's call, regardless of who you are, shakes things up. In her book, *A Mythical Life*, Houston (1996) wrote the following:

> *We exist on a flimsy spur of local consciousness overlooking the great expanse of being. Whenever we get shaken up or shaken loose, whether it be by going mildly mad or by exploding with paroxysms of God-awesome knowing, the surface crust of consciousness breaks like crackling ice and we fall into the depths from which we came. The habits of a lifetime, even one's most esteemed accomplishments, can dissolve in the waters of these depths. Consider what happened to Thomas Aquinas. There he was at the summit of his career, having produced works that addressed ever possible moral, theological, and philosophical question. This man of huge body and intellect, weighing, it is said, almost four hundred pounds, would sit on his poor donkey, with two secretaries riding at either side of him, dictating his Summa while eating endless bologna sandwiches. Who could be more substantive and certain than Thomas? Then, while celebrating Mass in a Neapolitan Church he had such a profound experience of unitive depth that he was unable to write, talk, or even tell of his experience – or much anything else for that matter. His good friend comes and begs him to tell him what happened. Thomas finally replies, "Reginald, I cannot. For what I have seen makes all of my work seem mere straw." Many have had this experience, some by virtue of grace, others by years of search and inner discipline, others by taking one or another journey of transformation...* (pg. 71)

Each of us must continuously engage in ongoing theological reflection and personal assessment. The will of God in our lives changes as we grow in grace and wisdom. It is easy, especially for a minister – lay and ordained, to feel s/he has a lock on God and God's will, when in fact we never really do. Through my MA in Ministry studies at another local Catholic institution I found myself graced with an opportunity to be propelled into a depth, as Houston described it, of unknowing. This gave me a chance to not only spend an entire semester studying the theology and liturgical practice of the Anglican / Episcopalian Church, but to really assess who I am and if it reflected the person God had created me to be. During my period of "mild madness" I met with the rector of the Episcopal cathedral, a holy woman and female priest. She imaged for me a *persona Christi*. In one of our conversations she asked me a very important question. "Do you feel you are being called to the Episcopal Church because this is who you are or are you running from something in the Catholic Church? Maybe God is calling you to be Roman Catholic in a new way." She left our conversation with the assurance that she would be willing to recommend me to the vocation office immediately if in fact I felt this is where God was calling me. But her question had penetrated something deep within. As I spent the rest of the semester studying and learning about Anglicanism I realized it is a beautiful tradition. It encompassed almost everything I loved about the Roman Catholic Church and they ordain women! It was in many ways a dream come true and was so tempting. However, deep down I knew in my heart I was running from something. I am not Anglican/Episcopalian, as much as I might sometimes wish to be! I am a Roman Catholic. In addition, there was one very big piece that kept calling me back - the community of St. Anthony's and Fairport Harbor. I could not bring myself to leave the people that I so dearly love. I discerned that what I needed was not to "jump ship" and go to another denomination, though I would be lying if I didn't say it was really attractive. What I needed was a renewal of my vocation within my own tradition, which is what this time away, the dark night experience, had given me. I felt renewed and reenergized. I reapplied to the D.Min program and the pastoral ministry formation program and was warmly reaccepted into both.

When I resurfaced at the seminary I was greeted with love and compassion by the directors in both programs. I jokingly thanked them for taking me back without "throwing me on the rack" first. With my motivation renewed I completed the pastoral ministry program within my original time frame and the D.Min program a semester early (even though I had taken a full semester off!) I came back to the programs aware that the same problems and injustices existed, but my anger had healed. I was ready to be Catholic in a "new way" and was able to again embrace the task I had been called to so many years earlier. I sincerely felt joyful.

Making up for lost time (really only one semester), I dove right into my studies and within a very short period of time met and fell in love with St. Hildegard of Bingen. I realized at that moment she had brought me back to the place where I belong. She would not let me "jump ship" and so I committed myself to walking my faith journey, regardless of how challenging it might be, with her. Hildegard of Bingen did not advocate for women's ordination to the priesthood. She actually wrote against it. Though she saw herself, as did others, as equal in dignity and authority, at times surpassing, that of the male clergy. Nonetheless, she felt her call to be a prophetic voice in the Church was because the clergy had been negligent in their role as leaders.

Priesthood and the role of the priest were defined differently in medieval Germany than they are today. For example, only a priest or bishop can now hear confession. In medieval times, however, a female abbess was granted permission to hear confession and absolve sin (Macy, 2008, pg. 41). It wasn't until the 13th century that the Church decided this ministry would be reserved for priests and bishops (ordained men) alone. It was also astounding that Hildegard was given permission by the Catholic hierarchy to go on four significant preaching tours in major cathedrals including Mainz and Cologne preaching not only to the laity but to the clergy. There are several instances where bishops or abbots wrote follow-up letters to her asking for a copy of the homily she preached because it had such a powerful impact on the clergy in a particular area. She wrote hundreds of letters advising clergy on issues involving theology, liturgy, and conduct. Hildegard's advice and prayers were sought by kings, popes, and many other people of authority. It cannot be assumed that when Hildegard wrote against the possibility of women priests that she was writing against female ministerial leaders, because she herself was a very strong female voice of authority in the Church, then and now. Her notion of priesthood was tied almost exclusively to the consecration of Eucharist which she felt needed to be reserved for an ordained man. So, what do I think about women's ordination?

Pope Francis has again opened up the conversation of exploring the possibility of reinstating the female diaconate. Pope Paul VI explored this question as well. The reality is, and Cardinal Walter Kasper has stated it at times as well (although not positively); women are already functioning in diaconal roles. Women have always functioned in these roles. Women are validly preaching and ministering and working as co-workers with the priests and bishops in dioceses across the globe, especially in areas where there are "priestless" parishes. While the non-admittance of women to any level of ordained ministry has been a great disservice to the Church, especially when women are invested so heavily in the life and mission of the Church, we find ourselves in a time of hope.

I cannot receive the indelible mark of ordination. The Church does not ordain women. However, I am deeply engaged in diaconal work. I dealt with my frustration by getting a tattoo, a symbol of an indelible mark, on my left foot which reads *ordinate feminas* because I believe women should be ordained to the diaconate. Not necessarily into the exact ministry that exists today – again, you can't put new wine into old wineskins – but ordained to a level of ministry that is in right relationship with the needs of the community and the call being felt by so many women. I do not accept the schismatic ordination of women in Roman Catholic groups that have broken away from the Church. To continue to divide Christ's body is a scandal. At the same time, I believe the

Holy Spirit is calling the Catholic hierarchy to reinstate women's ordination to the diaconate. Hildegard repeatedly warned the clergy of the spiritual consequences that result when the institution allows its own agenda to prohibit the movement of God's Spirit.

I believe that the Church will someday, most likely in our lifetime, admit women to the ordained ministry of the diaconate because I have faith in the power of the Holy Spirit in the Church. Jesus sent women out to preach and teach and minister. The early Church celebrated the role of female deacons and the Church of the Middle Ages embraced the strong leadership of Abbesses. Women leaders are a very crucial part of our Church's history. Women deacons are an integral part of our tradition, even if over the years they have been forgotten.

Is there a possibility I will be ordained someday? Most likely - no. Not unless I go elsewhere. When I made the decision to renew my commitment to the Roman Catholic Church I did so fully aware that I will spend the rest of my days as a lay ecclesial leader and I am at peace with that. I am exactly where God has called me to be. I am a "Moses leader" invested in doing what I can, in my context, to help bring the community to a new experience of Church. While well aware that I most likely will never be able to fully enter into the experience myself.

I am the person that I am today in large part because I developed within the Church. I have questioned, doubted, struggled, been hurt, and at times been pretty angry, but it is still my home and my family and I have committed myself to its mission. Out of respect for the magisterial teaching I am not a visible advocate for women's ordination, especially to the priesthood. But I do believe the Church needs to reinstate the female diaconate. The "indelible mark" on my foot is my prayer that someday it may come to fruition. It reminds me of my call to walk the difficult journey of faith, trusting in God's divine providence even in situations where human agendas sometimes get in the way. It also reminds me that I am walking on "holy ground" with so many other holy women.

Back to Hildegard
The homilies and letters of St. Hildegard capture her polished gift for preaching. She stood steadfast in her call to be a trumpet for God, risking serious consequences at times from the male leaders in the Church. She made it her business to "shake things up" and she did it well.

Preaching
When assessing the literary canon of Hildegard, a significant collection that emerges is her collection of homilies. Women are not permitted, under normal conditions,[40] to preach in the Catholic Church. The ministry of preaching is tied tightly to ordained ministry which, as mentioned above, is forbidden to women. In a study on lay pastoral ministers in Roman Catholic administration, Wallace (1992) recorded the following testimony from a female "pastor" interviewed about her experience with a seminary priest who had, with good intentions, invited her to come and "talk" at a Mass to share the ministry she was doing. When there is a situation where a woman is invited to preach, there is resistance among the clergy to actually call it preaching. The following interview describes an experience similar to what most female lay ecclesial ministers have had when asked to preach:[41]

---

[40] "Normal conditions" translated implies if there are male preachers available. In many part of the world, including here in the U.S., women are commissioned and functioning as preachers in places where there is a shortage of ordained clergy. Wallace (1992), completed a study on the role of women preachers/parish administrators in the U.S. in her book *They Call Her Pastor*.

[41] This is always the case when I am asked to "preach". The presiding priest will get up and say a few words on the Gospel, even though I too will be preaching on it, so that there will not be any accusations made that "Father let a woman preach." Often at a communal penance service I will be asked to preach because it is not Mass and the rite allows for a lay person to function in this type of para-liturgy. However, whenever one of the priests is scheduled it is announced that Father____ will be preaching. When I am scheduled, it is always announced that Dr. Sterringer will be offering a reflection.

He didn't say, "Preach." He said, "Talk about what you are doing." And I said, "When am I doing this, at the lunch?" And he said, "No, at Mass." I said, "What time in the Mass?" And he said, "Well, at the homily time." I said, "You say I'm preaching, then." "Well, no," he said, "I can't." I said, "I can't speak after the gospel without preaching or addressing. I can't just get up and talk about something that is divorced from the gospel..." So he said, okay, he would stand up and say something. So he did. And then nobody could stand up and say [a woman] preached at the seminary. Father _____ said three or four sentences first. (p.127)

This historical ban on women preachers is astounding, given the reality that some of the earliest biblical preachers were women; The Samaritan Woman (John 4), Mary (Luke 1:46-55), Phoebe the Deaconess (Romans 16:1), and of course Jesus commissioning Mary Magdalene to go and preach to the male disciples that Christ had risen (John 20:18). Mary Magdalene preached the first Easter homily, yet for centuries women have only officially been permitted to offer "reflections" or give talks. However, on occasion women have been able to break through the institutional boundaries, like Hildegard did, and have received permission to preach. Today, Pope Francis as affirmed that women have permission to preach at "para-liturgies" or word services, but not at a Eucharistic liturgy.

It is commonly understood that for a woman of the twelfth century to presume to have the gift of preaching, without ecclesial approval, risked being condemned a heretic and possibly even burned on a pyre. Hildegard, however, not only dared to preach, but was granted permission by the hierarchy to go on four preaching tours to some of the great cathedrals including Mainz and Cologne. How could a woman be granted this privilege? It is assumed Hildegard's reputation and political connections provided this privilege. However, there are some historical scholars suggesting that this was far more common in the twelfth-century than presumed. In a book entitled, *The Hidden History of*

Women's Ordination, Macy (2008) suggested that the role of religious women in the Middle Ages was far more powerful than it is remembered in traditional historical accounts. Medieval female saints, such as Hildegard, are often portrayed with a staff (crosier) which is carried today only by a bishop as a sign of his authority. Abbesses, according to Macy, were often ordained (although their function was not necessarily equal to the function of ordained clergy today), and as part of that office she would have been given permission to "instruct" women and men in the faith. Even in light of Macy's solid argument, the extent to which Hildegard was able to travel and preach was extraordinary for a woman at that time, especially with the blessing of the Church. Hildegard's preaching was apocalyptic, as was her visions. For example, in a homily preached against the Cathar heresy she described those who adhered to the Catharism as:

> *The very bowels of that unnatural beast which coughs up and spits out the most disgusting impurity. And just as the prophets preceded the Lord and prophesied the way of salvation, demonstrating that he was filled with all of the virtues of justice, so too do these precede the beast, embracing the filth and wickedness of all evils, going the way of the errant... The Devil fills these people with blasphemy, wickedness, and the falseness of all evil.* (Baird & Ehrman, 1998, p. 123)

Her homilies were filled with "fire and brimstone" often directed at the sins of the clergy and heresy. A comprehensive reading of her homilies would definitely halt most Catholic movements today in the area of ecumenism. She rails against any group teaching or following a faith outside of orthodox Catholic teaching. Based on her reaction to the Cathars, it is a stretch to assume she would "throw off the yoke of the magisterium" to embrace some of the more contemporary, non-Christian movements that have recently assumed her into their movement.

Hildegard's nuns collected and preserved fifty-eight of her homilies in a work entitled, *Expositiones Evangeliorum*, which today is in the Riesenkodex, in Wiesbaden, Hessische Landesbiblothek. Kienzle (2011) claimed, "They [the collection of homilies] establish Hildegard as the only known female systematic exegete of the Middle Ages" (p.2). Hildegard's homilies were referred to with praise in the late fifteen century by an abbot Johannes Trithemius (1462-1516AD) who stated she preached on texts that were "obscure" and could only be understood by someone "learned and devout" indicating she was a skilled homilist (Kienzle, 2011, pp.1-2).

Homilies in Hildegard's Letters
In addition to having her homilies preserved in a collection, some of them were sent to individual or communities, by request, in later letters. The literary style of the homilies preserved in the letters is different from those preserved in her collection. These homilies do not adhere line by line to a scriptural text, but are exhortations on certain pastoral issues, particularly the sinful nature of the clergy and the Church.

For example in a letter (149) the priest Werner, around 1170AD, requested a copy of a sermon she preached while in Kirchheim condemning the corruption and sinful behavior of the hierarchy. She responds to Werner by sending him a copy of the homily (149r). The homily tells of a vision, similar to that in *Scivias*, where Hildegard saw a beautiful woman, representing the Church. The woman, though dazzling, was covered in dirt. She spoke to Hildegard:

> *Those who nurtured me – the priests, that is to say – were supposed to make my face glow like the dawn, my clothes flash like lightening, my cloak gleam like precious stones, and my shoes to shine brightly. Instead they have smeared my face with dirt, they have torn my garment, they have blackened my cloak, and they have soiled my shoes. The very ones who were supposed to beautify me with adornments have all failed miserably. This is the way they soil my face: They take up and handle the body and blood of my Bridegroom while defiled by*

the uncleanliness of their lustful morals, poisoned by the deadly venom of fornication, and adultery, and corrupted by the avarice rapine of buying and selling improper things. They encompass His body and blood with filth, like someone putting a child in the mud among swine. (Baird & Ehrman, 1998, p.92)

The priest Werner requested the homily in order that he, and the clergy entrusted to his care, could "keep it ever before our eyes, lest we forget" (Baird & Ehrman, 1998, p. 91).

In another letter (15) around 1163AD , Phillip, at the time dean (but later named Archbishop of Cologne 1167AD), requested a copy of the homily she preached in the cathedral in Cologne:

Because we esteem your maternal piety, we want to inform you that after your recent visit to us, at God's command when, through divine inspiration, you revealed the words of life to us, we were greatly astonished that God works through such a fragile vessel, such a fragile sex, to display the great marvels of His secrets... We request that you commit to writing and send us those things that you said to us earlier in person, since given over as we are to carnal lusts, we all too readily ignore spiritual matters, neither seeing or hearing them. (Baird & Ehrman, 1994, p.54)

The sermons requested of Hildegard by various clergy indicate that in the twelfth century the Church sanctioned the preaching ministry of a woman.

Hildegard preached adamantly against the heresy of the Cathars. Logan (2002) outlines the movement as having begun in France, reaching the German Rhineland (Cologne) around the 1140's and by the 1160's were in Mainz, "where they came to the attention of Hildegard of Bingen, who sent an anti-Cathar sermon to Mainz in 1163AD" (Logan, 2002, p. 203). They were a serious threat to Catholicism. Their basic belief system (though it varied across regions) was dualistic. They saw the material world as evil and embraced extreme spiritual asceticism. For the Cathars, the soul was where God resided; the body was where Satan resided. They rejected the sacraments of the Church because they represented body and blood and were communicated through material elements; bread and wine. This teaching was in direct contrast to Hildegard's holistic understanding of God's abiding nature in the mind, body, and soul. In a homily written around 1171AD, entitled, *A Sermon on the Perverse Doctrine of Heretics*, Hildegard presents, from a vision of the *Living Light*, a cosmic journey through creation. She affirms the biblical teaching, "God formed man in His image and likeness, and he is His work and the garment of His divinity" (Baird & Ehrman, 2004, p. 170). She goes on to describe the relationship between the body and the soul – they are not exclusive of one another as the Cathars claimed – but intimately bound together:

> *The soul works through the body, and the body through the soul, and the soul is the viridity of the body... The soul is suffused throughout the body, and through rationality it serves the body, ministering to its appetites and nourishment... But those people who are called heretics... deny the most sacred humanity of the Son of God and reject the sanctity of His body and blood in the oblation of bread and wine... Thus like a viper he [the Devil] gnaws at all sanctity and honor of God with such people as his agents [the Cathars], and they follow him.* (Baird & Ehrman, 2004, p. 171, 173)

Hildegard's preaching against the Cathars was a testament to her strong faith in Roman Catholic doctrine. She was holistic and embraced creation as good and sacred (which was a bit radical for her time), but she did not budge on doctrinal issues involving issues of morality and faith. Her strong convictions regarding the teaching of the Church, captured in her actual writings, directly challenge some contemporary presentations of her theology, modeled by Matthew Fox. She was tough and she blamed the rise of heresy, not on the teachings of the Church, but on the laxity of the clergy. In Hildegard's mind, if the priests were living holy lives, and were modeling authentic leadership, there would be no need for heretical movements.

Trumpet of God

Hildegard's role as a preacher was prophetic. She called it as she saw it, regardless of the consequences. That took a lot of courage in her day and it continues to take a lot of courage today. She railed against injustice with words on fire with the Spirit. She was so confident in her call to preach, it could not be contained to Church sanctioned preaching tours, but it permeated her letters as well. When the abbot of Disibodenberg, Helengerus (successor to the abbot Kuno), sent a letter to Hildegard attempting to make peace between the two monasteries she responded with a powerful sermon (77r) warning him (and the monks) to head her words lest "God strike you with His terrible vengeance" (Baird & Ehrman, 1994, p.171). She did not hesitate to rebuke anyone, especially clergy, when she perceived they were failing to follow the Gospel.

For example, in letter (252) to an unknown abbot, Hildegard wrote:

Wisdom says, No one can call a cloud and the terrors of the storm "heaven." Here is the meaning of these worlds. Whoever willfully and avariciously seizes a pastoral office like a thief is by no means to be called "father." Such people act like Samaritans, who were divided into two parts, the one with idols, the other with the Old Law. One must immediately flee such things, and become a companion of the little ones of God. These worlds should be heeded! (Baird & Ehrman, 2004, p.50)

In another letter (261) to an unknown abbot, she wrote:

O shepherd, why do you shrivel and dry up amid the sweet aroma of balsam, that viridity which is to be offered to foolish minds that do not have the breasts of maternal   compassion to suck? When they do not have such comfort they grow weak. Give them the lamp of the King so that these, your sheep, are not scattered in adversity. Rise up in the Light. (Baird & Ehrman, 2004, p.56)

And in another letter (263) to an unnamed prelate she stated, "The present time [in the Church] is not a 'time of healing', but because of its serpentine morals... the age is full of sorrows resulting from its wounds... For the Church has been stripped of its righteous standing"[42] (Baird & Ehrman, 2004, p.57). She understood the serious responsibility of ecclesial leadership. The lax and unethical behavior of the clergy infuriated her and she did not hesitate to share it.

Correspondence
The most vivid picture of Hildegard shines not in her theological works, music, or even in her *vita*, but in her letters. She was a prolific letter writer and so much of her personal thought and feeling is captured in the letters.[43] Her theological works reflect what she was commanded to write down as it was revealed to her by the *Living Light*. Her letters, however, capture her personality, and some aspects of her life. Some of her letters reflect the wisdom and gentleness of a loving mother. Other letters are scathing criticisms of corrupt political and religious power. And some capture moments of human pain and weakness, such as she experienced with the loss of her beloved nun Richardis.

Hildegard not only wrote to many people (men and women) of very high ranking, but they wrote to her, at times initiating the

---

[42] This is a statement that captures the sentiment of the Catholic Church in the last several decades following years of "serpentine morals" which came to light in the sex abuse scandals. She uses the image of the "garments of the Church" being sullied by sin, yet she stated that the "Church is still faithful to her bridegroom" making it possible to restore righteousness and goodness, if the people are willing to be cleansed. The Catholic Church is not yet in a "time of healing" because it still has not fully taken responsibility (been cleansed) of the sins it committed. Hildegard's prophetic words, over eight-centuries old, come across as if they were written for today.

[43] Ferrante (in Newman, 1998) states that the letters reveal very little about Hildegard's feelings or life (p.92). However, the letters paint a profound picture of her thoughts, feelings, and even life events. Not necessarily in a systematic order, such as is recorded in her *Vita*, but offers an alternate lens.

conversation. Over four-hundred letters are preserved today in the Riesenkodex, which is believed by scholars to have been organized by her last secretary, the monk Guibert of Gembloux. The translator of her letters, Joseph L. Baird and Radd K. Ehrman spent years immersed in the project resulting in a three-volume set of letters published from 1994-2004 with introductory commentary. They organized the corpus of correspondence, not chronologically, but by theme and importance. Baird (2006) compiled a smaller work, *The Personal Correspondence of Hildegard of Bingen* including only seventy-five of her most important letters. There was a desire, even early on, to collect and preserve the correspondence. In a letter from the monk Guibert (109) around 1177AD, he asked for her to accompany him in this task:

> *Would you please send the present letter back to me, and whatever letters I or the brothers of Villers have sent to you at various times up to the present. For it is my intention to gather all of our letters, yours to me and mine to you, into one volume and to preserve them, not only for my consolation but also as a means of exciting divine wonder for His gifts to me in those who will be chance design to read them.* (Baird & Ehrman, 1998, p.48)

Most Hildegard scholars assume the authenticity of her letters, primarily the more significant ones, including the letters to Bernard of Clairvaux and the correspondence with Pope Eugenius III, both of which secured her permission to write theology. However, there is an academic argument suggesting her letters may have been later redacted or embellished by later sources concerned with moving along her canonization. In some cases it is questioned if they had even been written by her at all. Van Engen (2000) claims her letters were redacted to reflect her own "self-understanding which claimed or imagined approval from Bernard and Eugene (Kienzle, 2011, p.19). Certainly the excessive laudatory style of her letters, particularly by men who otherwise had little respect for women, raises some question regarding authenticity, or at least the extent of glossing/redaction. However, the argument is not widely accepted within the world of Hildegard studies at this time. As is the case with any historical document, authenticity must be examined in an ongoing way as new scholarship emerges. For this study the letters will be assumed authentic, not only because there is not substantial cause to assume otherwise, in addition, most scholars believe without the approval of Bernard and Pope Eugene III, Hildegard would have been punished by the hierarchy for having assumed the authority to write theology.

The tone of her letters shift depending to whom she was writing and the reason. However, a common form she used was to begin her letter with the acknowledgment that what she was about to write came not from her own knowledge, but directly from the divine source, the *Living Light*. She often began by stating she was a weak, unlearned, "poor little form" of a woman, who was writing simply to communicate a message revealed to her by a divine source. The content of her letters, however, reflect the words of a strong woman and a keen awareness of the political and religious context to which she was writing.

An exposition of the large corpus of letters exceeds the space available here. In addition to the volume of letters, the topics and situation are vast as well. Selections of Hildegard's letters will be discussed in this section by the themes, including praise and admonishment. There are also a couple of events, such as the assignment of Richardis in 1151AD and the Interdict in 1179AD that generated several famous letters which will only be briefly mentioned because they have been presented in other sections. The everyday letters Hildegard wrote were often in response to a letter she first received. On other occasions she offered her advice/admonition unsolicited. The excerpts selected are intended to offer a sampling of her writing style and agenda. The picture that emerges of Hildegard's correspondence has been painted with "broad strokes" creating space for future reading.

Letters of praise

Many of the letters writing to Hildegard were written by men and women praising her holiness and knowledge, and often seeking her advice. These letters came from abbots, abbesses, bishops, popes, kings, nobility, and at times unnamed clergy, nuns, and laypeople. Hildegard, as well, wrote many letters of praise, and was always more than happy to offer her advice, solicited or unsolicited. Many of these letters from clergy (bishops, abbots, and priests) requested Hildegard to expound on the meaning of theological points including the nature of the Eucharist, requested by abbot Wolfard (46), how to properly celebrate the Mass, requested by an unknown priest (297), the nature of the Trinity, requested by Eberhard, Bishop of Bamberg (31), and a rite for exorcism, requested by the abbot Gedolphus (68). Henry, Bishop of Beauvais, wrote a letter (32) seeking forgiveness from God through her:

> *Henry, by grace of God, unworthy thou I am, sends greetings to Hildegard, beloved mistress of St. Rupert at Bingen, whatever good the prayers of a sinner, uttered with a contrite and humbled spirit, can accomplish...For God's esteem for you is clear, even to me a sinner... we beseech you to implore the Lord in your prayers for forgiveness of our sins.* (Baird & Ehrman, 1994, p.99)

Hildegard responds to him describing a vision she had of the *Living Light* commanding her to share it with him:

> *I saw, as it were, the beautiful form of virtue, which was Pure Knowledge. Her face was extremely bright, her eyes like jacinth, her clothes like a silken cloak. And on her shoulders she had a bishop's pallium like carnelian... She summoned a lovely friend of the king, that is to say, Divine Love and they went together and knocked on the door of your heart, calling out: We wish to live with you.* (Baird & Ehrman, 1994, p.100)

In another letter (66) from an unnamed superior, Hildegard is addressed as the, "bride of Christ and most worthy mistress of the sisters of St. Rupert in Bingen" (Baird & Ehrman, 1994, p. 145). In this letter the superior requests her prayers and tells her that he is so impressed by her holiness that he credits her fully for everything he has said or done well. She responded to him in a less than laudatory manner (66r), "O man, you who love the world and are secular in your disposition, you are like a storm in your moral character... you limp along in your good works" (Baird & Ehrman, 1994, pp.145-146).

Based on the extant works available, Hildegard seemed to have a familiar relationship with Pope Eugenius III, with whom six letters exist, though there seems to have been additional correspondence lost (Baird & Ehrman, 1994, p.34). Pope Eugenius III is credited with having offered his approval for her to continue her theological writing, after having read an excerpt of *Scivias* at the Council of Trier (Baird & Ehrman, 1994, p.33). Hildegard's words to Eugenius shift from soft and flowery in letter 2, to a harsh warning in letter 3. In letter 5 she challenges his leadership skills, calling him to take better charge of his subordinates and to throw off all depravity. Her message is strong, yet she maintains, at least in the form of a literary genre, her having fear for having been charged with the task of revealing this message to him; "This poor little woman trembles because she speaks with the sound of words to so great a magistrate" (Baird & Ehrman, 1994, p.37).

In addition to receiving letters of praise or solicitation of prayers and advice from clergy, she also received letters from women, religious and secular. One of the most influential religious women whose letters are preserved in this corpus are those of Elisabeth of Schonau, a contemporary mystic and visionary like Hildegard. Elisabeth writes a letter (201) to Hildegard asking for support and guidance on how to deal with her visions which had become the topic of local gossip, not only among the laity, but the clergy as well. Hildegard responds (201r) that the devil is always lurking where God has chosen a vessel; "For God always scourges those who sound His trumpet, but according to His own good purpose. He foresees that their fragile vessel will not perish" (Baird &

Ehrman, 1998, p. 180). She challenges Elisabeth to stay strong, and humble, and trust that God will provide her with the strength to endure the challenges her visions will bring. In a subsequent letter or letters (202/203) Elisabeth greets Hildegard with resounding praise, "You are the instrument of the Holy Spirit, for your words have enkindled me, as if a flame had touched my heart" (Baird & Ehrman, 1998, p.181) before continuing into a long discourse condemning the problem of the Cathar heresy (which rejected the material world as evil), to which Hildegard would have agreed with Elisabeth.

There are several letters from unnamed abbesses, many of which are simply requesting prayers or theological insight. In a letter from an abbess she wrote, "We know, beloved lady that you have always had, and still have foresight into all things" (Baird & Ehrman, 1998, p.65). It seems as though Hildegard may have received more letters than to which she could even respond. In a letter (186) from an unnamed abbess, she wrote; "I have on occasion greeted you in a letter, saintly lady, but I have never received a response" (Baird & Ehrman, 1998, p. 149).

Letters of admonishment
Hildegard did not measure her words when confronting the corruption among clergy. Her courageous speech leaves one wondering how she managed to stay in good graces with the hierarchy. In a letter to Gunther, Bishop of Speyer (41r), Hildegard wrote:

> *Hear, do not hear the reason for God's admonition, lest he strike you with his scourge. In His zeal, God will strike down that heinous offense of yours, for even His priests and their companions are holding Him up to mockery... Now, O man, you are enveloped in great darkness.* (Baird & Ehrman, 1994, p.113)

Hildegard's letters clearly indicate clergy and religious were expected to be vigilant and obedient to the precepts of the Church.

She felt justified in her role to admonish them when they failed to uphold their role properly. Around the year 1170AD Hildegard wrote a response (149r) to an abbot Helengerus:

> *Now, listen and learn so that in the inwardness of your soul you will be ashamed. Sometimes you are like a bear which growls under its breath, but sometimes like an ass, not prudent in your duties, but rather, worn down. Indeed, in some matters you are altogether useless, so that, in your impiety you do not even put the malice of the bear into practice.* (Beard & Ehrman, 1994, p.164)

It is uncertain in many of these instances how her letters were received. As was mentioned at the beginning, there is some scholarly question regarding the possibility of glossing and later redaction, possibly in an effort to move forward her canonization. Even in that circumstance, the texts would have been most likely redacted by male clergy, and have subsequently been accepted by Rome, indicating magisterial awareness of the need for reform among the clergy.

In addition to clergy, she also addressed secular leadership. A famous relationship of Hildegard's was with the Holy Roman Emperor Frederick Barbarossa. King-Lenzmeier (2001) stated:

> *Hildegard's ability to manage one of the most difficult political figures of her time was nothing short of extraordinary. Considering that Frederick was neither a man of great patience nor of deep respect for the authority of the Church, his relationship with Hildegard was surprisingly smooth... He was obviously impressed with the seeress, and the combination of her unflinching character, meeting with her personally, and her accurate predictions may well have caused him to treat her as a vessel of God's providence.* (p.162)

The correspondence between the two of them suggests she met with him in person at some point in Ingelheim and predicted he would be named emperor. Hildegard writes several letters to him (312, 313, 315, and 316) one of which (313) she chastises him for his poor leadership:

> *O king, it is imperative for you to have foresight in all your affairs. For in a mystic vision I see you like a little boy or some madman living before Living Eyes... Beware therefore that the mighty King does not lay you low because of the blindness of your eyes, which fail to see correctly how to hold the rod of proper governance in your hand.* (Baird & Ehrman, 2004, p. 113)

Hildegard believed any properly obtained office, religious or secular, was an appointment by God. She railed against simony (which she felt may have been involved with the appointment of her nun Richardis at Bassum) or other forms of fraudulent leadership (the above excerpt may have been written to Barbarossa on an occasion of one of his appointments of an antipope). Most of her letters of admonishment were to leaders who were not properly fulfilling their role.

Major Life Events

Richardis von Stade came to the monastery at Disibodenberg to study under the tutelage of the holy Hildegard. When Hildegard saw in a vision that the *Living Light* was calling her to move her sisters out of Disibodenberg to Rupertsberg, it was the mother of Richardis, the Margravine of Stade, who made it possible. She endowed Hildegard's convent with the necessary resources. Unbeknown to Hildegard, the gift of the Margaravine of Stade was an exchange. Within a short period of the move, she informed Hildegard that she was requesting her daughter Richardis and granddaughter be moved from Rupertsberg to assume leadership roles in other monasteries. Hildegard was devastated. The correspondence between Hildegard, Richardis' brother, Hartwig the Archbishop of Bremen (12, 13,13r), the Bishops of Mainz (18,

18r), Pope Eugenius III (4), Richardis (64), and her mother the Margravine von Stade (323), preserve one of the most personal experiences of Hildegard's life. This small grouping of letters will not be discussed in detail in this section because they have been already presented in another place in this study; however, they are significant in that they reflect Hildegard's deep love, and subsequent pain, for her nun Richardis. In many of the letters Hildegard comes across confident in her role as a "trumpet" or voice for the *Living Light*. In this correspondence, however, she comes across scared and hurting. For example, in her letter to Richardis' mother (323) she wrote, "I beseech and urge you not to trouble my soul so grievously that you make me weep bitter tears, and not to lacerate my heart with terrible wounds" (Baird & Ehrman, 2004, p.120). This is a personal side of Hildegard not often present in her writings, but offers a glimpse into her personality. She was structured and rigid, but she also was emotional and irrational at times. There is always a tendency to put leaders, especially religious leaders, on a pedestal separating her/him from real life experiences.

Another event that generated only a few letters, one of which is probably the most well-known letter, was the interdict that had been placed on Hildegard and her nuns near the end of her life. Without permission from the clergy at Mainz, she allows an excommunicated soldier, who she claims had been reconciled to the Church, to be buried in the cemetery at Ruperstberg. She is commanded by the clergy to exhume the body and when she refused her convent was placed under interdict. The letters between Hildegard and the Prelates at Mainz (23), Christian the Archbishop of Mainz (24, 24r) present a woman who was clearly tired, nearing the age of eighty-one years old, but with a religious vigor much more profound than what is captured in her earlier letters. The tone in which she addressed the prelates at Mainz reflected an attitude of someone totally convinced of her position. She last line of her letter (23) ends with a stern warning, "This time is a womanish time...But the strength of God's justice is exerting itself, a female warrior battling against injustice, so that it might fall defeated" (Baird & Ehrman, 1994, p.79). The bishops of Mainz did not lift the interdict based on Hildegard's letter, or even her personal deliverance of it. Christian of Mainz wrote to her affirming that the interdict would be lifted if his brother clergy found the witness testimony of "reputable men" sufficient. One of these reputable men, a long-time ally and follower of Hildegard, was Phillip, the Archbishop of Cologne.

Voice of Authority
In many instances the letters preserved were written to or from an individual or community as a response to a pastoral or political concern. However, there are a handful of her letters that fall under a different genre. They reflect the authority of a pastoral letter, written by a bishop, council of bishops, or pope. For example, Hildegard wrote a letter (344) to *Secular People* sometime before 1153AD. It was not directed at a particular group, but seems to have been intended to be read universally by all secular people (this is the way the pope or bishops even today still address many of their pastoral statements). In this letter she wrote a lengthy exhortation on sin, violations against the commandments, but specifically she focuses on ruthless and violent homicide:

> *Therefore, O dear children, by the fact that you were lovingly created, hear and understand me. Why do you act so insanely and spurn Me out of the madness of your fervor? Why are you committing such criminal acts, destroying the flesh, killing a person like yourselves? This evil is the invention of the mind of the fallen angel, who wanted to destroy Me... Therefore I, the Piercing Light, say: O woe, woe, woe, for that homicide which arose at the devil's instigation in order to cast down My good work.... Even the earth mourns when a man kills a man, because its moisture drinks that blood.* (Baird & Ehrman, 2004, pp. 137-138)

Another set of her letters are not really letters at all. Baird and Ehrman (2004) collect them at the end of the third volume. They are reflections, meditations, and even a few sermons on a wide variety of topics ranging from visions (375,376,384), expositions of Scripture (383, 386), collection of songs(390), homilies (377, 381), catechesis on the Eucharist (388), meditations (374, 385) and even a warning about allowing one's ego to pervert the message of the *Living Light* (382):

> *It often happens thus when some inspiration comes forth from the Living Light, which is God, touching a person's spirit: If that person glories it in a way other than s/he should or if s/he climbs higher than s/he has the ability to do, the serpent laughs scornfully to himself about such a fool.* (Baird & Ehrman, 2004, p.174)

The odd collection of letters at the end of volume three reflects the character of journal entries written by a woman who never ceased to pass on to anyone who would listen, the will of the *Living Light* as she experienced it.

A Feather on the Breath of God
One of Hildegard's most famous quotes came from a letter she wrote to a cleric name Odo of Paris (letter 40r):

Listen, there was once a king sitting on his throne... Then it pleased the king to raise a small feather from the ground and he commanded it to fly. The feather flew, not because of anything in itself, but because the air bore it along. Thus am I, a feather on the breath of God..." (Baird & Ehrman, 1994, p.111)

This is a story that has been repeated throughout this book. It takes a lot of faith, trust, and a strong prayer-life to allow oneself to be directed by the Holy Spirit. "Let go and let God" sounds easy when in fact it can be quite difficult. It means letting go of our ego to allow the grace of God to guide and direct the journey.

St. Hildegard *ora pro nobis*

The sunrise, of course doesn't care if we watch it or not. It will keep on being beautiful, even if no one bothers to look at it.
- Gene Amole

My third tattoo is on my left forearm and it is a literally and symbolically a prayer intention. The words, *St. Hildegard ora pro nobis* (pray for us), are encased in a beautiful rose, similar to those that grow wild throughout Germany and, to my surprise, identical to the ones that are growing on each side of the steps leading up to The HILDEGARDEN.

I was compelled to get this tattoo shortly after I made the decision to get on an airplane alone and go to Bingen in the spring of 2015. I had never been out of the country and I knew I would spend almost a week by myself before I met up with my daughter Trisha. I did not even begin to pack my suitcase until a couple of days before I left because I still couldn't believe it was happening. I had no idea how to get from the airport in Frankfurt to the Hildegard Abbey in Eibingen, though I soon found out it would involve a train, ferry, and taxi! Having the story of Cain from the Book of Genesis in mind, I believed this tattoo would protect me along the way and it did.

If you remember the story, after Cain killed Abel, and sinned against God, he was expelled from his homeland East of Eden to make his way through this dangerous world. He feared God would abandon him, but God assured Cain that he was not walking alone. In his goodness God marked Cain with a seal to protect him as he journeyed. "And then the Lord put a mark on Cain so that no one that found him would kill him" (Genesis 4:15-16). I had all kinds of thoughts running through my head of how I might get lost, robbed, hurt, or possibly even killed in my travel. I was very nervous, but a part of me did feel "marked" and protected because I had faith that this trip was part of God's plan for me.

Journey to Bingen, Germany

In 2012, the same year Hildegard was named a saint and Doctor of the Church, I graduated from St. Mary's Seminary and Graduate School of Theology (our local diocesan seminary) with a Doctor of Ministry (D.Min) in the topic of women's leadership. My dissertation was entitled, *Celebrating the Roles of Women in the Life and Mission of the Church*. It included a historical survey of the diverse ways women have functioned in leadership roles in the Church throughout history, concluding with the ways women are functioning today, particularly in the Cleveland Diocese.[44] In my Doctor of Ministry (D.Min) research I met Hildegard of Bingen and immediately fell in love with her. I could not give her any more space in my historical survey than the other women, but I was determined to do further research on her when I completed that degree. I came to Union Institute & University knowing exactly what the focus of my research and studies would be for the next three years and I did not sway from my goal.

I have spent the last three years completely immersed in her story, trying to learn who she really was and what message she was communicating. I knew I would not be able to share her story in language the community could understand if I did not first immerse myself in her world so that I could understand it. In addition to collecting just about every book, article, video, music cd, and other resources available on her, I realized one day I would need to go to Bingen to walk in her footsteps. I was planning on making the trip after I graduated in 2016, but through divine providence (and the prodding of my daughter), I was able to go during the course of my doctoral research for this project. I boarded a plane to Frankfurt in May 2015, flying solo, and headed towards Bingen to spend some time at the Abbey of St. Hildegard.

---

[44] Our current bishop appointed a female chancellor and diocesan worship director, both of which are significant diocesan positions. Both of these offices have traditionally been staffed by clergy, and in many dioceses still are, however, Canon Law does not require an ordained minister to fill these roles. The bishop has stated that he appointed women to these offices for no other reason than they were the most qualified applicants.

As I began to think about my upcoming trip, many fears surfaced. I wasn't sure if I would be safe traveling alone. I thought about what my family would do in the event something happened to me. I was literally venturing into the unknown. I have read enough of Carl Jung to know that this was a journey that I not only had to take, but I had to take alone. In her book, *A Heroines Journey*, Murdock (1990) wrote:

> *The heroine crosses the threshold, leaves the safety of her home, and goes in search of herself. She journeys up hills and down valleys, wades in rivers and streams, crosses dry deserts and dark forests, and enters the labyrinth to find what is at the center of herself. Along the way she meets ogres, adversaries, and obstacles which she must avoid. She needs a lamp, a lot of thread, and all of her wits about her to make this journey.* (p. 46)

When I arrived in Frankfurt, Germany I had to take a train to Bingen. I found the station, purchased my ticket and boarded the train. About half way to Bingen the police officer making the rounds questioned why I had purchased two train tickets…

Figure 14

When I got off of the train everything felt surreal. I found someone to ask where the Abbey of St. Hildegard was located. He pointed to the opposite side of the Rhine River from train station. So I carried my luggage, for what felt like miles, to the ferry dock that would take me across the river to Rudesheim-Eibingen. Ironically the train had dropped me off right at the site of the original monastery of Rupertsberg located right beyond the tracks (see figure 14 above). Although I did not realize for several days that Hildegard had brought me right into Rupertsberg, just a couple of blocks from where she had landed with her sisters over eight-hundred years ago.

Figure 15

I found my way to the Ferry (a trip I would take at least two dozen more times over the course of the next nine days) and crossed over the Rhine River into Eibingen.

When I crossed the river I could not believe I had was actually standing in the land of St. Hildegard. Several hours from the time I landed in Frankfurt I had finally reached my destination. I could see the abbey a at the top of the hill through the grape vineyards (see figure 16) and the path was clearly marked (figure 17). I found a cab driver, interestingly from India, who loaded my bags and drove me up the winding road to the Abbey.

Figure 16

Figure 17

When the cab pulled into the steep driveway we were greeted by a Benedictine sister who was very warm and welcoming. She took me to my room which was simple, clean, and comfortable. The accommodations included a three meals a day, a large gift shop (which I was at daily), a vending machine in the hall with wine and beer from the Abbey (costing less than the bottled water!) and the opportunity to join the sisters in for Liturgy of the Hours and Mass multiple times throughout the day. I learned quickly that there was no wifi and no cell phone reception. My first morning I woke up at sunrise to the bells ringing and found my way through the stained glass halls into the chapel for morning prayer.

"Land of Hildegard"[45] in Germany

On my first full day in Germany, following Mass and an authentic German breakfast, I went in search of the "The Land of Hildegard" tourist center (see figure 18) across the Rhine River back in Bingen. The information office was able to help me organize my travels for the next several days. When I first entered the tourist center, the woman at the desk was very friendly and spoke English. She asked me what I was doing in Bingen and was surprised I had traveled alone. After I explained to her I was here to learn about Hildegard for a doctoral dissertation in leadership, she immediately responded, "You know, Hildegard was not a feminist!" I am not sure if it was because I was a woman, an American, or both, but her comment was interesting. I spent about an hour with her before I thanked her for all of her help, including having allowed me to take a photo of a map that the tourist group had created

---

[45] http://www.landderhildegard.de/

depicting what Rupertsberg most likely looked like in its day (see figure 7 pg. 26). She shared a tourist booklet with me that I was able to use to explain to cab drivers where I was trying to go.

Figure 18

Bermersheim
Over the next several days I traveled to Bermersheim (see figures 1-3 on pp.16-17) to visit the alleged place of her birth. I had boarded a train to Bermersheim on the fifth day of my journey confident that I knew exactly where I was going. When I got off of the train it was apparent that there were no cabs and that I was going to have to walk the remaining two miles, which would not have been too much of a concern except that the entire trip was through the woods and grape vineyards and I was not quite sure where I was at or if I would even make it back. The photo on the cover of this book is the situation I faced as I began my two mile hike. I was very nervous entering this path – I felt like "little red riding hood" – I had literally come over the river and now was heading into the woods. I assumed the tattoo of St. Hildegard on my arm would give the police a lead to return my body to the Abbey if I didn't make it out!

Figure 19

Finally, after walking for what felt like forever, I came upon a clearing in the woods (see figure 19) which led to a small town. I was so excited to see civilization off in the distance. Arriving in town I learned quickly that there were no stores or businesses and the few non-residential buildings were locked. Starting to panic a bit, I found someone who was kind enough to help me out. She looked at me with a bit of shock (I'm sure I did not appear to be a local) and asked, "Where did you come from?" I explained everything to her and showed her my little tourist booklet. I am sure she wanted to laugh, but she kept her composure. As it turned out, there are two Bermersheims and I was in the wrong place! She told me her son would drive me back to the train station (for the first time in my life I had to place total and complete trust in God and Hildegard that it was safe to go with this person) and I got in his car. After taking me back to the same train station I had gotten off of several hours earlier, he gave me directions to the Bermersheim of Hildegard birthplace. I got off of the train and again could not find an open store. I walked for another mile or so until I could locate a cab. Given the way the day had been going it was not a surprise that the cab driver I found was not very friendly. He did not understand where I was trying to tell him I needed to go. After driving for quite a while he stopped at a church and told me we had arrived but it wasn't the same church as in my picture booklet. To make a long story short, he began to cuss in German, called someone on the phone, started driving like a maniac (I was pretty sure he was either going to kill me in a car accident or throw me out the door on the side of the road) and then to my surprise we arrived at a church that matched the picture in the booklet! I jumped out to take pictures (courageously asked him not to leave) and then got back in the car to go back to the train station. An entire day's journey, including ferries, trains, $60 in cab fare, several miles of walking, and two near death experiences later, I had reached the Church in Bermersheim!

Disibodenberg
The trip to Disibodenberg, the monastery to which Hildegard was tithed as a child, was also challenging though not quite as scary as Bermersheim. There were cab drivers available at the train station when I arrived, which was a beautiful site in itself! The driver I connected with was not exactly sure where I was asking him to take me, but he was very nice. We found our way up the big hill to the ruins and he dropped me off promising to come back in two hours. I would have loved to have spent the day there, but two hours is what I had, plus I was not quite sure he was actually coming back. I had paid him for the trip and so again, I had to trust I would get back safely. Being a reasonable person, however, I did try to figure out how I would get down the big mountain I

was on the event he did not return. I wasn't sure what kind of German forest dwellers were lurking in the trees. Thankfully he did return and the experience of walking the ruins of Disibodenberg was the most profound spiritual experience I have had. To be on the very property, which still existed to some degree, where Hildegard lived for over two decades, the place where she learned music and herbal medicine, and where she prayed each day and studied scripture, was an experience I cannot fully describe. I did not want to leave. The woods, and the view and the environment were breathtaking. Figure 20 is an image of the ruins at Disibodenberg. Other images of Disibodenberg can be found on pp. 19-20 in figures 4-6.

Figure 20

Rupertsberg
A few days into my trip I stopped in a museum which had a selection of Hildegard's artwork illuminated on display. Following the tour I asked the gentleman where Ruperstberg was and how I could get there. He responded, "There is nothing left in Rupertsberg. It is not worth your time. Anyways, no one is there today. They only open up the remaining cellars on Sunday." I told him I needed to go there – I just wanted to stand on what I knew

would feel like holy ground. So he gave me directions and I began to walk in the direction he pointed. As I was nearing the location he showed me on the map I realized I was at the train station. I had gotten off of the train my first day at the place Hildegard had built her monastery. It is all built up today and very little remains of the original structure, aside from a few underground cellars that had been restored in the sixteenth century and were salvaged several years ago. They were discovered when they were blowing up the area to build the railroad tracks. As I neared Rupertsberg I felt the overwhelming presence of Hildegard even though it was congested and loud and a computer company was now utilizing the space. The view of the property from the opposite side of the Nahe River (see figure 21) is still beautiful.

Figure 21

When the cellars were discovered they had been damaged from the railroad work, but have been restored. They needed to determine that what they had discovered in fact belonged to the Rupertsberg Abbey that St. Hildegard built, which they did, and so a historical group was able to preserve what was left. The yellow house structure which now sits on the property (see arrow in figure 21) is currently a computer software company. It must be the only computer company in the world constantly visited and photographed by religious pilgrims! I was blessed the day I walked to Rupertsberg because the facilitator of the organization that maintains the few underground cellars happened to be on site. It was not a day that it was normally open, but by chance (I'm sure it was not chance at all but Hildegard) she was there. She gave me a private tour of the cellars (see figure 22) and shared with me the various ways they are used for Hildegard prayers services and talks. She also gave me a pocket size statue of Hildegard to carry in my pocket as I continued on my journey.

Figure 22

The cellar in figure 22 has been remodeled (not much is left of the original structure outside of a few beams) and displays a large statue of St. Hildegard (with her staff) and a picture of creation from her *Liber Divinorum Operum.*

Eibingen
While in Eibingen I not only attended prayer and Mass at Abbey, but I was also able to walk down the hill and attend Mass at the

Parish Church of St. Hildegard in Eibingen. This is the location where her second monastery was located before it was destroyed in the early nineteenth century.

Figure 23

Figure 24

In addition to several statues and other images of Hildegard, in the Church there are three stained glass windows depicting various herbs that she prescribed for healing in *Physica* (see figure 25) and a window with the title of her first book, *Scivias* (see figure 26).

Figure 25

Figure 26

The most remarkably attraction in the parish Church of Eibingen is Hildegard's reliquary and the large replication of her *Trinity in Unity* vision (see figure 27) from her book, *Scivias*.

Figure 27

Hildegard of Bingen began her public ministry at the age of 43 years old when she was commanded by the *Living Light* to write down her visions. To say the experience of being in the presence of her reliquary on the Feast of Pentecost during the week of my 43rd birthday was extraordinary would be an immense understatement. Ironically, I did not plan to be in Germany in Hildegard's Abbey on the day I turned 43 years old. It happened by chance, although, as I have already stated, I don't believe in chance.

St. Rochus
In addition to spending quite a bit of time in Bingen, Rudesheim-Eibingen, I was able to travel to the Cathedral in Mainz (the

diocese where Disibodenberg, Rupertsberg, and Eibingen are located). Hildegard wrote many letters to the prelates at Mainz during her lifetime, to the Cathedral in Cologne (where Hildegard preached, although it has been built up since she was there), and I went to Bremen (where her beloved nun Richardis' brother was a bishop). I spent many hours riding ferry boats down the Rhine River and taking trains along the Nahe River, both of which Hildegard traveled often. Rupertsberg sat on the corner of the Rhine and Nahe. I visited health food stores selling Hildegard natural products, and went to a beautiful little church in Bingen, St. Rochus (see figure 28), which claims to have some of the items from the chapel of Rupertsberg before it was destroyed.

Figure 28

While I was up at St. Rochus I visited the "Hildegard Forum" restaurant and gift shop. Between the Forum and the Abbey, I ate way too many Hildegard "cookies of joy", drank a bit of Hildegard spelt beer and too much Hildegard tonic (see figure 29 – I'm still not quite sure what was in the tonic but I brought back as much as TSA would allow me to), dined in restaurants claiming to serve "Hildegard inspired foods" and got up early with the bells to sit in Hildegard's Abbey for early morning prayer while the sisters sang the divine office, in much the same way as Hildegard herself had done. I set out each day with total and complete faith in God's divine providence (trusting in the supervision of St. Hildegard) and I successfully reached every destination on my journey. Each night I returned to the Abbey and prayed a prayer of thanksgiving. I had no idea how I safely made it back, but through the grace of God I had. While in the land of Hildegard I completely immersed myself in her world, and though it was brief, the experience was transforming.

Figure 29

When I returned home all I could think about was how I could bring a bit of what I experienced in Germany back home to share with the community to which I minister.

It is important to me to present Hildegard of Bingen in such a way that appeals to a wide audience. While she was a devout Catholic religious sister, and my ministry has been largely rooted within the Roman Catholic Church, Hildegard's message of wholeness and holiness extends beyond the confines of the Catholic Church. Without sacrificing the integrity of who she was, I want her to be accessible to a wide group of people so that her works might be appreciated, celebrated and emulated. One day while I was writing my dissertation I received a random text message from a parishioner, who at first I didn't recognize. He randomly and anonymously wrote; "Wow, I've been reading some of Hildegard's work. She is really deep. That is some heavy stuff.

Bring her down to a common level for us so that we can understand her." The text came at a moment when I was trying to decide how I wanted to present her – as a theologian or as spiritual director. I chose to go with the spiritual director. There is a lot of high quality theological texts available today on Hildegard of Bingen's work. I have discerned that my call is to make her holistic spirituality accessible to everyone.

When I returned from Germany I held several talks and retreats at St. Anthony's as well as other Catholic and Protestant Churches. The events were all well attended, by women and men, and her message was very well received. I believe the community needs her presence and I prayed for a way to meet that need.

Be a Child of the Light
In the beginning* *was the Word, and the Word was with God, and the Word was God. He was in the beginning with God. All things came to be through him, and without him nothing came to be. What came to be through him was life, and this life was the light of the human race; the light shines in the darkness, and the darkness has not overcome it. A man named John was sent from God. He came for testimony, to testify to the light, so that all might believe through him. He was not the light, but came to testify to the light. The true light, which enlightens everyone, was coming into the world.* (John 1: 1-9).

In December 2015, at a time when I was not expecting it, I had a profound religious experience. An experience not entirely unlike that of pilgrims who have traveled to holy places such as Fatima and Medjugorje and have experienced a strange happening in the sky. In Fatima and in Medjugorje it is believed that the sun danced. Up until this past December I was not convinced that was possible because it defies, at least as I had been taught, natural law.

When God breaks into our human existence in a way that defies the laws of nature we call it a miracle. I am not totally convinced that the way we define miracles is proper. I believe that miracles certainly do take place, but maybe not because they defy natural law. I am more inclined to believe that they represent a law or reality that we have not yet become awakened to. For Catholics the act of transubstantiation is not so much a miracle as it is a reality that we, in our limited human consciousness, cannot clearly define or understand.

To say a miracle defies natural law is to assume we have figured out, in its entirely, what natural law even is. Quantum physics, including string theory (a field far beyond my area of expertise), suggests there is much more to reality has been discovered. We have erroneously come to believe all that is real can be experienced with one of our five senses. But, what if we exist in a much more complex reality (including other dimensions) that are just as real and present but inaccessible by our five senses? A miracle may simply be a glimpse into a much larger reality of an existence that we, as finite human beings, are still awakening to. I am beginning to believe a "paranormal" experience could simply be a normal experience that we do not yet have the ability to explain. I had a "paranormal" experience recently.

My family and I lived in Eastlake, Ohio for almost fifteen years before moving back to Fairport Harbor. I would regularly walk around the area, especially down Vine St. for quiet time to pray and discern. I had an experience I will not soon forget one evening in early December 2015 while I was out walking. I decided to walk across the Lake County Captain's Field bridge, as I often did. I had been thinking a lot about my dissertation and how I could make a unique contribution to the field of Hildegard studies, when so much great work has already been done. I was praying for a sign to affirm for me that I had not wasted my time or energy in this venture. As I crossed the bridge I stopped to look at the sky. As I was looking at it I thought to myself, "Something doesn't look normal. There seems to be a second source of light off to the right." It is hard to see in this black and white photo, but it was there. I took a picture of the sky and kept walking.

Figure 30

A short while later, as I headed up a side street towards Euclid Ave. I was stopped dead in my tracks. I could not believe my eyes. The clouds had parted a bit and the second source of light, to the right of the sun, was much clearer than it had been on the bridge. I quickly pulled out my phone and took several photos. See figures 31 & 32.

Figure 31

Figure 32

As you might imagine, I was a bit shaken. "Freaked out" might be a better description. I was plunging quickly into a state of paranoia. It was unclear what I had seen, but I know it was real (that is why I pulled out my camera) and it was unlike anything else I have ever seen or been taught existed. It was not the moon, it was clearly a ball of brightly shining light. I watched the news and internet to see if anyone else had seen it or published any photos. The few days that followed I researched everything I could possibly find (most of which came from conspiracy theory sources) and by the end of the week I was convinced that the world was ending any day now because this fiery ball, that I was sure should not be in our sky, was visible. I showed a few people and the reaction of most were, "It must be photo-shopped." I can assure you it was not. I took the photos myself. So then, what in heaven's name was it?

After taking a lot of time to pray about it I decided I was going to embrace it as a manifestation of divine light. I began to see it as another form of the light that had infiltrated my bedroom porch that one morning almost two decades ago. There may be a solid scientific explanation for what I saw in the sky. It could have been a "sun dog" or a just a reflection. It may have been nothing at all, or it may have been a sign to start stocking the apocalypse supply room. I don't know.

What I do know is that Moses experienced a supernatural light – a bush that burned and wasn't consumed. Mary experienced a supernatural light – an angel telling her she would conceive in her womb the incarnated God. Paul experienced a supernatural light – one that knocked him to the ground and completely transformed his whole being. The Emperor Constantine experienced a supernatural light – one that formed a cross in the clouds of the sky. Hildegard experienced a supernatural light – one that would appear to her repeatedly throughout her lifetime, often leaving her bedridden for months. The young Portuguese children experienced a supernatural light when Mary appeared in Fatima. The young Croatian children in Medjugorje experienced a supernatural light, as have many pilgrims who have visited there since. And I, together with a friend who was with me, saw a supernatural light, breaking into the ordinary sky of Eastlake, Ohio.

"Hail, O Light." Upon us who lay buried in darkness and shut up in the shadow of death, a light shone forth from heaven, purer than the sun and sweeter than the life of earth. That light is life eternal, and whatsoever things partake of it, live... O pure Light! In the blaze of the torches I have a vision of heaven and of God.... – St. Clement of Alexandria

The HILDEGARDEN Honey Bee

"God has arranged all things in the world in consideration of everything else." -St. Hildegard of Bingen, Doctor of the Church

Bee – the only creature who came unchanged from Paradise.
--Hilda M. Ransom, *The Sacred Bee*

I have worked as a pastoral minister in a small parish community of Fairport Harbor for almost two decades. Over the years I have become so attached to this community, the thought of ministering anywhere else would probably devastate me. I love the people here in Fairport Harbor and in the Cleveland Diocese.

However, as I reflected on the role of lay female pastoral ministry outside of the "utopia" I have been blessed with here in Fairport Harbor, I became painfully aware that the work of the pastoral minister, though she works tirelessly on behalf of others, and of the whole, is often considered by the institution, and at times the community, to be disposable. This in part stems from the reality that she is a lay person and cannot share in the ordained ministry.

As you may have presumed from the title, my last tattoo is a honeybee. It is the only one of the four that is not overtly religious, though as I continue to grow in my faith I believe it is profoundly spiritual. While all of my tattoos were physically painful to varying degrees, this is the only one that almost drew tears. As with my first one, I offered up my pain in prayer. The full color honeycomb & bee tattoo that I have on my right foot serves as a profound symbol for me of the role of lay pastoral ministry. In the quote above from Hildegard she reminds us that every creature has been ordered in some significant way to the whole. In the words of St. Paul, no part of the whole is useless, and those parts that seem insignificant are often the most necessary. The honeybee, though she ceaselessly works, not necessarily for herself, but for others, has been treated as though she is disposable and our environment, including our food supply, is beginning to suffer the consequences. For decades we treated the honeybee as though we could get on without her. We are learning today that human beings would not last but only a few years without the tireless work of this tiny, and often feared, creature. I have reflected a lot on the parallel between the honeybee and the lay ecclesial minister, particularly female lay ecclesial ministry.

Human beings need the unseen, and often unappreciated work of the honeybee. Human beings would suffer a collapse (using hive language) if the honeybees no longer existed. There is an ecological movement today to preserve, protect, and celebrate the role of the honeybee as an integral part of our world. We are now coming to recognize that our sins against nature have consequences.

In much the same way the Church today, as Pope Francis has pointed out, needs to preserve, protect, and celebrate the valuable role of women in leadership and ministry within the Roman Catholic Church. For far too long the work of women in the life and mission of the Church has gone unseen and unappreciated. Pope John Paul II asked forgiveness for the many ways the Church has sinned against women over the years by failing to respect and honor the "female genius." Pope Francis has echoed those words. In reality, the Church would suffer a collapse without the dedicated work of female minsters. My love for honeybees stems in part for the way in which I can relate to their integral, but not always celebrated, role.

One of the realities of parish ministry is that a lay pastoral minister has no real canonical rights outside of the rights granted to all the laity. What this means is when a pastor retires, the next pastor has the ability (and often exercises it) to put his own staff in place. It is proper for a pastor to have the freedom to build a staff that is willing to collaborate with his vision, however, it creates a very unstable position for lay pastoral ministers who have invested years of time, money, and energy into formation and education to function in the parish. With the new directive which puts term limits on pastors, the security of the pastoral ministers role becomes even more uncertain. To put it in secular terms, there is no job security.

At St. Anthony's we are blessed with a wonderful pastor who has already been here with us for twenty-two years. If he retires when scheduled at age 75 (one response to the vocation crisis was to kick up the retirement age...) I will only be 53 years old. Naturally I have been thinking about what the future might look like. Whether or not I will be able to stay on this parish staff with a future pastor is to be determined. Even if I am able to stay, the likelihood of a future pastor giving me the space and ability to function as I have been is unlikely. From the perspective of credentials, I have become almost "overqualified" for parish ministry and it that is not always well received by an incoming pastor. A second issue would be that I have worked for the same pastor for many years and have been formed in his style of ministry, with his vision of leadership which does not always transfer well to another pastor coming in with another idea of what parish life should look like. The third reason, and probably the most significant reason, is that I am a strong, and often outspoken, leader. The reality of this context is that when a future pastor is assigned, one who is certainly going to be much younger than I, he will most likely "strip" me of the position I have held for so long.

It is difficult to discuss a reality such as this without sounding negative, however, my intent is not to be negative. I am simply stating an issue that I brought up in my D.Min dissertation and one that continues to be a concern. For the community that would mean they could possibly lose their pastor and pastoral associate, two people who have been intimately involved in their lives for many years, simultaneously. That is not to say that the next pastor would not be a wonderful addition and might possibly bring a whole new set of gifts and talents to the parish, but it would be a drastic change. Knowing how the community in Fairport Harbor responds to change, I did not want to see that happen here.

Abraham and Ruth

In my personal reflection I have come to understand the reality of lay pastoral ministry and ordained ministry by comparing the Hebrew stories of Abraham and Ruth.

Abraham – ordained ministry
In the Book of Genesis Abraham was called by God to leave his homeland, and be willing to give up his family (sacrifice his son), to follow in faith. It was a risk, but God promised Abraham he would be rewarded for his faith. Abraham was told he would inherit a great nation with as many descendants as stars in the sky (Gen 22:17). Abraham for me represents the promise of reward for those called to ordained ministry. The promise to be named a shepherd – a pastor or possibly a bishop - a father of many descendants, affirms one's call to say yes to the sacrifice required for discipleship.

Ruth – lay ecclesial ministry
Ruth, the Moabite, also said yes to her call, which required as much faith and self-sacrifice as Abraham, but without the same promise. Ruth, a pagan, offered herself fully in love to Naomi without any expectation of reward. She, like the honeybee, was "disposable" to the community, yet she too said yes.

While these two examples are in some sense a caricature, they capture an experience of ministry today. Ordained ministers share in a promise of reward (canonical rights and protection) not offered to the lay ecclesial minister who has committed her/himself as fully. Yet, in most dioceses, this has not inhibited the generous response of lay ministry. It has just raised the question of justice.

The HILDEGARDEN

I kept praying about how I could possibly stay rooted in the community long-term, administering pastoral care, helping people grow in wholeness and holiness, teaching others about Hildegard while applying my doctoral research, particularly my Ph.D. work, and still remain within the Catholic Church, which I have so faithfully served for so long. After much prayer the unthinkable happened. We were gifted with the opportunity to purchase a closed Catholic Byzantine Church two blocks down the street. When I called my husband Rick to tell him I wanted to put a bid on the property he did not believe me. Two days later, largely as a result of the support we received from my Uncle Dug, we were signing papers with the realtor. It will obviously no longer operate as a Catholic Church– it will be a retreat center focused in the spiritualty and leadership of St. Hildegard. It will be called *The HILDEGARDEN,* a spiritual community center offering programs to "grow the mind, body, and spirit." There will be no creed or doctrine. It is simply a place for people to come to heal and grow.

In addition, *The HILDEGARDEN* will make it possible for me to bring some of Germany here to Fairport Harbor! A short time after we purchased the property I was reflecting on the whole experience with a priest friend of mine and he pointed out that the front of the Church building of *The HILDEGARDEN* is similar in shape to the front of the Abbey Church of St. Hildegard in Rudesheim-Eibingen where I stayed last May (see figure 33). When we put the pictures side by side I was in awe.

Figure 33
St. Hildegard Abbey, Germany   *The HILDEGARDEN, Ohio*

The HILDEGARDEN is scheduled to open on September 17, 2016 (Hildegard's Feast Day). The center will offer a holistic venue of programs, not limited to Hildegard themed events, but certainly Hildegard will always be present. Programs will be focused on topics such as spirituality, meditation, holistic healing, various educational topics, natural nutrition, ecology, gardening, beekeeping (the center now has two hives in the back of the property), and of course programs on Hildegard herself. The center will collaborate with local businesses, such as the yoga studio. It will include a unique gift-store stocked with Hildegard themed items including books, videos, music, her "cookies of joy", and fennel tea. Of course there will be some bee-themed items available as well. Retreats and pilgrimages will be organized out of the center, including a future trip to Bingen, Germany to stay again at the Abbey of St. Hildegard.

The story of Hildegard will be shared at *The HILDEGARDEN* in a language that the community can understand. At times programs on the importance of eating healthy, other times a labyrinth walk, and on occasion an evening concert with local talent performing her music will be offered. With respect to who she was historically (including her theology, ecclesiology, and medieval world view) her charism will be presented in such a way that she speaks to all people. *The HILDEGARDEN* will be inclusive and focused, in a unique way, on sharing with others the healing power of the sacred feminine.

How will this retreat center be any different than already existing centers in regards to changing a paradigm of leadership in the Catholic Church? When my family and I purchased the Church building, it came with a house /rectory as well. We have since renovated the rectory and moved in. While the property is no longer functioning as a Catholic Church, the community has the opportunity to engage with a well-respected female Catholic minister living in a repurposed rectory, administering a facility (church building) that, for almost 100 years, was an active Catholic Church. While the purpose of this property has changed, it preserves much of its original character. This new image of what spiritual leadership can look like contributes in a positive way to a changing paradigm. The community begins to see a new way in which to situate an old story. It is an example of what happens when you pour new wine into *new* wineskins.

The work I have done over the years academically and otherwise is not necessarily going to change all that's unjust within the Roman Catholic Church. Pope Francis has been courageously highlighting many issues that need to be addressed, none of which will be healed overnight. The way in which the Church has conceived the roles of women and leadership has been so heavily influenced by patriarchy for centuries, it would be naïve to think that the building of one small retreat center, *The HILDEGARDEN*, is going to inspire universal action. Even in my own diocese I am sure there will be challenges along the way. There are many clergy who have not yet embraced lay ecclesial ministers, and particularly women ministers, as equal "co-workers in the vineyard of the Lord." I already had one young priest tell me, "You are walking a fine line with this... But I think you just might pull it off." I am not quite sure if he was being supportive or sarcastic, but either way he is right. I am walking a fine line and I do believe I am going to pull it off because it's not essentially my work, it is God's. I have opened myself up as a vessel. It has been clear every step of the way that there is a divine force, a power much greater than myself, directing and ordering this process. When the Holy Spirit moves, no one can stop its progress. That is what makes this an enchanted journey.

It may seem bold to assume that somehow I, "a little form of a woman" as Hildegard would describe it, have been called to question a patriarchal system so powerful and entrenched. To suggest that the non-admittance of women to the ministry of preaching and canonical leadership is the root cause of so many of the Church's pastoral problems. To imply that if we are going to raise up the visible leadership of women, as Pope Francis has repeatedly stated is necessary, then we need a new model. We cannot pour new wine into old wineskins. The Scriptures are clear - they will burst and both the wine and the wineskins will be ruined. It may be audacious to suggest all of the above, and yet, that is exactly what I believe is happening. It has taken me almost two decades of theological formation, and many unexplainable spiritual experiences, to be comfortable voicing my soul, as Sue Monk Kidd describes it:

> *In order to voice the soul we will have to balance our inner experience with our outer one. A mystic is a person who tends to have inward experiences of the Divine and who finds ultimate authority within that experience rather than in a source outside of herself. Prophets, on the other hand, are people whose spiritual energy moves externally into the world. They become voices, calling society to truth, justice, and equality. They go "out there" and struggle to bring about social and spiritual revolution. The point is, we can no longer afford to be one or the other. Conscious women are both.* (p. 203)

As I journeyed through decades of seminary classes, formation sessions, certification programs, theology and ministry degrees, endless hours of providing pastoral care, there has been something within that has continued to move me along. I often pray for the wisdom to discern if my call is valid or if I am being motivated by pride, ambition, or simply anger at being treated unequal by clergy and seminarians for so many years. But something deep down kept drawing me on, making me feel as if there was a task ahead of me that I could not yet see, but needed to be prepared for. That task, I believe, is *The HILDEGARDEN*. Everything I have done up to this point has prepared me for what is ahead.

I believe that in order for systemic change of any kind to come about it has to happen from within, like a seed planted in a garden. And it has to be nourished with love and respect. My goal in creating this retreat center is not to divide myself from the Church, but rather to offer a place where people can heal and grow, in whatever faith tradition, if any, they subscribe to. I will not be presenting a creed or doctrine, other than *viriditas.* I am not building a Church. My goal is to help people find new and creative ways to restore the moisture and greenness lacking in their lives in mind, body, or spirit. I feel this new space has been created to be cultivated as a garden in need of gardener leaders.

Hildegard saw God active in every part of the created world, through the force of *viriditas.* She also embraced a deep faith in the efficaciousness of the sacraments and challenged the clergy of her day to properly embrace their role. She creatively integrated her own spirit of eco-feminism together with hierarchal religion into one world view. She was a leader with a vision. In reflecting on the enormous contributions she has made to diverse fields, including music, art, theology, medicine, philosophy, administration, and even politics, the most appropriate description of her would be that she was a "well-watered garden."

The way in which Hildegard moved to action, not only her sisters and other subordinates, but those in positions of authority above her, was remarkable. Was she born with a unique gift or was it learned? Golden (2010) stated, "Historically, great leaders and great creators were believed to be born with unique and rare talent…Since then the theory has been replaced by the view that leadership skills can be taught and creativity… potentially can be found in everyone" (p.241). There was nothing remarkable about Hildegard's birth, but her having been immersed in the monastic environment from such an early age was unique. Her openness to receiving the gifts of the environment in which she grew provided an atmosphere where she could learn and develop creative leadership skills.

Hildegard uses gardening metaphors throughout her writings, not only in relation to *viriditas*, but often as an image of leadership. The gardening metaphor is used very often in the Scriptures, which she was intimately aware of, not only in the Christian Scriptures, but in the Hebrew Scriptures as well. In the Book of Judges there is a parable told involving a gathering of trees:

> *One day the trees gathered to anoint a ruler for themselves. They said to the olive tree, "Be our ruler." The olive tree replied, "But I would have to give up my rich oil, by with both the gods and people are honored, to go and hold sway over the trees." Then the trees said to the fig tree, "Be our ruler." But the fig tree replied, "But I would have to give up my sweetness and my excellent fruit, to hold sway over the trees." Then the trees said to the vine, "Be our ruler." But the vine replied, "But I would have to give up my wine that cheers the gods and people, to hold sway over the trees."* (Judges 9:8-13)

None of the trees were willing to give up the way they had been doing things to embrace something new, something creative. Houston and Sokolow (2006) wrote that in order for leaders to grow personally and professionally, leaders must be willing to be open to doing things differently; "behave in a different way" (p. 79). The consequence of failing to grow as leaders can be toxic. In a later biblical parable Jesus is recorded as having cursed the fig tree (Mark11:12-14) for not having produced any fruit.

The creative leadership of Hildegard demonstrated a way by which leaders in the Catholic Church could do things differently. She crossed over social, religious, and cultural boundaries, leading in a way that was extraordinary for a woman of her day and even for a woman in the Catholic Church today. She offered a new paradigm by which ecclesial leadership can be understood.

Using the same image of the trees, one of the New Testament letters asked, "can a fig tree produce olives, or can a grapevine produce figs?" (James 3:12) Hildegard captures this image in a letter (84r) she wrote to a Prior, "By no means would it be proper for a priest to perform the functions of a farmer, or a student to perform the tasks of a master" (Baird & Ehrman, 1994, p.187)

Hildegard saw a divine order, including an ordering of "proper roles" of not only women and men, but also based on one's socio-economic rank. She came out of an environment steeped in traditional Catholic theology, and she taught that God ordered everything and everyone in the world according to a divine plan. Tightly defining roles, based on gender, ethnicity or social rank, has opening the door historically to discrimination, oppression, slavery, abuse, and in the worst situation, genocide. Through a contemporary lens, Hildegard's adherence to divine order could be offensive and potentially problematic. This is, in part, why some contemporary writers opt to "write out" that aspect of her thought. It is more than a disservice to scholarship, and to Hildegard's work, to remove any aspect of her thought. It violates her integrity and it fractures her character.

Integration of the Dark Side
Hildegard was a product of her time, and that is evident in so much of her writings. The way in which she envisioned the world was marked by her experience of medieval monastic life. She was stubborn in her opinion and she embraced a world view that was ordered in a way that today would be considered by many as unjust and inflexible. The integration of Hildegard as a whole is fundamental to understanding her as a leader. Clendenen (2009), stated, "This lifelong process of integration, never fully accomplished in a lifetime, is conducted through the treacherous and deeply satisfying reconciliation of opposites from within oneself... to develop towards maturation" (pp.86-87). A mature depiction of Hildegard of Bingen necessarily requires an integration of her negative (dark side) with her attributes that are positive and light-bearing. This is true of all of us.

Hildegard preached a message of wholeness, integration, and beauty, and saw an image of God in every part of the created world. She was rooted in a holistic *greenness*, yet her theology was conservative, Christian-Catholic, and it cannot be immediately presumed that it would be radically different today. It is a nice thought to image her as a saint who would offer the world today a "feel good" spirituality, but that is not the theology she preached in her visions, letters, writings, music, or homilies. She preached fire and brimstone, yet there is something about her that draws people from all walks of life, all faith traditions, towards her message. She reveals, in an extraordinary way, a spirit of *viriditas*.

Hildegard as Gardener Leader

Hildegard was so diverse and so complex, the task of labeling her leadership style is difficult, if not nearly impossible. However, one metaphor that can be used to describe her, an image that she herself would have approved of, is that of a gardener. Alvesson and Spicer (2011) describe the gardener as one who facilitates growth: "In this literature, leadership appears as a beautiful thing: it fosters creativity, morality, authenticity, spiritual growth, and so forth… One of the guiding ideas here is that the best and most successful leaders are true to their authentic self" (pp. 76,80). This certainly describes Hildegard; however, again it is important to refrain from romanticizing this image. Alvesson and Spicer (2011) warn that the gardener image could plant seeds in one's imagination that this type of leaders oversees a "Garden of Eden" in his or her context:

> *The picture that emerges is that of paradise. It paints the picture of a sacred space that is uncontaminated by the crude laws of the real business [ecclesial] world and bureaucracy: a Garden of Eden, or delightful and peaceful place, in which leaders and followers are happy and realize their potential while being productive… In the Garden of Eden, employees under a 'gardening leaders' do not suffer the pain of toiling at the soil or industrial work: the leader as facilitator of growth protects a space in which people explore their talents and spirits… Of course, this picture is too good to be true.* (p. 88)

The gardener leader needs to be fully invested in caring for the garden. Gardens are full of weeds, pests, disease, and are always in need of pruning and watering. Even with the best gardener and the best care, sometimes the plants do not produce. In Vision One:13

of *Liber Divinorum Operum,* Hildegard stated that God created the whole world, the Garden of Eden, and everything in it with the "fullness of divine love" (Fox, 1987, p.18), yet because of the sin of the fallen angel Lucifer, human beings have fallen from this perfect state as well. Most of Hildegard's writings were directed towards her deep desire to "care for the garden" and restore the essence of *viriditas*. The role of a gardener leader is difficult.

In a letter (85r/b) Hildegard wrote to an abbot named Adam she advises him on the difficulties of a gardener leader. The need, as Hildegard always understands it, to be dependent upon the grace of God, the virtues, to overcome the temptation and threat of evil, the vices. Within the context of the letter she told a story:

> *A contorted figure said, Listen to me: A destructive wind and hail and fire and pestilence will come upon that garden, and will dry it out. But the young man answered: Not so, it will not be so, because I do not wish it and I will bring forth a pure fountain and will irrigate the garden. And the contorted figure answered: Ha! That is as possible as if locusts would eat through hard rock. And so that crafty figure brought winter into that garden and sought to dry up the herbs and the flowers. And that young man, caught up in playing his harp, did not see what was happening. But when he did take notice, he called the sun back with a loud sound... and the sun brought the viridity of summer back into that garden... and he cast the contorted figure down to the earth... Now you, O father [the abbot Adam] understand these words... The grace of God shines like the sun and sends its gifts in various ways; in wisdom, in viridity, in moisture. But wisdom can degenerate into grossness, viridity can fall under great labor, and moisture can turn into harsh bitterness... You have a garden of people, in which, as the representative of Christ you seek to plant many wholesome desires and good works. And through the power of His gifts, the grace of God pours out his dynamic good will upon those desires and those works, and causes the garden to grow green through the dew and the rain*

> *and the fountain of living water...But vices come from the devil... The crafty vices bring the cold cloud of ignorance upon this people, so that their wholesome desires and good works fail... Warned by these things, do not trust in your powers alone, but see to it that you flee to the grace of God, so that you may protect and admonish your people in every way.* (Baird & Ehrman, 1994, pp.195-196)

In another letter (132) she directs an abbot Manegold, who had been fretting regarding the state of his monastery and monks, "This is the way you look upon your garden: you rejoice when prosperity shines on it like the sun, and you grow angry when a cloud covers it over with excessive disturbance. But have patience in each instance" (Baird & Ehrman, 1998, p.75).

In a letter (106r) to the Monk Guibert, who later will work on the writing of her *Vita*, Hildegard put forth a beautiful image of a garden as the place where the virtues of abstinence, faith, patience, chastity, humility, and love (God) abide:

> *But, now, look to that glorious garden which love has planted, and gather to yourself every virtue in true humility and simplicity of heart. And although you find yourself among men of various states of mind, learn how patient and how long-suffering divine goodness has been to us all... May the Holy Spirit enkindle in you with the fire of His love so that you may persevere, unfailing, in the love of His service.* (Baird & Ehrman, 1998, p.41)

In thinking about how to renovate the sanctuary so that it maintains a sense of peace and tranquility, a place where people can come to grow, we first decided we would need a piano/organ in addition to a creative podium. In addition, I found a beautiful statue of a woman whom we will call Hildegard. It is a statue that to me represents wholeness and healing. It emotes a sense of peace. In the Scriptures when a character is nameless it invites the reader into that role. This statue is faceless inviting all people, women and men, into a place of healing and growth. She will go in the grotto (see figure 34).

Figure 34

The HILDEGARDEN will be a place where people can find the source of inner strength needed to grow their gifts and talents. It will be, in a metaphorical (and literal) sense, a garden, and my role, as I see it, will be to function as a gardener, just as Hildegard did. In their chapter on the metaphor of leaders as gardeners, Alvesson and Spicer (2011) wrote:

> *Just like a plant dies when it stops growing, people symbolically die when they fail to live up to their 'potential'.*

> *But personal growth is of course not just good for the person who grows. The crux of the matter is that personal growth is deemed necessary for organizational growth...This then, is what the metaphor of the leader as gardener today exemplified: someone who enables his or her employees or followers to grow.* (p.77)

The HILDEGARDEN is not going to change the whole leadership structure of the Catholic Church. And it will most likely not bring healing and reconciliation to every corner of Fairport Harbor. In fact, as with any new movement, there will most likely be a reaction, which can be negative and resistant to change. The way in which a leader responds to the reaction and resistance has a significant impact on the outcome. Houston and Sokolow (2013) offer advice (using language Hildegard would use) in responding to these reactions:

> *Metaphorically, the devil doesn't arrive in a blaze of sound and fury; most times, in fact he shows himself in small ways. Small mindedness is a large part of what brings down the world... By standing up to confront the small things, sometimes you can prevent the large things from taking place. Stop negativity at its source.* (p.63)

It will be important to continuously communicate the work of the center with those in positions of authority, as well as the community at large, in order to dispel misinformation regarding the intended use of the property. To maintain a positive attitude grounded in the mission of love. The goal is to create a center that facilities growth and healing in the spirit of an extraordinary woman, St. Hildegard of Bingen, offers an innovative model and it communicates, in a creative and engaging way, a different story.

An idea begins to become a reality when it is spoken, written, and shared. The energy shared between people influences its success. The energy that has been generated over The HILDEGARDEN has been remarkable.

Figure 35
The HILDEGARDEN by Patsy Gunn

The extent of the territory this center will reach, and the long term influence it might have, is at this point is undetermined (that will be the work of a future survey/study). However, it is my guess that when Hildegard ventured out of Disibodenberg to build Rupertsberg she could not have even begun to imagine the long effect that event would have on women and leadership in the Church today. She was moving a small group, twenty sisters, to a relatively small piece of land on the Nahe River (most people today have never heard of the river, unless of course they are historians or wine connoisseurs). She spent the last few months of her life at odds with the institution. While the interdict had been lifted, there were quite a few clergy in Mainz and in higher ranking offices still pretty upset with her. To think her message – including her homilies, letters, visions, music, leadership, and even food advice – would spread not only throughout all of Germany, but to the universal Church (outside of the Holy Roman Empire) would have been thought impossible. And yet here we are, over eight centuries later, celebrating her newly appointed status as a Saint and a Doctor of the Church. Just as Hildegard believed the voice of the *Living Light* called her to take a chance and build Rupertsberg, I believe I was called to build The HILDEGARDEN.

When a seed is planted, and the soil is right, the potential for growth can be extraordinary. *The HILDEGARDEN* is garden to which I have been called to tend. It is my vision that this center will provide the soil, and other necessary nutrients, to cultivate growth within the community here in Northeastern Ohio.

Figure 36

The HILDEGARDEN
630 Plum St.
Fairport Harbor, OH 44077
440-754-8002
office@thehildegarden.org
www.thehildegarden.org

I am St. Hildegard. I know the cost of remaining silent. And I know the cost of speaking out. – June Boyce-Tillman

Introduction to the Soliloquy
Over the years I have developed a very personal relationship with St. Hildegard. As I was considering a creative writing piece to accompany my dissertation, I was drawn to the idea of writing a soliloquy modeled after St. Augustine's. What is a soliloquy?

A soliloquy is a unique literary genre directed at drawing the reader into the mind of a character. This soliloquy of St. Hildegard of Bingen serves as a vehicle to pull the reader creatively into a personal experience of St. Hildegard through the mind of the author, Shanon Sterringer, who has spent the last several years fully immersed in the life and works of this remarkable twelfth century *magistra*. An introduction to the soliloquy is necessary before one delves right into its content because the soliloquy presumes one is already familiar with Hildegard and her ongoing experience of divine revelation through what she described as an encounter with the *Living Light*. Some background information on the nature of the *Living Light*, both within Western Christian tradition and also its significance in Eastern spirituality, is necessary in order to understand the source of light to which Hildegard refers. The introduction is in no way an exhaustive presentation of the *Living Light* as it has been embraced in the mystical tradition, but simply an effort to introduce the reader to its nature.

Hildegard of Bingen was a Roman Catholic German nun and her message needs to be viewed through that lens. For her there could be no separation between the secular and the sacred. To remove her from this medieval Catholic context is a distortion of her character and her message. However, the core message she offered extends itself beyond the confines of Catholicism to a universal application. This message, especially her call to awaken to the presence of the *Living Light* and the essential *viriditas*,[46] is profound. We live in a world suffering from a lack of light – a world marked by the darkness of greed, corruption, unbridled power, discrimination, and social injustice. A world in which natural resources, as well as human resources, are being exploited, contaminated, and used up at an astounding rate simply to fulfil an insatiable desire for short-term gain. We live in a world dying from a lack of *viriditas*. This is true not only in the secular world, but within religious contexts as well. It is light that dispels darkness; it is moisture (greenness) that dispels dryness. Though her message is wrapped in medieval Catholic thought, Hildegard has a profound message to share with everyone - the *Living Light* can illuminate our darkened world, if we are open to its presence.

There is material within Hildegard's writings that may not appeal to a modern mind or worldview including passages that are even offensive to contemporary culture. There is also material that may not seem relevant outside of a Catholic context. Some scholars have removed these parts of her writings to make her more palatable to a wider audience. In doing so, it has fractured her as a whole, causing a great loss to the richness of her character. Boyce-Tillman (2010) pointed out that Hildegard is often referred to as a "woman ahead of her time" but she is actually very much a woman *of* her time. She was, to the core, a medieval, German, devoutly Catholic, nun. She cannot properly be removed from her historical context. However, Hildegard saw light and beauty and greenness everywhere and she celebrated God's goodness. She also saw devils and evil and darkness and she suffered from those visions.

The intent of the soliloquy is to provide a literary work to inspire and nourish leadership, particularly female leadership in the Roman Catholic Church. The work is focused on shifting sick, ineffective paradigms of leadership in an effort to inspire true healing – in mind, body, and spirit. Leadership in a religious setting is defined by one's vocation or calling. It is described as a

---

[46] Literally translated "greening power." It is a theological concept Hildegard used throughout her writings.

response to a perceived need within the community. In his book, *Humble Leadership*, Standish (2007), describes leadership in the Church as the call to be "radically open to God – in which we lead from faith rather than fear, from a willingness to let God's will flow through us..." (p. 22). Discerning a vocation to leadership in this way requires self-reflection. One literary tool fundamental to the discernment process is the use of a soliloquy, or an internal dialogue – a conversation with oneself. Soliloquies have been used in a variety of different literary settings for a number of different audiences. Soliloquys are most famously found in the writings of Shakespeare (Hamlet, Macbeth, Romeo & Juliet), but have also been used by religious figures, notably St. Augustine of Hippo, to aid in the discernment process. The soliloquies of St. Augustine were inspirational to the writing of this soliloquy. A soliloquy makes visible the invisible questions, concerns, and fears of an individual. Through a lens of faith, a soliloquy is a manifestation of an internal conversation between the individual (mind, soul, and heart) and God (who resides within).

This internal voice serves to guide or direct one's actions, as it did for St. Augustine, a fourth century philosopher, who struggled with the decision to embrace Christianity. Before he took the step towards conversion he needed to be able to answer the question, "Is Christianity reasonable?" Augustine wrote two soliloquies discerning this question before being baptized and later becoming one of the greatest Doctors of the Church. His soliloquies demonstrate the thought process which led him to affirm that Christianity is in fact reasonable, at least as he discerned it, and therefore the soliloquy was an effective formational tool. In his soliloquies Augustine engaged in a dialogue with the Soul in an effort to better understand himself and God and the vocation to which he was being called.

Cary (2000), in a book, *Augustine's Invention of the Inner Self: The Legacy of a Christian Platonist* wrote the following:

> *Augustinian inwardness has its roots in the Plotinian Platonism and its doctrine of the divinity at the core of the soul. Plotinus himself says we must turn inward to find God because the higher part of the soul, continually contemplating, is identical to the divine Mind. Hence, turning into the soul's interior is turning to God, and self-knowledge yields knowledge of all that is divine, eternal and ultimate... When the soul does turn inward, therefore, it gazes not at a private space, but at the one intelligible world that is common to all: and likewise when the soul is united to the core and center of its own being, it is united to the one core and center of all things... It is a brilliant image: we human souls think we are many insofar as we look outward at the bodily world, like faces on the outside of a huge sphere. But if (perhaps with divine help) we could turn our gaze into the interior of the sphere, we would see that on the inside we are all one God.* (pp. 28-29)

This is a profound lens through which one can read not only the writings of Augustine, but other writings of spiritual leaders as well. The example of Augustine is so important to this particular soliloquy because it grounds the creative writing piece in the long-standing tradition of the Roman Catholic Church which is an institution that has often restrained the role of women leaders.

In addition to Augustine's example of a soliloquy, the visual work of Linn Maxwell, *Hildegard of Bingen and the Living Light* was foundational to this soliloquy as well.[47] In this film Maxwell embodies a contemporary voice of Hildegard who has come back from beyond to speak to our modern world, in a soliloquy style. The literary genre she employs bridges the gap between the twelfth and twenty-first centuries. The dramatized video presentation is under an hour in length, yet remarkably captures the spirit and nature of Hildegard. In the video the voice of Hildegard is presented in a very personal, contemporary, and somewhat humorous way. A similar technique will be applied to this

---

[47] http://www.hildegardofbingen.net/store.html

soliloquy, to both the voices of Hildegard and also the *Living Light*. In Hildegard's actual visions the voice of the *Living Light* was not personal as it is being depicted in this creative piece. I have taken some creative liberties presenting her experience of the *Living Light* in this informal style. Important to the writing of this soliloquy was the sharing of the author's own personal narrative. Nash (2004), in his book *Liberating Scholarly Writing: The Power of Personal Narrative,* described it in this way:

> *The central pedagogical question that guides me as I write this book is a simple one: How can I describe SPN (scholarly personal narrative) for my readers in such a way that it provokes, evokes, and invokes? I want to write a book that gets people thinking about scholarship in some fresh ways that is provocative without being combative. I want to write a book that evokes from my readers the wish to tell their own stories, and possibly get them to try to find matches and mismatches between their stories and mine... The invocation of conceptual and textual sources is, for me, the inescapable scholarly dimension of SPN writing.* (p. 10)

My experience of being a female minister in a male-dominated Church is filled with pieces and parts of stories that many others share, including Hildegard of Bingen. Like Nash it is the hope of this dissertation, through the use of a creative literary technique, that it might inspire others to embrace more fully their vocation to spiritual leadership in turn bringing about much needed change.

Format of the Soliloquy
The soliloquy is an example of an internal conversation one might have as s/he discerns the task s/he is being called to embrace. This piece is a contemporary conversation between Hildegard of Bingen and the *Living Light*. Using the example of St. Augustine's soliloquies this work will follow a similar style. However, it is important to note that Hildegard did not write a soliloquy of her own. This soliloquy is a creative writing piece consisting of a blending together of fiction and non-fiction. Hildegard's whole

life reflected an internal dialogue of light to light – her light and the *Living Light* and so in that respect it captures her essence. Portions of the soliloquy will be in Hildegard's own words excerpted from her writings and in those instances will be noted. Other portions will be casual conversation bringing the reader into more of a personal experience of Hildegard and her relationship with God. It will demonstrate a personified experience of one looking inward in order to better understand what is common to all, as was highlighted in the excerpt from Phillip Cary above. Hildegard is seeking guidance from the *Living Light* in order to discern how she is being called to intercede on behalf of leaders in the Roman Catholic Church today inundating her, as Catholics often do, with difficult questions regarding faith.

The soliloquy will have three voices. The voice of the narrator (N.) is necessary to set the scene and bridge gaps within the narrative. The voice of Hildegard (**H.**) will comprise of her own voice (using noted excerpted text as well as fictional dialogue presented by the author) and also the internal voice of the *Living Light* (*L.L.*) which resides within her soul seeking to help her see and understand her contemporary role in helping to move forward the leadership of women in the Roman Catholic Church today. At times the dialogue will be informal and playful while shifting back and forth between the formal tone of Hildegard's own writings and visions. The "scholarly personal narrative" of the author of this soliloquy, Shanon Sterringer, will be creatively brought into the text as well in the form of several intercessions or letters written to Hildegard following her canonization. The intent is to not only weave into the conversation a personal experience of the leadership of women in the Church today, but it also helps to provide some background information on where the interest in Hildegard emerged for the author. The soliloquy will be laced with history, theology, philosophy, and poetry from Hildegard's own writings and time period. One of the most obvious characteristics of Hildegard of Bingen is that she created her own style of writing, music, theology, art and leadership. For example, her music, which is considered "genius" in many circles, is often described as having nothing to which to compare. It is often described as resembling Gregorian chant but it is not Gregorian chant. It is entirely unique from anything that existed before or following, yet it is remarkable. It is the hope of the author to create an experience, with this soliloquy, to share in the same creative spirit that radiates from Hildegard's own work. It is an attempt to make a medieval German saint accessible to those seeking her guidance and intercession today. It is through the revelation of the *Living Light* that we come to recognize our personal call.

What is the Living Light?
From a faith perspective the *Living Light* is energy; an energy that existed long before there was a heaven or an earth. The *Living Light* is the energy from which all that exists was born and someday will return. Science calls the spark of energy which caused life in all its forms to spring forth the *Big Bang*, Western religion calls it the *Word of God*. This primordial force has been personified in the ancient Jewish Scriptures as Holy Wisdom, *Hagia Sophia*. Many believe that through this light everything that exists not only came to be, but has been sustained:

> *For Wisdom is mobile beyond all motions and she penetrates and pervades all things by reason of her purity. For she is an aura of the might of God ... the refulgence of eternal light, the spotless mirror of the power of God, the image of his goodness. And she, who is one, can do all things, and renews everything while herself perduring; and passing into holy souls from age to age, she produces friends of God and prophets... For she is fairer than the sun and surpasses every constellation of the stars. Compared to light, she takes precedence... God of my fathers, Lord of mercy, you who have made all things by your word... with you is Wisdom, who knows your works and was present when you made the world... Send her forth from your holy heavens and from your glorious throne dispatch her... She preserved the first-formed father of the world when he alone had been created; and she raised him*

> *up from his fall... Wisdom delivered from tribulations those who served her.* (Wisdom 7:24-29; 9:1,9; 10:1)

The belief that the *Living Light* not only called forth creation, but continues to animate the great web of life can be found in diverse spiritual traditions. This sacred force is neither male nor female, but pure energy (spirit) stirring in the minds, hearts, and souls of every creature.

The *Living Light* has manifested itself in every culture, age, and religious tradition. For example, in the Judeo-Christian tradition it was manifest in the burning bush that was on fire, but not consumed, as it spoke to Moses in the desert proclaiming, "I am who am" (Exodus 3:14). It was this energy force that Christians believe came upon the Blessed Virgin Mary making her the *Theotokos*, Mother of God (Luke 1:35) and later appeared to Saul (renamed Paul) through a blinding vision to convert from a life of violence to a mission of love; "On his journey, as he was nearing Damascus, a light from the sky suddenly flashed around him" (Acts 8:3). It is believed that the *Living Light* became incarnate in the person of Jesus who proclaimed, "I am the Light of the world, whoever follows me will have the light of life" (John 8:12).

In the Eastern non-Christian religious traditions the *Living Light* has often been described as the energy that moves one towards an "awakening" experience. Sufi Llewellyn Vaughan-Lee (2013) describes it in this way:

> *Our light is part of the light of the world, and as the alchemists understood, it has a unique role in realizing the true potential of matter. It is through our light that this light hidden in matter can be released. And when this light hidden within the world, the lumen naturae, is released, the true purpose of creation will once again become visible... Life will awaken to its divine nature.* (p.69)

Some suggest that it is the presence of the *Living Light* that people encounter when they have a near death experience. The *Living Light* has moved about the earth from its inception endowing those open to it with great gifts of wisdom and knowledge necessary for transformation and elevation of consciousness. "Those attuned to what is really happening can participate in this rebirth... The light of the world can communicate directly with our individual consciousness and together they can recreate life" (Vaughan-Lee, 2013, p.30).

The *Living Light* continues to speak to those open to her presence today. Cynthia Bourgeault (2008), an Episcopalian priest and wisdom teacher described an experience she had of the *Living Light*:

> *All of a sudden I felt myself suffused in golden light... and I heard a voice distinctly say, "Shhh... all will be well." While I certainly could not understand the message itself, I understood that warm golden light... I discovered in that moment that there was something in me that knew. It didn't know what it knew, exactly, but it knew that it knew.* (p. 7)

It is believed by many that the *Living Light* is the force that has guided prophets and mystics throughout the centuries bestowing gifts of abundant grace. The *Living Light* is often identified with the Holy Spirit (in the Western Church *Spiritus Sancti* and in the Eastern Church *Hagia Sophia* or Holy Wisdom). In the mystical tradition (Christian and non-Christian) the *Living Light* is often understood as a manifestation of oneness – a higher level of consciousness.

In his text *Alchemy of light: working with the primal energies of life,* Sumi Llewellyn Vaughan-Lee (2013) describes this primordial light in the following way:

> *But within the heart of every human being there lies hidden another light which reveals a world beyond the one perceived by our ego-consciousness. This is the light of the*

> *Self, which is a direct knowing of God. It is this light that draws us back to God that calls us on the search for Truth, and reveals the real nature of life...When this light within the heart is awakened; we begin to experience a whole different world.... The light at the core of the world has always been present, but hidden, waiting to awaken, just as our own light lies hidden in our own heart until it is awakened.* (pp.16-17)

Growing in awareness of the presence of the *Living Light* is an experience that continues to unfold throughout our lives. It is not so much a moment as it is a process.

It is the position of Hildegard of Bingen, as well as the author of this book, that the sacred source of *Living Light* inherent within each person is the font from which the gifts of knowledge, wisdom, understanding, counsel, awe, piety and fortitude spring forth empowering one to respond to the call (vocation) to leadership. It was through this experience that Hildegard of Bingen mustered the courage to respond to her call to prophetic leadership. Her openness to the *Living Light* infused in her a knowledge and understanding of the world inaccessible by the empirical methods of her time. Hildegard's writings reflect knowledge well beyond what was known in twelfth century Germany. This is not only reflected in her theological writings, but her medical texts as well. One must ask how a cloistered woman, who had been tithed as an anchoress at the age of eight years old with no formal education, could produce an advanced (and in many ways scientifically correct) description of the way in which various organs and systems within the human body function and interact, centuries before human beings had the technology to understand and describe it?[48] How do we make sense of the volumes of theological writings penned by Hildegard, all of which she insistently claims came not from her own knowledge, but were

---

[48] Similar questions have been raised by some scholars in regards to the extraordinary genius of Leonardo DaVinci and the "code" that some feel is embedded in much of his work.

the result of knowledge inferred in her by repeated experiences of the *Living Light* which she saw not from her external eyes, but her internal eye?

In the introduction of her first work, *Scivias*, Hildegard wrote a declaration in which she stated the following:

> *And behold! In the forty-third year of my earthly course, as I was gazing with great fear and trembling attention at a heavenly vision, I saw a great splendor in which resounded a voice from Heaven, saying to me, "O fragile human, ashes of ashes, and filth of filth! Say and write what you see and hear. But since you are timid in speaking, and simple in expounding, and untaught in writing, speak and write these things not by a human mouth, and not by the understanding of human invention, and not by the requirements of human composition, but as you see and hear them on high in the heavenly places in the wonders of God... Thus, therefore, O human, speak these things that you see and hear. And write them not by yourself or any other human being, but by the will of Him who knows, sees and disposes all things in the secrets of His mysteries." Heaven was opened and a fiery light of exceeding brilliance came and permeated my whole brain, and inflamed my whole heart and my whole breast, not like a burning but like a warming flame, as the sun warms anything its rays touch. And immediately I knew the meaning and exposition of [many mysteries]... And I spoke and wrote these things not by the invention of my heart or that of any other person, but as by the secret mysteries of God I heard and received them in the heavenly place.* (Hart & Bishop, 1990, pp. 59-61)

Recent scholarship has suggested that the visions Hildegard described were the result of her having possibly suffered from a serious condition of chronic migraines. Others have suggested her visions were induced by mind-altering substances (such as mushrooms[49] which are recorded as having medicinal qualities in her work on herbal remedies). And some have hinted at the possibility of her profound visionary experiences, including the physical and mental suffering that followed, as symptoms of what is known in the ancient Hindu tradition as a *kundalini* awaking experience (Maddocks, 2003). Regardless of what circumstances brought upon her visions, she steadfastly attributes them to an ongoing experience of *The Living Light*. It is through this experience that she begins to identify the nature of her relationship with God and others and her call to creatively lead her community.

The *Living Light* is present in each person. However, for one to recognize the presence of the *Living Light*, s/he must be focused on developing her senses beyond the five senses associated with the material world. "Learning how to look" takes a concentrated effort facilitated by meditation, and for a person of faith, concentrated prayer. Vaughan-Lee expresses it this way, "The veils that cover our daily life prey on our attraction to complexity and our mistrust of the simplicity of life. They distract us from what is most basic, most universal and most real" (2015, p. 113). Hildegard lived a monastic life from age eight to eighty! She would have spent countless hours immersed in discernment including long periods of silence as was commanded by the Benedictine Rule (H. Feiss, 2000). In addition she spent many hours in solitude praying, singing, and reflecting which may have provided the spiritual nourishment necessary for her soul to become fertile ground through which the seeds of mysticism (dependent upon the development of the inner senses) could come to fruition.

In their text, *The Physics of Angels*, Matthew Fox and Rupert Sheldrake (2014) describe the presence of a *Living Light* personified as angels. Interestingly, when they discuss the creation of the world, they challenge the long-held notion that when God

---

[49] See the article *Mushrooms and mysticism* http://www.huffingtonpost.com/mark-kleiman/mushrooms-and-mysticism_b_39881.html

created light, that it was referring to the light we experience as the sun and moon. Our sun and moon did not yet exist when the world came to be, and would not exist for almost ten billion years after the Big Bang. The light they claim God commanded to come into existence was the physical presence of the *Living Light* captured in angelic beings. Quoting from Hildegard, they write:

> *The original fire out of which the angels burn and live, that is God himself. The fire is every glory out of which the mystery of mysteries comes forth. The angels surround God in their glowing fire, for they are living light. They do not have wings like birds but are still hovering flames in the power of God... When he spoke the words, "Let it be," there existed illuminated beings.* (p. 134)

Imagining the revelation of God as the *Living Light* speaking to Hildegard in the form of an angelic being certainly was familiar within Roman Catholic tradition, medieval cosmology, and the world view of Hildegard herself.

Traditionally Roman Catholic theology has preserved and formed its followers with an image of God that is exclusively male. Many are unaware that the catechism states, "God is neither male nor female, but pure spirit" (CCC #239). The exclusive use of male nouns and pronouns when describing God has created a distorted image of God within Roman Catholic tradition. We tend to impose our own human attributes (good and bad) onto God rather than allowing God to be God –"I am who am, says the Lord" (Exodus 3:14). God is pure energy or light. There is no darkness in God. The *Living Light* – the energy force which animates all of creation – is genderless. However, for this soliloquy, the *Living Light* will be referred to using feminine pronouns.

Hildegard Awakens
As the soliloquy begins, Hildegard finds herself awakening from what feels like a long, restful sleep, unsure of where she is at or what she is happening…

Soliloquy of St. Hildegard

Hildegard Awakens
N. It is early in the morning on the 17th day of September in Bingen, Germany. Stirred from a restful state, Hildegard rises from her bed, which was unlike any she had ever slept in before. Overstuffed and fresh, as though she had been sleeping on a cloud. She looks about the room with an overwhelming sense of peace. The room, filled with fresh air coming from a gentle breeze and sunlight peering through the white iridescent curtains, was unfamiliar to her. The screen-less window propped slightly open allowing the sound of an outside fountain to slightly animate the room. The walls painted with a white brighter than Hildegard has ever seen with furniture built from the most beautiful wood. The rooms of her monasteries were always so dark and dreary, this room, by contrast was so light and airy. She notices a table adorned with green plants and herbs radiating the greening essence of *viriditas*[50] and her Psalter sitting majestically in the corner, as though waiting for her to pick it up and play.

H. Where am I? It doesn't feel like Rupertsberg, or Eibingen either. Is this my monastery? Where are my gardens?

N. Peering out the window she looks for her herbs.

H. Are those my herbs? Are any of my sisters here?

N. Hildegard begins to walk the room wondering if she in some sort of heavenly anchorage[51] or if someone else is around?

---

[50] *Viriditas* literally means "greening power". However, in Hildegard's writings she uses the term to denote a much more significant reality. *Viriditas* literally is the life-force sustaining all of creation.
[51] An anchorite was a room attached to a monastery. To embrace the life of an anchoress was popular in the middle ages, especially for women because while it involved a life of solitude, it freed her from marriage or another form of male dominance.

H. Is Jutta[52] here? Maybe Volmar[53] or Richardis[54] is here!

N. Hildegard's excitement is quickly deflated as she realizes she is in this room alone. She moves over to the window and looks again outside. Her eyes, taking a moment to adjust to the light, recognize a river – maybe it is the Rhine - but it seems further away than she remembered. Walking around the room Hildegard reluctantly sits down on a chair near the window, confused and overwhelmed by what she is feeling.

H. Am I in heaven? Where is everyone else? Maybe I have been asleep waiting the glorious day of Christ's coming! This must be the waiting room – St. Peter will be calling my name any moment! After all I lived a virtuous life and followed the voice of the *Living Light*. I recorded everything I was instructed to. I stood up against the evils of my day, risking the well-being of myself as well as my sisters.

N. Sitting still for a moment Hildegard has another thought; maybe she isn't in heaven at all.

H. What if I am in Purgatory! Maybe I am here because of that fight, okay fights, with the Abbot Kuno.[55] But those were not my fault...

---

[52] Jutta of Sponheim was a relative of Hildegard's family. Hildegard was entrusted to Jutta's care when she was tithed at the age of eight years old. Jutta was rigidly aesthetic, following the Benedictine Rule to such an extreme extent that it probably caused her early death.

[53] Volmar was Hildegard's priest, confessor, secretary, and friend for over sixty-years until his death in 1173 AD.

[54] Richardis was her most beloved nun, the source of her greatest moments of joy and her most devastating pain. Richardis was "ripped from her" in 1151AD when she was named Abbess in a convent in Bassum. Hildegard felt the appointment was the result of the political ambition of her noble family. The letters preserved from that experience shed honest light on Hildegard's human side. Richardis only functioned in Bassum for less than a year before she died prematurely, causing a wound in Hildegard that never fully healed.

N. Hildegard stands up and begins to walk the room anxiously. She is starting to get upset.

H. He was so stubborn. He did not believe I was being guided by the *Living Light* – he was so jealous of me and of my connections – especially when Pope Eugenius III and the Emperor Barbarossa would write to me, not him. I cannot possibly be being punished for that. Maybe this is just another one of my visions[56]. Maybe I am just hallucinating– my sisters keep telling me I should stay away from the mushrooms![57] Oh how I wish the *Living Light* would appear and instruct me on what to do. But, if the *Living Light* speaks I will have to write down what I see and hear and will be commanded to share it with others. How can I do that when I do not even know where I am at? Who am I supposed to share it with? There is no one even here. This is all too much for me, a weak and feeble

---

[55] The abbot Kuno was assigned to lead the male monastery at Disibodenberg around the same time Hildegard was chosen to lead the female monastery. Many of the contemporary films and writings take "historical liberty" in depicting Kuno as the abbot from the time Hildegard was tithed. Regardless, Hildegard and Kuno did not get along well and the source of their tension reached a height when Hildegard saw a vision instruction her, and her nuns, to move out of Disibodenberg (with their dowries) to build their own convent at Rupertsberg.

[56] Hildegard experienced visions of great theological mysteries – the incarnation, salvation, the trinity – through what she describes as the *Living Light*. She does not begin to write, however, until the age of forty-three when she is commanded in a vision; "write down all you see and hear". She also possessed a profound understanding of science and medicine, beyond that of her day. She claimed her knowledge came directly from her visions.

[57] It is believed by some scholars that Hildegard used mind-altering mushrooms (which she refers to in her text *Causes et Curae*) which may have contributed to her visions.

woman. [58] Maybe I should lie back down. Now I really am starting to get a headache![59]

N. She decides to go back to bed, maybe she will fall back to sleep. She begins to wonder if she is sleeping now. This could all be just a dream. As she works her way back over to the bed Hildegard notices a table with a pile of letters. She proceeds to make her way over to them. She tries to adjust her eyes from the light as she looks at all of the stacks.

H. What is all of this? I wrote a lot of letters in my lifetime[60] but nothing like this. It will take me years to read all of these. There must be thousands of letters here. Look at this one addressed to *The Sybil of the Rhine*[61] - they must have the wrong address. There is no one here named Sybil. But, why are so many addressing me St. Hildegard? I am not a saint - I am simply a *feather on the breath of God.*[62] Although I did work hard at reforming the lazy clergy and decaying Church in my day! Maybe I am being named a saint for tolerating Kuno for so long!

N. Hildegard picks up a letter and notices the date.

---

[58] Hildegard frequently referred to herself in this manner in her writing. It is debated as to whether or not she believed she was weak, or if it was a literary technique to keep her in good graces with the patriarchal powers at that time.

[59] Many scholars today believe Hildegard suffered from severe migraine headaches. This may have been the illness that kept her bedridden for long periods of time. Others believe this might have contributed to her keen sense of light and also even possible may have set a context for her visions.

[60] There are over 400 letters of Hildegard's correspondence preserved and translated. These letters include a wide range of recipients including popes, emperors, abbots, nuns, lay people, and some anonymous.

[61] She was often referred to as the "Sybil on the Rhine" due to her gift as a seer / prophet.

[62] She referred to herself as "a feather on the breath of God" (letter 40r to Odo of Paris).

H. What year is it? 2016AD! That means it has been 837 years since I fell asleep in the presence of my sisters and Br. Guibert at Rupertsberg[63] I am supposed to be in heaven enjoying the company of my beloved Volmar and Richardis, and of course my dear Jutta. I'm not sure what I'm supposed to do with all of these letters. What is with this stack marked "intercession"? How am I supposed to intercede for people? I am a philosopher, a musician, a doctor, an herbalist, an artist, a theologian, a visionary, an advisor to kings and popes, an abbess and now they want me to take on the role of intercession! I am one woman! How can I possibly take on another role? The male hierarchy is always pushing more and more work on us women! It must still be a "womanish time!"[64] People are always seeking my advice.

N. Pulling up a seat, Hildegard begins to sift through the letters. A large grey envelope catches her eye. Opening it up, she begins to read it out loud.

H. *Dear St. Hildegard of Bingen,*
My name is Shanon and I believe you have been sent to me by God to keep me motivated in my vocation to lead, minister, teach, write, and work for change in an institution that is flawed on so many levels. I have been taught all my life that the saints walk with us on our journey of faith and so I am seeking your intercession as I stumble along my journey. I fell in love with you several years ago and to this day I continue to be amazed at what you accomplished. When I feel I am growing weak or overwhelmed I look to your example to draw strength and encouragement.

---

[63] Ruperstberg was one of 2 monasteries Hildegard founded after she moved her sisters out of Disibodenberg in 1151 AD.
[64] She used the term "womanish time" when referencing why God would impart sacred knowledge of such great mysteries to a woman rather than to the male clergy.

You are probably wondering why I would be so enamored with you and your work – while you are certainly growing in popularity, I believe I am your biggest fan! I have virtually every book, song and video published on you. My days are totally immersed in reading, listening, and reflecting on your works. I even have a couple of tattoos in your honor - Hildegard of Bingen, ora pro nobis and Viriditas! I imagine you must be thinking the tattoos are a bit over the top, but your influence on me has been that profound. I am sure the undertakers will have fun one day trying to figure out what those are all about! Maybe I should share with you a piece of my story.

I grew up in a unique context, quite different from yours, nonetheless unique. The experience often left me feeling alone. My family moved a lot creating a context where I was never able to set down any deep roots. I believe it is in that loneliness that I was able to develop a strong relationship with God that has brought me to this place of ministry and leadership within the Church today. It gave me the eyes to see a world beyond what I could always experience.

I was not tithed as you were, but like you my life changed drastically when I was a young child. My dad died when I was 7 years old and so I grew up without my father. I imagine my love for the Church (and my ability to tolerate its exaggerated patriarchy) is in part due to the fact that I missed my father so much during my childhood. When I was in my mid-twenties I discerned a call to ministry and began my formal studies. Like you, I did not have a sound education as a child and I too have felt the consequences of my lack of early education. I have been a full-time student for most of my adult life, studying at numerous institutions including many years full-time at the local Roman Catholic Seminary (earning several graduate and post-graduate degrees). It is surprising that they even let me, a woman, into those programs! In many instances I was the only woman in the class – and I had to work twice as hard to receive the same grades and respect as the men in my class going on to

ordination! And they were definitely not always nice to me along the way – but you know how that goes… In spite of them, I have written two master's theses and two doctoral dissertations! My written work has taken decades, just as yours did – and I imagine I will be writing for decades to come. I am so close, and yet feel so far away from producing my "great work" which has been a seedling growing in my mind for years. It has begun to sprout, but has not yet fully blossomed. Over my years in the seminary and parish work I have spent many hours with clergy, seminarians, and lay Catholic leaders. My experience as a minister has been both rewarding and exasperating. My relationship with the institutional Church is very much a "love-hate" relationship, which I am sure you can relate to.
Like you I am a letter writer. I have corresponded (positively and negatively) over the years with bishops, priests, nuns, political leaders, ecclesial administrators, and others in positions of authority. I have stood up for injustice – especially where the clergy are concerned – but I have not had the privilege or opportunity to correspond with the Pope… I may, however, send him a copy of my book!

You have inspired me in so many ways. I believe in the healing power of viriditas and am well-invested in learning more about holistic health and herbal/natural medicine. I even studied at a natural nutrition school to better understand your writings on these topics –I appreciated the wisdom gained in that program! My daughter is a wonderful nutritionist. You would love her – if I could only get her to meet you… Anyways, thanks to you, spelt flour and fennel are staples in our house! We even named our garden in your honor - the "Hildegarden" and it is abundant in herbs and greens. And your music – there is nothing quite as healing as your chants. I have listened to Ordo Virtutum so many times I have it memorized –as does everyone around me! I see so many parallels in what I do and what you did! Just last year I found myself directing two parish religious education programs (one that I had been at for many years and the other which was a new position). As I ran back and forth throughout the week (the parishes are geographically close – one on each side of the river!) I could not help but see a parallel to you as you ran back and forth across the Rhine River administering both at Ruperstberg and Eibingen. I also am a professor at a religious university and find myself teaching and preaching often – mostly women, not with fire and brimstone like you did, but I try to bring people, especially those who have wandered away (or have been hurt by the Church), back to the faith.

Like you my Latin is poor – although I have tried so hard over the years to improve it! And my love for the Scriptures, particularly the Wisdom literature and my Christology, is strong like yours. Now, if I had just been born with your gift for music that would have been awesome! I cannot even carry a tune... although I have a dulcimer sitting in my room waiting to be played!

I was so blessed this past summer to have been able to travel to Bingen to visit your holy places. I boarded a plane and traveled to Bingen alone (the first time I have ever been out of the country) to stay with your sisters in Eibingen. When I arrived in Frankfurt I found my way by train and foot to your abbey. It was the scariest, most exciting experience, I have ever had! As it turned out – and this was pure coincidence, I was in your monastery for daily Mass praying with your sisters as I celebrated my 43rd birthday! The same monumental birthday that propelled you into your public ministry and the writing of your first major theological work, Scivias.[65] *It did not really hit me that I was going to be in your Abbey for my 43rd birthday until I was actually there. Even more astounding, I was there in your parish Church, with your relics, on the Feast of Pentecost! The priest did not preach as powerful a homily as you did on the Feast of Pentecost when you warned the clerics at Trier of God's*

---

[65] The first book Hildegard wrote. It was completed around 1151 AD (after ten years of writing). She published it upon completion after receiving permission from Pope Eugenius III and Bernard of Clairvaux in 1148 AD to write.

vengeance![66] *At least I don't think he did… I don't understand much German, but the people were smiling and I'm sure the people in Trier when you preached were not!*

The experience of being with you this year while I discern what path the Living Light is calling me to walk has been nothing less than incredible. I believe you were walking the journey with me while I was there traveling between Disibodenberg (the ruins are overwhelmingly beautiful – I can't image the glory of it in its day), Bermersheim (I thought I might actually die on this trip – but that's for another letter!), Cologne, (I'm not sure what it looked like when you preached there, but it was the biggest cathedral I will ever see!) Mainz (I was hoping to meet a prelate but there were none around), Ruperstberg (I'm not sure you would like what's going on there these days), and of course Bingen (again, not sure you would like it there today- aside from the many stores carrying Hildegard tea and cookies!) and Rudesheim-Eibingen (if I were to ever move from Ohio this is where I would want to live – beautiful area surrounding your two churches). The week I spent walking in your footsteps was transforming and continues to draw me in to your spirit. I wanted so much to just stay in Germany in your presence. Well, actually I wanted to get back to my family – what I really wanted was to bring Germany back to Ohio!

---

[66] In letter 223r Hildegard responded to the request of the Provost in Trier to send a copy of the homily she preached while she was there in 1160 AD. Her response began with, "I, a poor little form of a woman with neither health nor strength, nor courage, nor learning, a woman totally subordinate to my superiors. I heard these words from the mystical light of a true vision…" She continues on for several pages railing against the sins of the clergy (not with the voice of a weak and unlearned woman) and warns them of the days to come, "God does not excuse [especially the clergy], without vengeance the failure to follow His precepts" and that he will cleanse the Church like a "Gardener will cast unwholesome weeds out of His garden" and then the righteous "all the wholesome plants" he will save (Baird & Ehrman, 1998, pp. 18-23).

The reason for my prayer today is this – I am getting tired and worn down. The Church, as you well know, can be exhausting and downright frustrating! I am speaking here for myself, but I know I speak as a voice for many women leaders, and some men. The Church desperately needs a new model of ministry. The Church continues to identify leadership with priests – whether they are good leaders or not – and many are not. We are in dire need of spiritual leaders. I am engaged each day with families and individuals who are so grateful for my care – and I draw strength from them. But some of the clergy here are so insensitive and difficult to work with. They do not respect the ministry of women; they can be so self-absorbed and arrogant! I would like to say that you cannot imagine the arrogance, but after reading your letters I believe you most certainly can imagine!

I have had my share of "Kuno" experiences and they are wearing me down. Today in my diocese there are more lay ecclesial ministers (mostly women) functioning in parishes than there are clergy – women with graduate and post-graduate degrees, often surpassing the education and formation levels of the ordained clergy. Almost every parish staff in my diocese has at least one full-time female minister working long hours engaged in clerical work, and yet the clergy continue to act as though women are naturally inferior. I know you taught that women were weak and fragile, but you certainly were not! I don't believe there has been a woman before or after you with the courage to speak the prophetic words you spoke to so many clergy who had fallen from their vocation Yes, there is a hierarchal structure, and maybe it serves a purpose, but so many women are being subordinated unfairly and unjustly. This subordination is not based on one's call, commitment, or even competency, but simply on one's sex. There are dioceses throughout the world that are suffering from such a lack of ordained clergy where women have been appointed "parish life coordinators" (aka "lay pastor")[67] running every aspect of parish life, but without the faculties to celebrate sacraments... I know how you felt about women's ordination, but it is a different time and the leadership of women is so desperately needed. The clergy are not feeding the sheep – it is again a "womanish time" as you used to say. Women ministers are caring for the flock – many of the shepherds have "retreated to the caves of their own desire."[68]

Not all – some are working hard. I have been blessed with a "Volmar" who has given me the gift of education – teaching me philosophy, scripture, and patristics; he has tried desperately to teach me Latin; and he has given me a secure place within the institution to write and minister and even preach when appropriate. He is truly a gift. However, he is rare! Outside of my "utopia" so many of the clergy I have encountered have been so blind to the gift women bring to leadership in the Church. Clericalism is rampant.

How did you do it? How did you continue to stay strong when constantly confronted with so much injustice, especially among the clergy who are called by the nature of their office to lead as Christ led – as servant leaders – but rather lead as if they are elite members of a good old boys club, expecting not to serve, but to be served? How did you keep yourself focused on your vocation, in spite of so many obstacles along the way? I want so much to persevere in the face of injustice, to be a transformational leader, as you did. But, they can be so frustrating.

---

[67] Ruth Wallace (1992), *They Call Her Pastor*

[68] Excerpt from a powerful homily (letter 15r) Hildegard preached to the "shepherds of the Church" in 1163 AD at the cathedral in Cologne. "You are a bad example to others, since no rivulet of good reputation flows from you, so that, with respect to the soul, you have neither food to eat nor clothes to wear, but only unjust deeds with the good knowledge. Therefore, your honor will perish and the crown will fall from your head. Thus injustice calls forth justice, and it seeks out and searches for every scandal...Poor little timorous figure of a woman that I am, I have worn myself out for two whole years so that I might bring this message in person to the magistrates, teachers, and other wise men who hold the higher positions in the Church"(Baird & Ehrman, 1994, pp.54-63).

It is for this reason that I have dedicated my academic career to you and your work. It is my hope that I might be able, through my own dedicated service, and your example, bring about much needed change in the Church, at least in the Church of my diocese. But, I just don't know how to do it.

Our current Pope Francis has repeatedly challenged the clergy to throw off the yoke of clericalism and to embrace mercy, yet here in my diocese, and in others nearby, it seems to be worsening. I know I have been called to model something different, called to work to change the paradigm, but I don't know how to do that and so I ask for your intercession. I have considered every possible way and nothing seems viable. I know I have been called to a task, I have a vocation, and I just don't know how to accomplish it. Please help me discern the voice of the Living Light so that I can find a way through, what feels like a stone wall, in order to make a difference.

BTW – I have found so much joy in reading your letters. There are a few that make me laugh every time I read them! You were something else!
Yours in Christ,
Shanon

N. Putting down the letter Hildegard begins to feel overwhelmed.

H. **What is going on? What does she mean I'm a saint? How am I supposed to help this woman? I understand how frustrated she is, but how can she be ministering in a parish? Since when do they allow women to do that? I could understand a convent, but a parish? Where did she get my letters? And what is BTW? This is all too much for me, I am just a weak and fragile woman.**

N. Putting her hands to her head Hildegard begins to massage her temples. She definitely has a migraine now. Looking about the table she spots two large envelopes with a Vatican seal.

H. What are these? Two letters - one dated May 10, 2012 and the other October 7, 2012 from Rome? What did I do now? They cannot possibly still be upset about that soldier. The interdict placed on my convent was lifted centuries ago! How many times do I have to tell them – the man was reconciled to the Church![69] When are they going to let it go! Hmm... This says it is a letter from Pope Benedict XVI. Benedict XVI? I knew many popes in my day, and wrote letters to a few... But I haven't heard of this one. I do know of Pope Benedict the IX and the X but they did not follow the voice of God![70] I hope Benedict XVI isn't like them! I guess I should open the letters to see what kind of trouble I am in now!

N. Opening the first letter Hildegard reads it out loud.

H. This is a letter from The Congregation of the Causes of Saints. That's interesting....

---

[69] During the last year of Hildegard's life, she and her sisters were placed under an interdict for burying a man in the monastery grounds who had been condemned of heresy. She claims he was reconciled to the Church. The interdict prohibited the nuns from singing and receiving Holy Communion. The story is preserved in her *Vita* (Silvas, 1994, pp.) and her reaction to the prelates in Mainz is preserved in a letter (23) that she personally delivered – on foot at the age of eight-one, to them. In her letter she wrote: "Seized by no small terror, as a result, I looked as usual to the True Light, and, with wakeful eyes, I saw in my spirit that if this man were disinterred in accordance with their [prelates in Mainz], a terrible and lamentable danger would come upon us like a dark cloud before a threatening thunderstorm... And so, O men of faith, let none of you resist Him or oppose Him, let He fall on you in His might, and you have no helper to protect you from His judgment" (Baird & Ehrman, 1994, pp. 76-79).

[70] Both were deposed as anti-popes.

Vatican City, 10 May 2012
"The Holy Father today received in audience Cardinal Angelo Amato S.D.B., prefect of the Congregation for the Causes of Saints. During the audience he extended the liturgical cult of St. Hildegard of Bingen (1089-1179) to the universal Church, inscribing her in the catalogue of saints."

WHAT! That woman from Cleveland wasn't joking! I am officially a saint! How can this be? I ... a saint! I cannot believe it. I am not sure what is more shocking – that I am a saint or that it took those men in Rome 834 years to do a job that should have been done centuries ago! I wonder what miracles I performed to have received this honor?[71] Maybe it was the healings from my infirmary. What is this second letter? This one says it is an Apostolic Letter – that sounds important. Maybe they realized they made a mistake. Maybe they rethought their decision to name me a saint... Maybe they found the angry letter that I wrote to the Abbot...

N. Opening the second letter from the Vatican Hildegard reads it out loud.

Vatican City, 7 October 2012
A 'light for her people and her time': in these words Blessed John Paul II, my venerable predecessor, described Saint Hildegard of Bingen in 1979, on the occasion of the eight-hundredth anniversary of the death of this German mystic (1). Hildegard's eminent doctrine echoes the teaching of the Apostles, the Father and writings of her own day, while it finds a constant point of reference in the Rule of Saint Benedict. For these reasons the attribution of the title of Doctor of the

---

[71] To be canonized there needs to miracles verified by Rome associated with the person after their death. However, in the case of Hildegard Pope Benedict waived the normal requirements for canonization, including the miracles, because she had already long been revered a saint in Germany. There are miraculous healings recorded in her *Vita* from when she was alive and offering medical services in her infirmary (Silvas, 1994, pp.181-210)

Universal Church to Hildegard of Bingen has great significance for today's world and an extraordinary importance for women. In Hildegard are expressed the most noble values of womanhood: hence the presence of women in the Church and in society is also illumined by her presence, both from the perspective of scientific research and that of pastoral activity. Her ability to speak to those who were far from the faith and from the Church make Hildegard a credible witness of the new evangelization.

By virtue of her reputation for holiness and her eminent teaching, on 6 March 1979 Cardinal Joseph Höffner, Archbishop of Cologne and President of the German Bishops' Conference, together with the Cardinals, Archbishops and Bishops of the same Conference, including myself as Cardinal Archbishop of Munich and Freising, submitted to Blessed <u>John Paul II</u> the request that Hildegard of Bingen be declared a Doctor of the Universal Church. In that petition, the Cardinal emphasized the soundness of Hildegard's doctrine, recognized in the twelfth century by Pope Eugene III, her holiness, widely known and celebrated by the people, and the authority of her writings. As time passed, other petitions were added to that of the German Bishops' Conference, first and foremost the petition from the nuns of Eibingen Monastery, which bears her name. Thus, to the common wish of the People of God that Hildegard be officially canonized, was added the request that she be declared a "Doctor of the Universal Church".

Today, with the help of God and the approval of the whole Church, this act has taken place. I declare Saint Hildegard of Bingen, professed nun of the Order of Saint Benedict, to be a Doctor of the Universal Church" (7).

Now I know I must be dreaming! Women are not named Doctors of the Church! I have never heard of such a thing![72]

---

[72] Hildegard is the 4th woman in the history of the Roman Catholic Church to be named a doctor. Catherine of Siena, Teresa of Avila, and Theres of Liseux are

And by a German Pope nonetheless! They want me to believe that I am a Doctor of the Church so that they can turn around and condemn me of heresy! They want to accuse me of being guided by my own ambition – of failing to embrace Queen *Humilitas*[73] Kuno must be behind this! I am not going to fall for it! I don't know what to do – I need some guidance. I need the *Living Light*.

N. Walking over to her bed, Hildegard kneels down and proceeds to make the Sign of the Cross. She begins to pray…

PRAYER
H. "O God, you defend those who believe in you. Keep me safe in your omnipotence. I find shelter under your wings, and honor you in thanksgiving and praise. Never do I lift my eyes to a God who disappoints me and does not know me (*LDO*).[74] I wander aimlessly in the shadow of death, a pilgrim in a strange land: the destination of my travels is my only comfort. I should be a companion of angels, O God, for I was fashioned in clay by your living breath. But should not I then recognize and sense you? Pain has befallen me, for the tent of my body turned its eye to the north. Alas, I was held prisoner there and robbed of my light and the joy of wisdom. And driven from my inheritance, I was led into slavery. Where am I and how did I get here? Who will comfort me in my prison? How can I break these chains? Who will care for my wounds, anoint them with oil and show me mercy in my pain? O heaven, hear my

---

the others who received the title in the twentieth century, long after the time Hildegard lived.

[73] Humility was considered by Hildegard to be the "highest virtues" the antithesis of pride, which for Hildegard was the sin of Lucifer (the fallen angel) and the root of Original Sin for human beings. In her play *Ordo Virtutum*, the soul is only able to conquer the temptation of the Devil by drawing strength from the virtues and following (obediently) the example of Queen Humilitas.

[74] *Liber Divinorum Operum* (Book of Divine Works). The third of Hildegard's trilogy of theology books written around 1163 AD.

cry! The earth shall tremble with me in mourning, for I am a pilgrim without comfort and help" (*Scivias* 1, 4).

OPENING CONVERSATION WITH the LIVING LIGHT

L.L. Hildegard of Bingen! How is it that you do not recognize or sense me? I have been present with you from the time you were a small child, calling you to walk with me as a child of the light (Ephesians 5:8). I, the Living Light, am always with you. I am the source by which you drew your very sustenance. I am here with you.

N. Eyes still closed; Hildegard can see and feel the presence of the *Living Light*. She experiences an overwhelming sense of peace penetrating her entire being, just as she remembered.

H. Of course I recognize you. I am just so confused. I do not understand why I am here or even where "here" is. Am I in Rupertsberg? Where are my sisters?

L.L.. You are in Eibingen, Hildegard, in the New Abbey of St. Hildegard in Rudesheim – up the hill from your beloved monastery at Eibingen. This beautiful abbey was built in 1900AD and your sisters are here. Actually, your sisters that you knew in your lifetime are long deceased, but many others have joined your convent since that time and have labored to preserve and maintain your writings, music, art, and your legacy – they are here. Your memory, music, writings, artwork, and religious spirit are kept alive here in this monastery. Pilgrims travel from all over, especially around your feast day, to draw inspiration and strength from your legacy.

H. Why am I in a new abbey? What happened to the monasteries I built with my own hands?

L.L. Ruperstberg suffered over the centuries Hildegard. There was a fire in the 14th century that destroyed much of what you built. It was rebuilt and then destroyed in 1632 AD during the thirty year war with the Swedes. Your remains were smuggled to Eibingen by way of Cologne by your sisters. Today there remains just a couple of underground cellars that have been renovated and are used now for prayers services and Hildegard events.

H. Cologne! That is a long way across the river! Why did they go so far out of the way to bring me to Eibingen?

L.L. That was the only way to ensure the safety of your reliquary. Once your remains arrived, they were enshrined at your monastery in Eibingen. The convent was destroyed in a fire in 1932 AD and a new one was built where your remains are still preserved to this day in the sanctuary under a beautiful reproduction of your Holy Trinity miniature. Pilgrims come from all over to show you honor. On your date of death, September 17th, your remains are carried in procession from the Parish Church up the enormous hill to the New Abbey, which is why you are here today!

H. So, they woke me up carrying me up the hill? Did one of the priests drop me? They do tend to drink too much spelt beer!

L.L. You always did have such a sense of humor! No, no one dropped you. You are awake because you have work to do.

H. What do you mean work to do? All I ever did was work! I'm tired. I need to rest. My head is pounding. I am a weak woman…

L.L It is again a womanish time in the Church Hildegard! Your wisdom and example are very much needed. The Church is in crisis and the people are looking to you for an answer.

H. What do you mean by the "Church is in crisis"? It couldn't be any worse than when I was alive!

L.L. *Much has improved, but there are some serious issues. It has been deeply divided by ethnicity and creed, not to mention ambition and greed! The credibility of the Church has been devastated by power and corruption among clergy, most seriously in the sexual abuse scandals. Years of bishops moving priests around rather than removing them from active ministry. So many lives have been devastated. The clergy have abused their power and have hurt so many of the faithful. Many have left the Church altogether or are simply not participating. They no longer believe in my presence – they have lost awareness of viriditas, in part because those entrusted with preserving and passing on my mysteries have failed to do so. They have allowed their own agendas and sinful tendencies to tear apart the Church and corrupt my message. The number of vocations of ordained and religious has plummeted. Schools and parishes are being closed at an unprecedented rate in dioceses across the developed world, including Germany. Many parishes are operating without priests and in some areas children have never even seen a religious sister. Lay women are doing so much of the ecclesial work, just as you did Hildegard, and yet the Church does not recognize their leadership with the same dignity as that of the clergy, though they should be. I continue to stir in the hearts of those who believe in me and I am calling forward a new generation of leaders in the Church – just as I did when I called you so many years ago - but the style of leadership is changing and the Church needs an example. They need someone to show them a healthier way.*

H. You said that they no longer believe in you and are not participating. Are they not afraid of being accused of heresy?

L.L. *The Church has changed Hildegard. Certainly one can be accused of heresy, but the fear of punishment no longer exists. To think there was ever a time that one was forced to have faith is in itself scandalous. Human beings were created out of love with the gift of free-will which never forces love. The Church should never have forced it either. I want people to do good and follow me because of love – not fear.*

H. Wow! I wish I would have had the freedom people have today! I would not have had to grovel for permission from Bernard of Clairvaux[75], Pope Eugenius III, and of course the Abbot Kuno to write down my visions. Thanks to my love for Queen Humility, I was good at groveling, but how I despised it!

L.L. The challenges you overcame contributed to your greatness Hildegard! Plus, you knew just how to speak the language of the hierarchy!

H. So, if the people are free today to believe and write as they wish, why are they calling upon me?

L.L. They are not free Hildegard. They no longer fear physical punishment for their beliefs, but they are suffering spiritual and emotional pain unlike anything in the past. They are drying up – they have lost their moisture, their viriditas.[76] Institutions are controlled by consumerism and commercialism. There is little concern for the common good or for the earth. All of my creation - nature, animals, and even human beings - are being abused and exploited for short-term gains. It is becoming difficult for them to see and hear me in their midst. They are not open to my presence the way you always have been. The clergy are still drawn to

---

[75] The earliest letter in Hildegard's collection was written to Bernard in 1146-1147 AD requesting his permission to write: "Now, father, for the love of God, I seek consolation from you, that I may be assured. More than two years ago, indeed, I saw you in a vision, like a man looking straight into the sun, bold and unafraid. And I wept, because I myself am so timid and fearful. Good and gentle father, I have been placed in your care so that you might reveal to me through your correspondence whether I should speak these things openly or keep my silence, because I have great anxiety about this vision with respect to how much I should speak about what I have seen and heard" (Baird & Ehrman, 1994p.28).

[76] This echoes the word she wrote in a letter (201r) to the medieval mystic Elisabeth of Schonau she wrote, "Thus the Church of God has withered, for it lacks moisture. Withdrawn from the love of God, it has grown cold" (Baird & Ehrman, 1998, p.182).

power, prestige and money and they have turned the Church into a business. Clericalism, as Shanon said in her letter to you, is rampant. The Church depends heavily on the charisms of the laity, often times lay women, to keep the Church authentic, yet women are prohibited from fulfilling dignified roles, including ordained ministry. As always, the clergy are not tuned to me – they invest enormous amounts of time and energy arranging liturgical services in my name but fail to actually let me speak. They look at me, Hildegard, but they do not see. They hear, but they do not listen (Matt 13:3). They have lost the ability to see the presence of my light within the community and even within themselves. Their mouth says yes, but their actions say no and that is the way of the evil one (Matt 5:37). They are not caring for the garden as they've been entrusted to do.[77] The leadership in the Church is in need of transformation – you were a transformational leader.

H. I'm not sure what I transformed. I preached, and wrote, and admonished, but even up till the end it seemed as though my words were falling on closed ears. From what you are saying, it seems not much has changed in nine centuries!

L.L. Actually, Hildegard, a lot that has changed. There is a growing awareness among many of our interconnectedness – many people are becoming strong voices for those who are abused, exploited, and discriminated against. Many have awakened to realize that they cannot survive without the gifts of the earth and are trying to find more sustainable ways to live. But the human condition is still such that it is weak and is constantly being drawn away from the purpose and plan God has ordained. Greed, injustice, power, war, selfishness – all of this is dominating the

---

[77] Hildegard repeatedly uses the image of a garden as a metaphor for the Church. God is THE Gardener, but those in positions of leadership are called to be gardeners as well and in addition the individual person, in Hildegard's thought, is like a garden. In a letter to unnamed Dean she wrote, "Cut down the weeds... Plant the seeds of fruitful virtue in your garden" (Baird & Ehrman, 1998, p.120-121). In a letter to an abbot named Adam (85r/b) she wrote a beautiful exhortation on the role of a *Gardner Leader*.

minds and hearts of otherwise good people. I was thinking of the homily you preached against the Cathars[78] - the Devil indeed continues to deceive many within the world today[79], often times in my name and to those unsuspecting! But I am The Living Light and am present with them continuing to call them into right relationship with me, each other, and all of creation. I am Love and am confident that my love will prevail if only my words can be heard. Do you remember the words I gave you to share - **"Earth does not cast off earth, nor spurn that which is like unto itself. Rather it builds it up to the best of its ability. Therefore consistent with the aid and mercy of God, it behooves you to observe wisdom and bring back the wandering sheep to the fold. Then God will spare you in your sins, because you are all one earth.** *"[80] They just need to be reminded that they are all from the same earth – the same source. The social sins of the day – greed, discrimination, violence, human trafficking – they are not only hurting others, they are hurting themselves. They are fracturing the whole of my creation.*

H. The devil has that effect on this world... He is always causing division – causing people to look from light towards darkness. Even when they know better – his power is strong. After a vision of you I believe I wrote, "The Devil and his followers, who turned away from the supreme God, not wishing to know or understand it. Therefore they are outcast

---

[78] A heretical sect that threatened the Catholic Church during Hildegard's time. The Cathars rejected the sacredness of the human body, or any part of the created world, thus rejecting the incarnation and sacramental life of the Church. Hildegard took it upon herself to be a "trumpet of God" against this movement.

[79] "Within your midst, the ancient serpent is building towers in their ears, that is, those who are like the Sadducees and like those who call Baal God, and do not know the just God, so that by the cunning of a deceitful spirit, he sometimes appears to them like a spark, either black or stormy, or bright and local... And this is a diabolical and deceptive thing, for deceptive spirits sometimes disguise themselves" (Baird & Ehrman, 1998, p. 124)

[80] From a letter (219) she wrote to a community of monks (Baird & Ehrman, 2004, p.9).

from all good, not because they did not know it, but because in their great pride they despised it"[81]

L.L. *Yes you did write that! And in the same vision you also wrote,* **"Be converted and do penance! Thus as you rise from your evil habits that iniquity by which you had been soiled will not sink you deep into the ruin of death, since you cast it off in the day of your salvation. Therefore the angels will rejoice over you, because you have abandoned the Devil and run to God".** *They ask for your intercession Hildegard, not because you have the power to change them, but because you have the words of Wisdom – my words – that have the power to change them. You are a trumpet for God! You can get their attention – teach them how to look and how to listen to the voice of the Living Light. Remind them of the splendor of my virtues. They need to be reminded of their dignity and their vocation. Especially those called to leadership. There are too many leaders in the Church following their own agendas rather than mine.*

H. Tell me about it! I was just thinking about the letter I wrote to the prelates at Mainz when they forbade me and my sisters to sing the hours and receive the Blessed Sacrament! Not because we had done anything wrong, but because of their own pride and arrogance!

L.L. *I remember that! I still laugh when I think of the look on their faces as they read it!* **"Therefore, those who, without just cause, impose silence on a church and prohibit the singing of God's praises and those who have on earth unjustly despoiled God of His honor and glory will lose their place among the chorus of angels, unless they have amended their lives through true penitence and humble restitution! Moreover let those who hold the keys of heaven beware not to open those things which are to be kept closed nor to close those things which are to be kept open, for harsh judgment will fall upon those who rule, unless they**

---

[81] Scivias Book 1, Vision 2.

rule with good judgment!"[82] *Sometimes those tough words need to be spoken to transform the minds and hearts of leaders! Do you remember how you ended the letter? I still laugh!*

H. "This time is a womanish time… But the strength of God's justice is exerting itself, a female warrior battling against injustice, so that it might be defeated!"[83] **I was so angry – I think I stomped all the way from Rupertsberg to Mainz to deliver that letter! And they still didn't listen. Thank goodness for my friend Philip**[84] **– without him I may have died without the sacraments! I am being called back again to warn them, as I did during my day, of the consequences of their behavior?**

L.L. If only it was that simple Hildegard! It is not so much a warning. As I said before, I do not want anyone following me out of fear. I know some of the visions you received were filled with frightful images – although your sisters did tell you to lay off of the mushrooms! Seriously though, there is a lot in the world to be afraid of – but I do not want my message to be delivered in fear. You have been awakened to invite them to become more aware of my presence in the world. To encourage them to live lives rooted in viriditas. To inspire in them, through the example of your courage, to work at creating a world rooted in justice. I want them to grow in joy and love for me and for each other! I want them to see that there is a better way – an accessible path within themselves that leads to life. You are being called back to shine my light – to bring them hope. Your genius can help them to better appreciate the need to recognize the sacredness of all creation. To bring them back to a place where they can become whole – in mind, body, and spirit – in the essence of viriditas which is all around them if they choose to open their heart to its presence. You

---

[82] Letter 23 (Baird & Ehrman, 1994, p.79)
[83] Ibid.
[84] It is believed Philip of Heinsberg, who would later become the Archbishop of Cologne, stepped up in Hildegard's defense and was instrumental with the prelates of Mainz in lifting the interdict (Baird & Ehrman, 1994, p.82).

can help them, tap into their mystical gifts, to overcome so much of what divides and destroys them. Inspire them to be open to my song and to serve with humility.

H. O Frondens virga, in tua nobilitate stans sicut aurora procedit: nunc gaude et letare et nos debiles dignare a mala consuetudine liberare atque manum tuam porrige ad erigendum nos.[85]

L.L. Ahhh your music Hildegard is so transcendent! The path to wholeness calls us into a deeper awareness of the transcendent which speaks in song. I just love your work on the virtues.

H. *Ordo Virtutum* – one of my finest pieces! One must place their trust in queen *Humilitas*[86] if s/he is to lead with integrity.

L.L. Indeed! If we could just get more of the clergy to embrace the virtues the Church would be in much better shape! If the clergy want to be respected as shepherds they need to integrate attitudes of authenticity and integrity. It is not enough to just go to seminary – they know how to "talk the talk" but they are not "walking the talk."[87] The signal that they are sending to the faithful is inauthentic. Their message does not carry the spiritual authority necessary to draw people towards me. When their pride blocks out my Light their message is invalidated. They need to renew their vocation, not by adhering to the "letter of the law" which they tend towards, but by embracing justice. You articulated it beautifully in one of your visions; **"Hence you must think every hour about how to make so great a gift as useful to others as to yourself by works of justice, so that it will reflect the**

---

[85] Newman (1988/1998) "O leafy branch, standing in your nobility as the dawn breaks: Now rejoice and be glad, and deign to set us frail ones free from our bad habits, and stretch forth your hand to raise us up" (p.121).

[86] In her morality play, *Ordo Virtutum,* Hildegard portrays the devil being conquered through the virtues, of which humility is queen. A youtube presentation of the play can be found at https://www.youtube.com/watch?v=WBGgRSPyUFQ

[87] Houston & Sokolow, (2013), *The Wise Leader, p.* 44).

splendor of sanctity from you, and the people will be inspired by your good example to praise and honor God." [88]   *This is a treasure endowed on the Church for centuries, yet for some reason it often remains buried and unused. You walked the talk Hildegard. You challenged injustice where you saw it, especially among leaders - even when it came with a personal price. The Church needs more leaders willing to do the same today. The Church needs Hildegard leaders!*

H. Speaking of the Church, I received a couple of letters from a Pope Benedict XVI telling me that he had canonized me and named me a doctor of the Church! Imagine that! I never heard of a woman doctor of the Church! Is Pope Benedict XVI still around?

L.L. Yes, he is still around and he had some wonderful things to say about you! However, he is not the Pope anymore.
N. Hildegard, now becoming quite anxious begins to ask a series of questions.

H. What?! Do we have an anti-pope? I had this same issue with Emperor Frederick Barbarossa – he kept appointed anti-popes to office![89] Although he was so happy that I predicted his appointment as the Holy Roman Emperor that he continued to protect me, even when I yelled at him... Are the end-times at hand? Is there the antichrist ruling? I warned of this day![90] "For the son of perdition will come raging with the arts he first used to seduce, in monstrous shamefulness and blackest wickedness. For he runs wild in acts of vile lust and shameful blasphemy, causing people to deny God and tainting their minds and tearing the Church with the greed of rapine! For the son of perditions will try to seduce people by evil

---

[88] *Scivias* Book Three, Vision Ten.
[89] Letters 312-316 (Baird & Ehrman, 2004, p. 112-116)
[90] Many of Hildegard's visions and homilies were apocalyptic in nature and she repeatedly warned of the coming of the antichrist. Hildegard's antichrist imagery mimics the descriptions found in the biblical Book of Revelation.

deceptions, and at first speak to them flatteringly and gently, but then try cruelly to pervert and force them!"[91] Looking through these old newspapers piled up here there does seem to be a lot of weird things taking place – war, unusual weather, talk of aliens? The antichrist must be slithering about!

L.L. Whew those are some strong words Hildegard! No wonder you suffered from so many headaches! Calm down... Yes the world is experiencing some weird events right now. And there are some that feel the end-times are at hand, although there were many that felt the end-times were at hand in your day and in times before. Don't you remember what was in people's minds at the turn of the century when you were born? They were sure the world was ending and yet here we are centuries later! There are some that are fearful that the current Pope Francis might be the antichrist because of his radical acceptance of everyone – not only those who follow Catholic Christian teaching. He embraces people of all faith traditions (and even atheists) and insists they are equal in dignity as children of God and can be saved – even if they don't subscribe to the Christian faith. It is a very radical stance for a Catholic Pope!

H. Radical – I think he just might be the antichrist! How could an atheist be saved? That is not what you revealed to me in my visions. Maybe he is presenting the world a "fake" greenness!

L.L. I know this is shocking for you to hear Hildegard. You were a faithful servant and you passed on my message just as I revealed it to you. You lived at a different time – 12th century Germany spoke a different theological language than the world speaks today. I revealed myself to you in a language that you could understand. Not only that - if you had preached the message Pope Francis is preaching today, you would have surely ended up on a pyre, regardless of how many powerful friends you had! Are you okay, Hildegard?

---

[91] *Scivias* Book Three, Vision Eleven

H. Yes, I'm just thinking of something I wrote, "O servant of God, you who are an ornament in Christ's service, do not fear the heaviness that rises in you..."[92]

L.L. Change is hard Hildegard. People have such a myopic view of who I am and how I can be active in the world. And then the doctrines they create are so rigid. They don't allow much room for me to move about as I will. Look at your experience Hildegard. I called you to be my trumpet – which you did well - even though it was not normally accepted. I used you in a way that broke through social, cultural, and religious boundaries, challenging preconceived notions. When I reveal myself in a way that doesn't match a preconceived notion or that stretches one's mind and heart to be more open and inclusive (like Pope Francis is trying to do today) it can be overwhelming. Looking at the look on your face I think you are a bit overwhelmed right now!

H. So, as long as you are shattering my preconceived notions of the world and how you are active in it – what's the deal with the aliens? Why so much talk from the Church on it today?

L.L. The world as you experienced it Hildegard is microscopic in relation my macrocosmic reality. I am all that exists – not only that which exists in the world you knew but throughout all the universe. When I appeared to Moses in the desert and proclaimed "I am that Am"[93] it was in the form of Light (a bush that burned but was not consumed). And when I descended upon the disciples on the Feast of Pentecost – and upon you in your visions – again I appeared as Light. When I tell my followers "I am the Light of the World"[94] the depth of meaning is not often grasped. I am Light and in my light all things – galaxies, stars, planets, humans, and even microbes – come to be. The power of my light cannot possibly be contained in one tiny atmosphere or even one small universe.

---

[92] This is an opening greeting she wrote to a priest (Baird & Ehrman, 2004, p.93).
[93] Exodus 3:14
[94] John 8:12

Pope Francis, and his team at the Vatican Observatory, know that if I am truly omnipotent and omnipresent then I must exist outside of the immediate world within which they live. The material world expands far beyond earth and its solar system and the Pope, and his Jesuit brothers, have been discussing quite openly the likelihood of my having created extraterrestrial life. The reality of aliens raises numerous theological questions – shattering preconceived ideas of who I am and how I create. This has gotten people a bit ruffled. It certainly does not help the situation that the Vatican's telescope the most powerful telescope in the world[95], was named L.U.C.I.F.E.R. by its creator![96]

H. Okay – that's enough. This is more than I can handle. We both know who Lucifer was and what Lucifer did! God bestowed on Lucifer the highest honor – the brightest light – and Lucifer used that against God dragging not only other light beings (angels) down with him but humans as well![97] How can the Vatican possibly be okay with this? I am trying to be open-minded here, but this is too much. This has all of the markings of the antichrist!

L.L. As you know Hildegard, the name word Lucifer means "light-bearer" and so maybe someone thought it was funny, but it is not being received that way. Apocalyptic fears are escalating and in some cases it may be justified. However, as is always true, fears are fueled by uncertainly and lack of faith. No one knows the day or the hour[98] that the end time will come - it may be upon us and it may not be. Faith assures us that regardless of what is to come, "all will be well."[99] Your role today is not to warn of the coming of the anti-Christ or even to be concerned with aliens. I have

---

[95] http://www.vovatt.org/
[96] http://www.arcticbeacon.com/greg/headlines/university-of-arizona-vatican-and-jesuits-name-new-telescope-lucifer/
[97] See *Scivias* Book Three, Vision One for her vision on the fall of Lucifer.
[98] Matthew 24:36
[99] This is a famous line from another medieval mystic, Julian of Norwich (1342-1416 AD).

called you back inspire in the people a vision. They need a vision of me – not one marked by fear – but marked by love. They need an example of leadership rooted in faith and love, an example of authentic, creative, gardener leadership! They need to be reconnected to the Living Light. They need leaders who can draw them to a life deeply rooted in viriditas.

Leadership in the Church is not only in need of renewal, but is so desperately in need of a new vision. The vision I endowed in you, that you so faithfully shared eight-hundred years ago, was a vision that was necessary at that time. Today, the Church – and the world – needs a new vision. A vision still marked by virtue, charity, and justice, nonetheless a vision that speaks the language of people today. A vision that speaks to all people - not only Catholics – but also Catholics! So many Catholics in the Church today are hanging on to a past that no longer exists. They are so afraid to let go of what was – they are unable to embrace what can be. Especially those called to ecclesial leadership roles. "People who want to maintain tradition at all costs often want to maintain those traditions from the past that make them feel safe and secure, and they react instinctively and angrily to anything that threatens their security. They resist change in a church because change means living in uncertainty and ambiguity which are among the worst feelings these people can imagine. They would rather have the false clarity and certainly that being closed to God provides, rather than the ambiguity and uncertainty that taking new, God-inspired paths can bring."[100]

H. I remember the words you once spoke to me when I feared the path of ambiguity: "*I am the Living Light, Who illuminates the darkness. The person whom I have chosen and whom I have miraculously stricken as I willed, I have placed among great wonders, beyond the measure of the ancient people who saw in Me many secrets; but I have laid you low on the earth, that you might not set yourself up in arrogance of mind. The world has*

---

[100] Standish, 2007, p.20

had in you no joy or lewdness or use in worldly things, for I have withdrawn you from impudent boldness, and you feel fear and are timid in your works. For you suffer in your inmost being and in the veins of your flesh; you are distressed in mind and sense and endure great pain of body, because no security has dwelt in you."[101]

L.L. Yes! I recall that being an instance of "tough love" pushing you beyond your fears to trust in my providence. I know the message that I bring today is challenging – it always has been – but it is a message of hope and love. Your steadfast faith in me, regardless of the uncertain path ahead, is what is inspiring so many to seek you and share your message today.

H. Speaking of which, I cannot believe the stack of books and videos people have written about me! What is all of this? How long it must have taken to transcribe all of these books – and what on earth does this silver circle do?

L.L. Thanks to the invention of the printing press it really did not take long at all to print these books! They do not have to be copied by hand anymore! Believe it or not – people can "read" your books by listening to them on their phones! You probably don't know what a phone is... And the silver circle is a disc – it plays music and videos. It is actually quite remarkable – I imagine there are even a few discs in this pile with your morality play, Ordo Virtutum on them. There have been some wonderful presentations of that play in the last few years. And the films – you must watch "The Unruly Mystic" produced by Michael Conti[102] *and "Hildegard of Bingen" by Linn Maxwell*[103] *and also her new one "Trumpet of God" – she really captures your character! I laughed and laughed! Both are exquisite works of art! You were somewhat forgotten for about 800 years Hildegard, except of course by your sisters in Eibingen and a few loyal groups in Germany. But, over*

---

[101] From the "Declaration" in *Scivias*, (Hart & Bishop, 1990, p.60).
[102] http://theunrulymystic.com/
[103] http://www.hildegardofbingen.net/

the last half a century that has all changed! You have become quite famous – inspiring books, videos, music, live plays, and even a line of herbal health care products!

H. I will be sure to watch the films as soon as I figure out how to work it... I'm still so overwhelmed with all of this. And this stack of letters! Women and men, laity and clergy, have been petitioning me every day for centuries, even before I was canonized, asking for guidance – just the same as when I was alive only more! It will take me forever to go through these! There are several from women who are pretty upset with the way they are being treated by priests and the magisterium today. I don't think they realize how much better they have it than I did! At least they won't end up on a rack or worse!

L.L. Yes, a lot has changed since the 12th century Hildegard, and women do enjoy a much freer, and safer, existence in the Church than you did. However, the Church is certainly still heavily patriarchal and clericalism remains an issue. Women today must still learn how to "play the game" – just as you did - with the male power structure if they are to function within the institution. While they enjoy more freedom than did women in your day, they still do not have the freedom to directly confront the injustice they face, not without serious consequences. If they go against the patriarchal structure, which is formed in a concept of complementarity[104] – which ironically you are credited with having established - they will lose their jobs, be ostracized from the community, and in some cases even excommunicated. Regardless of their competence, training, education, and even their vocation,

---

[104] Complementarity is the teaching that women and men are created "equal but different" in the image of God. While they share the same dignity, the roles which they can fill are divinely ordered by natural law. This theological construct is the foundation for the non-admittance of women to ordained ministry. Prudence-Allen (1985) book, *The Concept of Woman*, called Hildegard the "founder of gender complementarity." A philosopher and systematic theologian, Prudence-Allen is one of the few women appointed to the Vatican International Theological Commission.

they are treated as subordinates. I know you understood my message in your day to be that women are subordinate, and are not equal in vocation to male ministers, but that is not correct Hildegard. They are every bit as equal and deserve to be treated with the same dignity and respect as the men. The Catholic Church is not going to ordain them, at least not anytime soon, and some are very angry. Others have been so patient – continuing to faithfully tend the garden even in less than ideal circumstances.

H. I am reminded of something I wrote to a woman late in my life, "In a true vision I saw and heard these words: Heavy downpours of rain destroy good, aromatic plants, and cause useless weeds to flourish. Gentle rains, however, bring forth good herbs that produce abundant fragrance."[105]

L.L. They need an example of leadership from which they can draw motivation. Leaders in the Church today need to be attentive to the needs of their diverse flock, and that includes the needs of their female flock. The Church needs leaders that can move it to grow and develop while at the same time respecting its rich tradition. Right now it appears that the Church is growing, but many feel its leaders are not meeting the needs of the followers.

H. Another vision comes to mind! "The Light which fully lives says: You, O human being, hear: There was a certain valley that sometimes dried up and sometimes burst forth in flowers. It did not, however, consistently produce wholesome plants, and though it was beautiful for people to see, it was not very useful for sustenance."[106]

L.L. Wow - I do speak words of Wisdom! You were an authentic leader Hildegard and you provided nourishment to those starving for Light. You were real, even though in your recent rise to fame people want to present you as if you weren't... You continued to feed the sheep even when storms raged and droughts ensued. You

---

[105] Baird & Ehrman, 2004, p.46
[106] Baird & Ehrman, 2004, p.123.

found a way around the obstacles placed in front of you. You brought Light to a world stumbling in darkness. Your leadership example is very much needed in the world today – for women and for men. That is why you are here. Your example inspires others to search for me and to engage in creative leadership.

H. The Church is very different than it was when I was a *magistra*. BTW - I still think I should have been an abbess![107]

L.L. BTW – you are quick at picking up slang! Speaking of which, remember the woman in Cleveland, she wrote you a follow-up letter – I think you should take a look at it.

H. How do you know? Oh, yeah… Let me see if I can find it… Okay, here it is. This one is dated January 28, 2016.

Dear St. Hildegard,
I write to you today, on the Feast of St. Thomas Aquinas, and also the fourth anniversary of my lay ecclesial ministry certification.

I do not know how to tell you thank you enough for the way in which you have inspired me. After first seeking your guidance I went in search of the Living Light and what I found has been amazing. In my prayer I opened myself in faith that I would somehow find the wisdom and knowledge to creatively lead as you did. For a moment (a long moment) I could not see a possible path through the patriarchy, clericalism and traditionalism that has been stonewalling any type of authentic growth in my ministry and my context. I was slowly slipping into a state of despair. All of my years of ministry, formation, and theological training seemed to have been in vain. Unless I left

---

[107] Hildegard was never named an abbess, but was named a *magistra*. This is important to note because an abbess had a significant amount of canonical authority, including independence from the authority of a male abbot. Hildegard, and her sisters, remained under the authority of the abbot of Disibodenberg until after Hildegard's death.

the Roman Catholic Church to minister elsewhere (which I will admit was at times tempting), I just could not see a way for me to "change the paradigm" in my context. Then it happened. I woke up one morning (only about a week ago) and had a vision – not quite the same way you had yours – nonetheless it was a vision.

I had an overwhelming feeling that a path was unfolding and I chose to follow. As I got dressed for work a voice told me I would build a retreat house in your honor. I was inspired to buy a closed, vacant Byzantine Catholic Church one block away from the parish I have ministered in for almost two decades. I went to morning Mass and prayed that if this was to be my path I would need some assistance. I did not know how I was going to pay for it or even if my family and community would respond. I knew it was crazy (just as moving out of Disibodenberg to Rupertsberg was a bit crazy!) yet I had an undeniable feeling that it was meant to be. Within one day – ONE day - the decision was made! I was graced with a benefactor (my uncle), my family was excited, and the Byzantine community accepted my bid. By day two the papers were signed and the deal was sealed. On day three we had a plan in place. All of this took place within three days! My head is spinning as you can imagine! This facility will be named, The HILDEGARDEN and like Rupertsberg and Eibingen, will serve to help the community grow in mind, body and spirit.

The HILDEGARDEN will provide a context for me to empower others, particularly women, to awaken to the presence of the Living Light within and around. It will be a place where ALL people can grow spiritually, regardless of their faith tradition, ethnicity, gender, sexual orientation, social or economic status. This will be a diverse and beautiful garden! We will offer programs, retreats, speakers, and of course a unique gift-shop promoting your genius! I will, of course, have to interpret your writings and style to be applicable for the twenty-first century, but I will do my best to maintain the integrity of your true character! I will certainly be looking for many opportunities to show off the pictures I took when I traveled through your "stomping ground" in Germany last year!

The HILDEGARDEN will be a forum through which I can share with others a more inclusive and holistic approach to faith, modeled after your leadership example. It is my hope that engaging in this type of creative action, while remaining an active pastoral minister in the Catholic Church, might positively draw the attention of the "powers that be" in such a way that helps to bring about a new paradigm for women and leadership.

As you well know, there is always the possibility the effort could take me in the opposite direction and may put me at odds with the institution. That, however, is not my intention. My intention is to be an agent of healing within an institution, and a community, that has in many ways lost its connection to viriditas. I hope to offer programs and workshops that help others discover the gift of the Living Light within – just as I have discovered that gift through my relationship with you. I ask that you bless The HILDEGARDEN as a sacred place, a site on the "Hildegard trail" – I will be bringing some of Germany back to Ohio! It is my hope that it might be a center through which mind, body, and spirit can be healed and viriditas restored. As I begin this new venture I beseech you St. Hildegard of Bingen – ora pro nobis!

In Christ,
Shanon Sterringer

H. Wow! I do not even know what to say. The HILDEGARDEN sounds wonderful. But, I don't understand. I have been asleep – how could I have responded to her?

L.L. You did not respond. I responded. Your role as an intercessor is to simply help one to open her/his inner senses to my presence. Your works and your example Hildegard inspired her to be open to my voice that guides and directs her. It is important that you are here because the world has become aware of your example. Women and men can draw from you the wisdom and knowledge and most importantly the inspiration that they need to lead creatively. Getting your message out there is important because it is really MY message and it facilitates a growing awareness of my presence. Even at this point, Hildegard, you are simply "a feather on the breath of God..."

N. Hildegard, closing her eyes begins to tell a story.

H. **"Listen, there was once a king sitting on his throne. Around him stood great and wonderfully beautiful columns ornamented with ivory, bearing the banners of the king with great honor. Then it pleased the king to raise a small feather from the ground and he commanded it to fly. The feather flew, not because of anything in itself, but because the air bore it along. Thus am I, a feather on the breath of God..."**[108]

L.L. *That is certainly my favorite story Hildegard and no one tells it quite like you! You are a feather on the breath of God and so is anyone who is willing to allow my voice to guide her/him on their path.*

H. **So, what exactly am I supposed to do?**

L.L. *Just be you! Continue to inspire others to share you with others. You would not believe how many people today are listening to your music. When your music is sung the angels in heaven – and on earth - are surely dancing! And how desperately the world needs your song! So many people have been renewed through your spirit from Germany to the United States. Some are sharing your message in a way that you may not be comfortable with – but they too desire to renew viriditas in a world that is in many ways drying up. The Church, of course, has claimed you for their own – which is wonderful – but as you well know, patriarchy deals with powerful women by controlling them – forcing you into obedience and subordination. The work of those outside the*

---

[108] Letter 40r to Odo of Paris (Baird & Ehrman, 1994, p.111).

Church, even if it is not always faithful to your character, is important because it restores your wings when the hierarchy clips them. Be present to all - within and outside of the institution - who are working so hard to share your story.

H. That I can do!

L.L. Maybe you should share with Shanon the letter you wrote to Brother Guibert when he kept pestering you to answer all those questions! He was a persistent little guy! What did he write, four or five times at least!

H. Persistent he was! Haha - remember he thought I had died before I answered his questions? Although I may have had something to do with that rumor... But he still wrote to my sisters asking if I left my response![109] **When he learned I was alive he immediately wrote; "For, although I do not deserve it, I earnestly hope and desire, God willing, to be nourished by the breasts of your maternal consolation for a long time still"** [110] **– and then asked if I was finished with his questions! He was relentless! Shanon has written me a lot of letters – I think there are a few more there that I didn't even open yet - but she isn't pestering me quite in the same way Guibert did!**

---

[109] "If, however, the blessed mother [Hildegard] is really dead, please write back to inform us on what day she parted the body... Moreover, please be kind enough to send back to us both the present letter and the one I sent her on the previous Lent, along with the appended questions and whatever answers she had given to any of them before her death" (Baird & Ehrman, 1994, p.45).

[110] The "thirty-eight questions" were sent to Hildegard by Guibert on behalf of the monks at Villers. Guibert sent numerous requests to Hildegard to answer them (102-109). "And so, O mother and lady, while you have life and wisdom, I beseech you to press on with the work you have undertaken of answering those questions" (Baird & Ehrman, 1994, p.47). Guibert sent four letters requesting Hildegard to answer – in letter 108 he had heard a rumor she was dead and sent an inquiry to the nuns at Rupertsberg – on learning she was still alive he sent another request in letter 109 asking her again to answer his questions! Finally she answered the questions in a separate document. A critical translation is available by Kienzle (2014).

L.L. That was pretty funny about Guibert! I was thinking you should share with her the image that you shared with Guibert of the garden being formed in love. It would be a beautiful image for her to reflect on in her own ministry and also to share with others at The HILDEGARDEN – do you remember it?

H. I think so...
For it was that same Love which planted a glorious garden redolent with precious herbs and noble flowers – roses and lilies – which breathed forth a wondrous fragrance, that garden on which the true Solomon was accustomed to feast his eyes. This garden designates those virtues that God Who is true Love established in the rod of Jesse, that is to say, in Mary, who flowered in chastity and brought forth that most noble flower... But, now look to that glorious garden which love planted, and gather to yourself every virtue in true humility and simplicity of heart. And although you find yourself among men of various states of mind, learn how patient and how long-suffering divine goodness has been to us all... And, with vigilant eyes, commend the sincerity of your mind again and again to the omnipotent God, lest you begin to sleep in doubt and be an upright knight of the true Solomon, who loves and crowns you... May the Holy Spirit enkindle you with the fire of His love so that you may persevere, unfailing, in the love of His service.[111]

L.L. Those are beautiful words Hildegard.

H. Yes, they are. I am definitely going to check out The HILDEGARDEN on September 17 – I hope they will be serving my *cookies of joy!*[112] **I would love to see some spelt beer**

---

[111] 106r (Baird & Ehrman, 1994, p.41)
[112] Using the ingredients in Hildegard's work *Physica*, contemporary "Hildegardians" have developed a recipe for cookies that end up being present at virtually any Hildegard gathering anywhere! Hildegard stated that the grain/flour Spelt, "creates a happy mind and puts joy in the human disposition" (Throop, 1998, p.13) and also when Nutmeg, Cinnamon, and Cloves and are

there as well, but that may be asking a bit too much! Cookies would be good. I am looking forward to seeing how I will inspire the community in Fairport Harbor!

L.L. I will be there as well.

N. As the *Living Light* begins to fade Hildegard starts going through the rest of her mail. She can't believe how popular she has become. She gently put the mail down and began to think about her life[113] – being tithed at the young age of 8 years old. She was so scared to leave her mom and the familiar town of Bermersheim[114] - all of her friends where there. The years she spent in solitude with Jutta in Disibodenberg[115] praying and singing and praying and singing and praying...[116] She loved Jutta, but she hated what she did to her body.[117] God created her so beautiful – why did Jutta not understand God loves beauty! Oh, and the endless struggles she faced with the monks and Kuno, and at times her own sisters. She remembered the difficult decision to move out of Disibodenberg to build a monastery at Rupertsberg[118] – and the gratitude she had felt for the Margravine of Stade for making that happen. The joy she felt when *Scivias*[119] was completed and the anticipation of starting her next book. And the heartbreak she tried so hard to forget when Richardis was ripped

---

combined and baked into a cakes (and eaten often) they "make your mind cheerful" (Throop, 1998, p.21). Some Benedictine monasteries sell them factory packaged.

[113] An account of her life is recorded in the *Vita de S.Hildegard* translated by Silvas (1994).

[114] There is no solid historical evidence to support Hildegard's birth in Bermersheim but tradition records it there.

[115] Hildegard most likely entered the community at Disibodenberg at the age of sixteen when she "took the veil."

[116] Benedictine Rule requires prayer (much of which is sung) seven times a day.

[117] Jutta was an extreme ascetic who practiced corporal penance including wearing a spiked cilice.

[118] In 1150 AD Hildegard received permission to build her own monastery at Rupertberg.

[119] 1151 AD

from her[120], as a child is ripped from her mother. She felt the anger she had harbored for the clergy who were abusing their office,[121] and the joy she felt when she could heal a patient in her infirmary.[122] How glorious it was to restore the monastery at Eibingen[123] and to go on four preaching tours![124] And the issue with prelates at Mainz so late in her life! The soldier she buried in her monastery grounds – he had been reconciled to the Church! She knew the issue with the bishops wasn't so much about the soldier as it was with her! The bishops, and the abbot, were angry because they suspected she had heard his confession.[125] They never really knew who heard his confession, they only suspected it was her. Thank goodness for the word of the soldier's priest and her friend Philip (who she still couldn't believe became the Archbishop of Cologne!) How dare they tell her she couldn't sing or receive sacraments! Burying the dead is a corporal work of mercy – she was doing the work of the Church! And to take away the right to sing – singing is the way in which heaven and earth communicate. It is the voice of the angels. Who were they to take

---

[120] 1151 AD The Margravine of Stade, Richardis' mother, demanded she be released from Rupertsberg to serve assume a position as an abbess in Bassum.

[121] She wrote hundreds of letters, homilies and visions reacting to the sins of the clergy.

[122] Many healings are recorded in her *Vita*. Her medicine is recorded in *Physica* and *Causea et Curae*.

[123] The monastery in Eibingen was destroyed in 1802 and rebuilt on a new location in 1900 where it is still a vibrant Abbey of St. Hildegard today. The property where the original monastery was is now a parish Church where Hildegard's reliquary is preserved.

[124] Hildegard was the only known medieval woman to be given magisterial permission to preach to congregations of lay and ordained, women and men.

[125] It is not documented that she in fact had heard the confession, but it is not out of the realm of possibility. Most scholars presume she may have heard his confessions because in the 12th century it was the practice for an abbess to hear the confessions of her nuns, and at times pilgrims that came to the monastery (Macy, 2007). The battle with the prelates at Mainz was most likely over her authority and less likely concerned with the soldier. Within a few centuries the Catholic Church would declare that the sacrament of confession could only be administered by an ordained (male) priest. That law still holds true today.

away the voice of the angels! Talk about arrogance! She feels herself getting angry – a homily is brewing! Taking a deep breath she remembers it doesn't matter now. It's in the past. She needs to let it go. The interdict was lifted and her sisters were able to sing her vespers. The last few months she spent at her beautiful Ruperstberg was enchanting. She remembers lying in her room, listening to the birds fluttering through her herb gardens. She could hear the sounds of the Nahe River right outside her window. In spite of all its challenges, she lived a good life. The angels rewarded her with a glorious light show in the sky the moment her soul left this world for the next.[126] She never imagined she would be coming back…

---

[126] The description of the sky when she died sounds like a modern day ufo sighting! In her *Vita* Guibert recorded, "For in the early dusk on Sunday, two arcs of brilliant and varied color appeared in the sky over the room in which the holy virgin gave up her happy soul to God…There emerged a bright light in the form of a full moon. It extended itself widely and seemed to dispel the darkness of night from that dwelling. Within this light a glowing red cross became visible, at first small, but later increasing in size, in which one by one, small crosses took shape… They had spread themselves over the sky… and they seemed to bend toward the earth where the dwelling was in which the holy virgin had passed away, and so cast a brilliant light upon the mountain" (Silvas, 1998, p.209).

Hildegard of Bingen and the Hierarchy Today

In 1979 by Pope John Paul II referred to Hildegard as "a light for her people and her time" and opened up her cause for canonization. Thirty years later, in 2011 Pope Benedict XVI contacted Mother Clementia in the Abbey of St. Hildegard in Rudesheim-Eibingen and asked her to "assemble a team of Hildegard experts at Eibingen to prepare her official biography, bibliography, and an outline of twelve theological themes for his proclamation" (Newman, 2013, p.38). He asked that the work be done quickly and with the "utmost discretion" because he did not want it leaking to the public until he made the proclamation. Hildegard of Bingen was canonized by Pope Benedict XVI on in May 2012 and named a Doctor of the Church in October 2012.

As is customary, an apostolic letter was promulgated by Pope Benedict XVI in the event of Hildegard's canonization. He described her in this way:

> *The teaching of the holy Benedictine nun stands as a beacon for homo viator. Her message appears extraordinarily timely in today's world, which is especially sensitive to the values that she proposed and lived. For example, we think of Hildegard's charismatic and speculative capacity, which offers a lively incentive to theological research; her reflection on the mystery of Christ, considered in its beauty; the dialogue of the Church and theology with culture, science and contemporary art; the ideal of the consecrated life as a possibility for human fulfilment; her appreciation of the liturgy as a celebration of life; her understanding of the reform of the Church, not as an empty change of structure but as conversion of heart; her sensitivity to nature, whose laws are to be safeguarded and not violated. For these reasons the attribution of the title of Doctor of the Universal Church to Hildegard of Bingen has great significance for today's world and an extraordinary importance for women. In Hildegard are expressed the most noble values of womanhood: hence the*

presence of women in the Church and in society is also illumined by her presence, both from the perspective of scientific research and that of pastoral activity. Her ability to speak to those who were far from the faith and from the Church make Hildegard a credible witness of the new evangelization. (October 7, 2012)

This declaration, affirming her role in promoting the sciences, pastoral care, creativity, and sacred feminine, secured for Hildegard a continued position of authority in the Catholic Church today.

In her day Hildegard was concerned with the abuse of power and neglect of office that was rampant among the clergy. She addressed it among the laity as well, but, as her letters indicate, she was most concerned with the clergy. Pride, for her, broke a person off from the whole resulting in a drying up of viriditas. Benedict XVI (2012) stated:

Hildegard also saw contradictions in the lives of individual members of the faithful and reported the most deplorable situations. She emphasized in particular that individualism in doctrine and in practice on the part of both lay people and ordained ministers is an expression of pride and constitutes the main obstacle to the Church's evangelizing mission to non-Christians. (Benedict XVI, 2012)

The current situation within the institutional offices of the Church, including the terrible sex-abuse scandals, financial mishandlings, exaggerated clericalism, and the lack of concern for the ecological crisis would certainly be on her preaching and writing agenda. The elevation in her canonical status allowing her to preach a message of healing and wholeness to the Catholic Church today.

There is a question that arises regarding Hildegard studies today. There seems to be two Hildegards – the Hildegard of the magisterium and the Hildegard of a contemporary spiritual movement pioneered by Rev. Matthew Fox. How do we bring together the two Hildegard's who have surfaced in the last couple of decades, both claiming her to be an example of leadership for the Catholic Church today? An honest reading of Hildegard's writings, particularly her systematic theology, presents a woman very much in agreement with the teachings and style of the now retired German Pope Benedict XVI.

While he is not often recognized as a "green pope" in the way Francis is, Benedict XVI's document, *The Ten Commandments of the Environment* made a strong statement regarding the need to integrate concern for the earth into spirituality. His having named Hildegard a saint and Doctor of the Church, and his many pastoral statements leading up to that moment, reflect his deep love and respect for her.

Rev. Matthew Fox, also a cleric deeply in love with Hildegard of Bingen, and a long-time adversary of Pope Benedict XVI, presents a figure of Hildegard that does not accurately represent who she was or her theology. It is likely if she were alive today she would write Fox a series of scathing letters admonishing him for his views, especially those that resulted in his excommunication. At the same time, she would probably also have written Benedict XVI a few letters as well, especially at the height of the sexual abuse crisis, admonishing him for his failure to protect those entrusted to his care. Both Benedict XVI and Fox have something to say about who Hildegard was, and both offer an image of her that is inviting and needed. However, the hierarchal interpretation of Hildegard is much more faithful to her historical character and removing her from her historical context does create a distorted image of who she was and what she taught. So, where does Pope Francis fit into this conversation?

Pope Francis is filled with the spirit of *viriditas.* Pope Francis has been on a crusade to reform many of the abuses among members of the hierarchy in the Church. He has been a strong voice against clericalism of clergy – echoing the tone of the letters Hildegard herself wrote. For example, on December 21, 2015 he presented the following message to the Roman Curia at their Christmas gathering:

> *Forgive me for not standing up as I speak to you, but for some days I've been suffering from a cold and not feeling too well.... I am pleased to offer heartfelt good wishes for a blessed Christmas and a happy New Year... I wanted to stress two important and inseparable aspects of the work of the Curia: professionalism and service, and I offered Saint Joseph as a model to be imitated. Then, last year, as a preparation for the sacrament of Reconciliation, we spoke of certain temptations or maladies – the catalogue of curial diseases; today instead I would like to speak about "curial antibiotics" – which could affect any Christian, curia, community, congregation, parish or ecclesial movement. Diseases which call for prevention, vigilance, care and, sadly, in some cases, painful and prolonged interventions. Some of these diseases became evident in the course of the past year, causing no small pain to the entire body and harming many souls, even by scandal. It seems necessary to state what has been – and ever shall be – the object of sincere reflection and decisive provisions. The reform will move forward with determination, clarity and firm resolve, since Ecclesia semper reformanda...*[127]

He structured his message in much the same way as Hildegard did hers; first referring to his weak state (in his case he had been sick) and then by offering a scathing critique of the diseases that have infiltrated the curia. In a non-related meeting with a group of Jesuits challenged the hypocrisy of clericalism and the negative effect it has on the formation of priests and the church at large:

> *This is hypocrisy that is the result of clericalism, which is one of the worst evils... The training of priests, must be a work of*

---

[127] http://www.associationofcatholicpriests.ie/2015/12/pope-prescribes-curial-antibiotics/

> *art, not a police action. We must form their hearts. Otherwise we are creating little monsters. And these little monsters mold the people of God. This really gives me goose bumps.* [128]

Like Hildegard, Francis recognizes the need for reform among the clergy, and he sees the sickness that develops when an institution is out of balance.

Pope Francis sent shock waves throughout the world, Catholic and non-Catholic, when he published his groundbreaking encyclical, *Laudato Si* in May 2015. This letter was written to the entire world calling an immediate need to direct attention to the dire state of the environment and the consequences that will ensue. If the document was not strong enough, he followed it up with an environmental "lightshow" projected on the front of the Vatican on December 8, 2015 (The Feast of the Immaculate Conception), a decision still reaping negative repercussions from traditional Catholic groups. He speaks, like Hildegard, with the voice of a prophet.

At the same time, his adherence to the canonical teaching of the Church (particularly where "natural law" is concerned), has drawn criticism. His position against women's ordination and same-sex marriage has been viewed by some as an indication that he is not really an agent of change, but is simply a "company man" or worse, a mere politician. Francis is bringing a new, holistic perspective to the faith, but like Hildegard, he is operating largely out of a framework of sex complementarity and he sees a divine order to the created world. For Catholic theologians, natural law is not subject to dialogue and so expecting Pope Francis, or Hildegard, to proclaim a teaching contrary to what has been preserved in the tradition, is next to impossible.

How then can her newly appointed status, and the charismatic leadership of Pope Francis, usher in any kind of real, systematic change? Both bring with their leadership a new paradigm. Both

---

[128] http://www.usatoday.com/story/news/world/2014/01/04/pope-francis-priests-vatican/4316775/

demonstrate an example of leadership that, while still strongly rooted in tradition, is different. It is fresh, full of *viriditas,* and joyful. Both emphatically recognize the presence of God in the created world. Both are painfully aware of the damage that is done when clergy, religious, and lay faithful, do not embrace their call with integrity and justice. Both have prophetically challenged consumerism, greed, and an insatiable desire for worldly pleasure, resulting in systems that are not only sinful, but unsustainable. Both Hildegard and Francis see evil running rampant in this world. Yet, both communicate a message of hope and goodness.

What does their message have to say to female leaders in the Catholic Church today? Pope Francis is not going to be calling for the ordination of women anytime soon.[129] He has publically affirmed continuity with the teaching of previous popes:

> *On women priests, that cannot be done. Pope St. John Paul II after long, long intense discussions, long reflection said so clearly. Not because women don't have the capacity. Look, in the Church women are more important than men, because the church is a woman. It is "la" church, not "il" church. The Church is the bride of Jesus Christ. And the Madonna is more important than popes and bishops and priests. I must admit we are a bit late in an elaboration of the theology of women. We have to move ahead with that theology. Yes, that's true.*[130]

Yet, he has repeatedly stated that women play a foundational role in the leadership of the Church and their roles need to be more visible and their voices need to be heard. Based on her letters and other writings, Hildegard of Bingen would agree. The role of

---

[129] The recent news of Pope Francis' decision to explore the possibility of ordaining women to the diaconate is complicated will most likely take years to research. The canonical role of the deacon in relation to the priest is vastly different in regards to authority and may or may not necessarily directly involve leadership depending on the role the deacon assumes in a parish and/or diocesan context.

[130] http://ncronline.org/blogs/ncr-today/pope-francis-reaffirms-ban-women-s-ordination

women's leadership in the Catholic Church is shifting; however, that shift is necessarily going to take place within the framework of the institution. There is room for a new paradigm to emerge, but the framework is, at this point, rock solid, built on centuries of tradition. So, how does a leader begin to chip away at a structure so deeply rooted? Begin to tell new stories.

Bolman and Deal (2008) wrote, "Effective organizations are full of good stories [tradition]. They often focus on the legendary exploits of corporate heroes [saints]" (p.260). Hildegard of Bingen was formed in an environment shaped by stories. Stories of great saints, like Disibod and Rupert shaped by the hierarchal institution within which they emerged. Her worldview, which was structured and orderly, reflected the stories she had been told. Pope Francis is in many ways telling the same story, but with a new voice, new characters, and a new style. As the story is retold by new characters, ideologies can change. The process of reshaping a story, creating a new narrative, is slow and arduous. With patience, and the invested effort of good story-tellers, the shape of the structure will slowly change. This brings us back to the important (though not necessarily historically accurate) work of Matthew Fox, as well as others seeking to share her story.

The work of the magisterium in canonizing her and naming her a Doctor of the Church has been essential to her mission. Just as she needed the approval of Bernard of Clairvaux and Pope Eugenius III to begin her public ministry in the twelfth century, she needed the approval of Pope Benedict XVI to being her public minister in the twenty-first century. Her newly elevated status allows theologians and female leaders in the Church to use her writings and her example to support much needed change in the Church today. And the work of theologians such as Matthew Fox is necessary because it brings to the table a fresh perspective as well as a popular context for her to become known. Yes, there are "two Hildegards" circulating through churches, bookstores and popular media today, and both are necessary in their own ways.

However, there was only one Hildegard of Bingen and it is her story that The HILDEGARDEN[131] will seek to share.

Figure 36

---

[131] The HILDEGARDEN is an upcoming retreat center, scheduled to open September 17, 2016 in Fairport Harbor, Ohio. The center has emerged as a practical application of this doctoral project. It is a spiritual center grounded in the vision of Hildegard of Bingen and will offer programs and retreats focused on "growing the mind, body, and spirit".

Hildegard of Bingen and Catholic Women Leaders Today

Hildegard of Bingen has been a subject of research here in the United States within the world of academia for about forty years. Starting with the liturgical work of Peter Dronke (1970) followed by the work of Barbara Newman, who pioneered Hildegard's theology of the sacred feminine in a Ph.D. dissertation she completed at Yale (1981). In the last thirty years most of Hildegard's works have been translated, although some works are still lacking critical editions. And most recently in the last ten years or so, there has been an enormous amount of secondary sources, scholarly as well as popular, flooding the market; biographies, commentaries, anthologies, and even fictional works. Yet, her theological thought was so deep and her personality so complicated, pulling together a cohesive presentation of Hildegard that is faithful to her original character while being applicable to spiritual experience today is an ongoing challenge, though not insurmountable.

In the world of Catholic devotions it would be expected, especially given her conservative theological views, that she would be well-known. In reality, however, she is still quite unfamiliar in most parishes and dioceses aside from some who may have possibly heard her music. It is possible that she has not yet fully emerged, outside of Germany, as an important figure because her sainthood is still so new.

In regards to Roman Catholic leadership Hildegard has the potential to play a key role in the development of a new paradigm for the role of women in ecclesial leadership, particularly in her role as a preacher. Due to the non-admittance of women to ordained ministry in the Catholic Church, women have also been prohibited from preaching. The heavily patriarchal structure has led to systematic neglect and at times abuse of the gifts and experiences women bring, and have always brought, to Roman Catholic leadership. Hildegard challenges the Church today to reexamine how women have participated in ecclesial leadership historically, as she did, and how those roles might influence ecclesial leadership today. "What does a non-ordained leader look like in the Roman Catholic Church and how can we better utilize the gifts and talents of those called to this vocation?" These are questions many, including those in the highest ranking Vatican offices including Pope Francis, are asking but to which they are not applying tangible solutions. Searching out alternative models of leadership within the Roman Catholic Church opens up the door for growth and development – this is where Hildegard can be effective.

Some of the narratives by which the Catholic Church operates have been employed for thousands of years, in part because they are believed to be divinely ordered. The practice and beliefs are so deeply entrenched, they seem at times impossible to even budge. A change in the narrative script is possible, even a significant change, with some creativity. Systemic change can only come about if it stays, to some degree, rooted in the tradition. This is where Hildegard becomes so important. A project such as this equips the community, especially the leaders, with the tools necessary for understanding the experiential impact a change in leadership style can have.

Hildegard held both power and authority. She was sanctioned by the institution to function as a *magistra* and in that role became a preacher, theologian, artist, visionary, philosopher, and healer. This was a sanctioned role bestowed on her by legitimate authority. Her power, however, did not come from the same source. Her power came directly from her experience of the *Living Light*. From this divine source she mustered the courage and the strength to lead – not manage or administrate – but lead. She was a "situational leader" in that she could adapt her style depending on whom she was dealing with, but she has the potential to become a "transformational leader" as her vision becomes realized in a contemporary leadership context. She moved throughout a patriarchal system with relative ease, because she exuded spiritual authority.

In an article entitled, *What do we Mean by Authority?* Gerard Mannion discusses the ongoing struggle in the Roman Catholic Church between the *de jure* notion of authority - those that possess authority by divine right - and the *de facto* notion of authority – those whose authority is actually recognized (Mannion, 2002, p.20). For instance, the pope and bishops claim the right to possess power over their subjects and Canon Law reflects that power. In reality, there is very little recourse for enforcing the law, outside of controlling those who work in some way for the Church – ministers, teachers, staff members. Mannion suggests that the domineering model of authority is not effective because authority in the Church is only legitimate if the adherents accept it (Mannion, 2002, p.22).

Many have asked the question, "Why would a woman invest so many years in an institution that does not ordain women? Why doesn't she go to a Church that will ordain her?" I personally have been asked that question many, many times. It is a vocation. And for a Catholic woman, it is a vocation to the Catholic Church. It is certainly always a temptation to seek out a Church that treats women with the property dignity and respect and recognizes our call. However, being a Catholic is as much a cultural reality as it is religious. It is not that simple to just walk away from dysfunction or injustice, much in the same way a person can't walk away from her/his dysfunctional family. Certainly in situations of abuse it is necessary, but in other instances many are called to stay within the institution and work for change. Many women are called to this role and many obtain graduate and post-graduate degrees in order to gain the training necessary to minister well. Through the urging of the Catholic institution itself, there are a significant number of educated, seminary trained women functioning in leadership roles in dioceses nationally as well as internationally: "Even church governance, long the last bastion of clerical monopoly, has been infiltrated by lay professionals" (Beal, 2011, p. 153). The codified law still reflects a *power over* approach, yet the experience on the local level is increasingly *power to,* raising the question posed by the theorist above regarding whether or not these positions reflect opposite approaches or if they can be understood through the lens of a new power paradigm.

The most rigid way in which power is exercised within the Roman Catholic Church is through Canon Law. Most Catholics, aside from the clergy and lay ministers, have never seen the Code of Canon Law or its 1752 canons (laws). However, dioceses and parishes are closely governed by its laws. The non-admittance of women to ordained ministry is clearly outlined in the Code, as are the ways in which women can function in leadership and administrative roles. Understanding Canon Law, not only today, but in the Medieval Church within which Hildegard of Bingen ministered, is necessary to understanding the institutional history of power (dominance) in the Roman Catholic Church. Using the seminal work of Max Weber (a theorist referenced in all of the articles reviewed), Catholic canon lawyers are asking the same questions in regards to the "substantive rationality" and "formal rationality" and their relationship to power and authority in the Church. In general, canon lawyers are searching for a "new type of law" which encompasses authentic authority in the Roman Catholic Church (Beal, 2011, p. 145). Authentic power, however, is not limited to codified law and can often be found outside of the law. Spiritual authority, as was modeled by the mystical theology of Hildegard, has the ability to move a community beyond the law. In biblical language this would be described as the spirit of the law as opposed to the letter of the law. The degree to which the law is enforced in a particular Catholic context depends heavily on the hierarchy in that local context. [132]

That all being said, there has been a great deal of theological development in the way in which the Roman Catholic Church views women's roles both in the Church and in the secular world. The Church is advocating an "equal but different" position, but is calling for justice for women in the workplace (they never seem to acknowledge the vulnerability, however, of female pastoral ministers...). There have been some significant voices over the last several decades regarding the issue of gender in the Roman Catholic Church including Elizabeth Johnson, a well-respected Catholic theologian and Phyllis Zagano, a strong advocate of reinstating the female diaconate. In her book *Women and Catholicism,* Zagano (2011) examines three contemporary case studies presenting issues regarding women and liturgical ministries, women in relationship with priests, and women as priests. She is writing out of the conviction that the Church, in spite of some progress, is still struggling to reconcile its attitude regarding women and the sacred, which is certainly the case.

Hildegard of Bingen was an example of extraordinary leadership at a time when women's roles were far more limited than they are today. Women religious (more commonly known as nuns) enjoyed a significant amount of freedom and authority, but women in general were very oppressed and controlled. Looking at the conflict that exists within Roman Catholicism today regarding the roles of women in ecclesiastical offices sheds some light on the conflict that must have existed in the twelfth century. One example is the hesitancy of the Church to acknowledge women preachers. Women are preaching, at Eucharistic services as well as para-liturgies (non-Eucharistic services), yet the words that are often used to describe what she is doing is "reflection, talk, message" rarely are the words "sermon, homily, or preaching" used to describe her ministry. Hildegard was a strong preacher and the Pope Benedict XVI acknowledged that she was a homilist (as did many popes, bishops, and clergy in her day). Her role as a preacher has allowed her to successfully transcend the gender boundaries of her day, in spite of her insistence on the theological construct of complementarity. It is possible that through her women today might be able to transcend those boundaries, if the Church can bring itself to validate the role of women preachers, even though they are not ordained.

In addition to her role as a preacher, Hildegard has the power to offer a new paradigm. How does that happen in a Church that does not do anything quickly or rashly? Those who have been blessed to have heard her story, like myself, need to find creative ways to make her story accessible to others. In their text, *Reframing organizations*, Bolman and Deal discuss four key frameworks from which change can unfold within an organization. Using the *symbolic frame,* they highlight the importance of storytelling:

> *Stories, like folk or fairy tales, offer more than entertainment or moral instruction for small children. They grant comfort, reassurance, direction and hope to people of all ages...Stories are deeply rooted in the human experience... 'Through storytelling our people can know very clearly what the company believes and what needs to be done...' Effective organizations are full of good stories. They often focus on the legendary exploits of corporate heroes* (2008, p. 260)

All religious institutions began with a story. The Roman Catholic Church is particularly fond of stories (millions of pages have been written on the saints and traditions). The majority of stories preserved and retold are the stories of the men who have shaped the patriarchal Church into what it is today. The women's stories are often left out or relegated to the sidelines, yet they are just as foundational and need to be told.

The story of this medieval heroine, St. Hildegard of Bingen, is the story of a powerful woman who was a genius on a number of levels, her advice, prayers, approval, and forgiveness were sought out by men and women from all levels of authority and social-economic classes. She befriended popes and kings, and had the spiritual power to chastise them when they were not fulfilling their duties. Her story is of a woman determined to preach the word of God and stand up against the injustice of her day, even at the age of eighty-one years old. The story of this heroine is one of a woman who accomplished more in her lifetime than what seems humanly possible. Hildegard's story is powerful. Her story needs to be told and not just in the world of academia, but within Catholic leadership circles and among the townsfolk.

How are stories told? They are told in a variety of ways, one of which is through acting out a character or role. Stories are performed in liturgy, in the workplace, in the classrooms, in everyday life. Performance is an essential part of the story-telling process and it is fundamental in defining identity. The roles of clergy, for example, are learned by children from a very young age by the way in which the clergy perform a particular function. The priest, the male deacon, and the altar boys sit in the sanctuary vested for liturgy, and for centuries men were the only ministers permitted to perform in these roles. In some parishes they are still the only ones permitted to perform in these roles (even though the Church declared in 1994 – yes only twenty two years ago) that females were permitted to function as liturgical ministers (just not in the roles reserved for ordained clergy).[133] What happens when a woman or a girl wears a vestment and sits in the sanctuary, even if she is only functioning as an acolyte?

It offers to the community gathered an experience of a new performance. The performance of a mixed community of male and female ministers (even if our roles are distinct) communicates a different story than that which was composed of all men. I had an experience last year that affirms this notion. I was at a Confirmation Mass with no female servers. There were a lot of men in the sanctuary, the ordained clergy and about six male servers ranging from young to old functioning. As I sat in the pew I felt frustrated by the message it was communicating,

---

[133] It probably is important to note that technically the law (Canon 230, paragraph 2) states that only in the absence of a male a female may function – although that is not the practice in most parishes. The "may" is dependent on the will of the bishop or pastor. A bishop or pastor has the right to refuse to allow girl altar servers and some dioceses still do not allow it. If the bishop states it is permitted the pastor has the option to not allow it. If the bishop states it is not permitted, the pastor does not have the option to allow it.

but I didn't say a word. After the Mass I was behind an older couple walking to their car. They didn't realize I was behind them. The gentleman seemed as frustrated as I was and said to the woman, "Why the hell can't they come into the twenty-first century already! There were no women up there – like a good old boys club. It's ridiculous!" When he turned around and saw me he seemed embarrassed. He apologized for being so blunt. I assured him there was, "No need to apologize…"

Whether or not the hierarchy is ready to change, the people are changing. They love their faith; they love the Church, but they want it to be authentic and just. The identity of women leaders in the Roman Catholic Church is changing in many places, quicker in places where there are a lack of clergy. A leading voice in the area of the current trend of changing roles of women in the Church today is Wallace (1992), *They call her Pastor*. This book documented the results of a study surveying the experience of female pastoral ministers administering parishes (basically functioning as pastors) and the parishioners in various places throughout the United States. Her first chapter begins with the question asked by some who read her work, "A woman in charge of a Catholic parish? You've got to be kidding me" (Wallace, 1992, p. 1). Following the extensive study conducted for her book (1992), Wallace has written several articles including, *The social construction of a new leadership role: Catholic women pastors* (1993). In this article she presents the results of her survey which revealed in 1991 there were 241 parishes being administered by non-priests. Of the 241 parishes 74% of them were being run by women. Her survey suggests that women pastoral leaders are more collaborative in their approach suggesting that they bring a different experience of leadership. The women leaders studied also tended more towards *power to* (empowering others) leadership whereas in many of the cases the ordained male pastors who preceded them tend more towards *power over* (domination) leadership. Wallace (2000), *Women and Religion: the Transformation of Leadership Roles,* presented the need for the Church to transform women's leadership profile providing women with a stronger voice in the decision making process of the Church (Wallace, 2000, p. 507). Pope Francis (2013) has called for the same in his encyclical *Evangelii Gaudium*:

> *Lay people are, put simply, the vast majority of the people of God. The minority – ordained ministers – are at their service. There has been a growing awareness of the identity and mission of the laity in the Church. We can count on many lay persons, although still not nearly enough, who have a deeply-rooted sense of community and great fidelity to the tasks of charity, catechesis and the celebration of the faith. At the same time, a clear awareness of this responsibility of the laity, grounded in their baptism and confirmation, does not appear in the same way in all places. In some cases, it is because lay persons have not been given the formation needed to take on important responsibilities. In others, it is because in their particular Churches room has not been made for them to speak and to act, due to an excessive clericalism which keeps them away from decision-making... The Church acknowledges the indispensable contribution which women make to society through the sensitivity, intuition and other distinctive skill sets which they, more than men, tend to possess. I think, for example, of the special concern which women show to others, which finds a particular, even if not exclusive, expression in motherhood. I readily acknowledge that many women share pastoral responsibilities with priests, helping to guide people, families and groups and offering new contributions to theological reflection. But we need to create still broader opportunities for a more incisive female presence in the Church. Because "the feminine genius is needed in all expressions in the life of society, the presence of women must also be guaranteed in the workplace" and in the various other settings where important decisions are made, both in the Church and in social structures demands that the legitimate rights of women be respected, based on*

the firm conviction that men and women are equal in dignity, present the Church with profound and challenging questions which cannot be lightly evaded. The reservation of the priesthood to males, as a sign of Christ the Spouse who gives himself in the Eucharist, is not a question open to discussion, but it can prove especially divisive if sacramental power is too closely identified with power in general. It must be remembered that when we speak of sacramental power "we are in the realm of function, not that of dignity or holiness". The ministerial priesthood is one means employed by Jesus for the service of his people, yet our great dignity derives from baptism, which is accessible to all. The configuration of the priest to Christ the head – namely, as the principal source of grace – does not imply an exaltation which would set him above others. In the Church, functions "do not favor the superiority of some vis-à-vis the others". Indeed, a woman, Mary, is more important than the bishops. Even when the function of ministerial priesthood is considered "hierarchical", it must be remembered that "it is totally ordered to the holiness of Christ's members". Its key and axis is not power understood as domination, but the power to administer the sacrament of the Eucharist; this is the origin of its authority, which is always a service to God's people. This presents a great challenge for pastors and theologians, who are in a position to recognize more fully what this entails with regard to the possible role of women in decision-making in different areas of the Church's life. (11/24/2013)

While the Pope Francis has maintained the Catholic Church's position against the ordination of women to the priesthood (and many are saying that this demonstrates that the Pope really has not initiated any real systemic change), he is calling for a visible, participatory leadership role for women, equal to (though different) from the ordained men.

How do we begin to teach – women and men – that women are called to be equal "co-workers in the vineyard" not subordinate "helpmates" when they are still being formed in a context that by its performance tells them otherwise?

We change the way in which we tell our story.

Post Script

There is a cartoon image circulating on social media with Alice in Wonderland sitting on a stump with Dorothy from the Wizard of Oz. She looks at her and says, "I have seen some weird shit." I love this image because over the last several years I too have seen some weird s*it. The "God moment" experiences I have encountered have at times been comforting and assuring of my call. At other times they have completely freaked me out. It is a joke at the office that I have some sort of "super-power" because weird happenings seem to follow me, and I am not the only person to witness them. My journey has been enchanted because it has revealed to me a reality beyond what is traditionally understood as normal. I have been "waking up" to something much bigger and more profound and it has been spiritually, emotionally, and even physically transforming. The first response to an awakening experience is to assume you are going crazy and believe me, I have considered that.

Over the years I have learned that when you are open to the Spirit of God, to the *Living Light*, you will be transformed. You will be called down a dark and uncertain journey and you will see some weird s*it. You will most likely suffer persecution, misunderstanding, and possibly even physical harm. You will question everything you have ever been taught and you may even feel lost or abandoned for a time. However, if you are grounded in love, goodness and truth, you will not only find what you need to sustain you along your way, but you will most certainly encounter a "happily ever after" experience.

The Sacred Scriptures promise, "With faith the size of a mustard seed, you can move mountains" (Matthew 17:20). I can personally attest to that. What has unfolded in my life over the last couple of decades can be compared to "moving mountains" – not because of any special gift that I have, but because of my faith. The ultimate destination of my path is not entirely clear, but I am confident that I am exactly where I am supposed to be and that everything I have done in my life up to this point has prepared me for the present task.

Over the last couple of decades I have been waking up to the reality that we have been placed on this planet, at this time, for a reason. We are the "light-keepers" charged with bringing the light of goodness and love into a world darkened by sin, greed, corruption, and evil. Each one of us is born with the spark of divine light – created in the *imago Dei, image of God*. When we are baptized we receive a candle lit from the Christ candle as a symbol that the light is entrusted to us to be kept burning brightly. With so many worldly distractions, it is far too easy to forget who we are and why we are here. Jesus proclaimed, "YOU are the light of the world" (5:14) and are called to walk as children of LIGHT (Ephesians 5:8). We are called to be light. Hildegard of Bingen responded to that call in the way to which she was able in 12th century Germany. She has resurfaced today, I believe, to call us to respond in the way that we are able in 21st century United States.

I am not sure where this journey is leading. In some ways it is still dark and uncertain, especially as it calls me to ask some very difficult questions and examine some long-standing ideologies. "Happily ever after" comes a day at a time. Every day is marked by both light and darkness. But, I am a "light-keeper" in search of truth, painfully aware of the possible consequences; "They persecuted me, they will persecute you" (John 15:20). However, based on what I have experienced up to this point, I am confident that I am in good company (earthly and celestial) and will be protected against the "monsters" that are yet to surface; "But, not a hair on your head will be destroyed" (Luke 21:18). We are created by God, in God, and are created for greatness. Wherever you are at right now on your journey – be sure to let your light shine.

"God's tabernacle is built on whatever is good and just. Rise up to the light, therefore, and you will live forever."
– Hildegard of Bingen in a letter to the Abbot Wolfard of Albon (1153-1154AD)

References

Authority and Power

1) Beal, J.P. (2011) Chapters 5 & 6, In Lacey, M. J., & Oakley, F. (Eds.), *The crisis of authority in Catholic modernity*. (pp. 135-191). Oxford: Oxford University Press.

2) Butler, S. (2002). Chapter 3, Embodiment: women and men, equal and complementary. In Johnson E. (Ed.)*The Church women want*. (pp. 35-44) New York: Herder & Herder.

3) Ciulla, J.B. (2004) Leadership and the problem of bogus empowerment. In J.B.Ciulla (Eds.), *Ethics: The heart of leadership*. 2nd edition, (pp.59-82). West Port, CT: Praeger.

4) D'antonio, W. V. (1994). Autonomy and democracy in an autocratic organization: The case of the Roman Catholic Church. *Sociology of Religion, 55*(4), 379. doi: 10.2307/3711978

5) Eichbauer, H. M. and Pennington, K. From Gratian's Concordia Discordantium Canonum to Gratian's Decretum: The evolution from teaching text to comprehensive Code of Canon Law. Thesis. The Catholic University of America, n.d. *ProQuest Dissertations and Theses* (2010): 387. *ProQuest Dissertations & Theses Full Text*.

6) Fox, M. (2001). *The Pope's war: Why Ratzinger's secret crusade imperiled the Church and how it can be saved.* New York: Sterling Ethos.

7) Gordon, R. D. (2002). Conceptualizing leadership with respect to its historical–contextual antecedents to power. *The Leadership Quarterly, 13*(2), 151- 167. doi: 10.1016/S1048-9843(02)00095-4

8) Gordon, R., Kornberger, M. and Clegg, S.R. Power, rationality and legitimacy in public organizations. *Public Administration* 87(1) (2009): 15-34. doi: 10.1111/j.1467-9299.2008.01743.x

9) Hardy, C. & Clegg, S. R.. (2006) Some dare to call it power. In Clegg, S.R.,Hardy, C., & Nord, W., (Eds.), *Handbook of organizational studies,* 2nd ed.Thousand Oaks, CA: Sage. 754-775.

10) Halter, D. *The Papal "No": A comprehensive guide to the Vatican's rejection of women's ordination.* New York: Crossroad Pub., 2004.

11) Haugaard, M. "Rethinking the four dimensions of power: Domination and empowerment." *Journal of Political Power* 5.1 (2012): 33-54. doi: 1913739

12) Lacey, M. J., & Oakley, F. (2011). *The crisis of authority in Catholic modernity*. Oxford: Oxford University Press. [Chapters 5 & 6: pp. 135-191]

13) Mannion G. (2002). What do we mean by "authority"? In Hoose, B. (Ed.) *Authority in the Roman Catholic Church: Theory and practice.* (pp.19-36). Aldershot, Hants, England: Ashgate.

Gender and Identity

14) Ecklund, E. H. (2003). Catholic women negotiate feminism: A research note. *Sociology of Religion, 64*(4), 515. doi: 10.2307/3712339

15) Estar, R. M., & Arcana, J. (2001). Women's power stories (Master's thesis, The Union Institute). *ProQuest Dissertations and Theses,* 180-180 p. Retrieved August 16, 2014, from Dissertations & Theses @ Union Institute & University.

16) Gee, J. P. (2000). Chapter 3: Identity as an analytic lens for research in education. *Review of research in education, 25*(1), 99-125. doi: 10.3102/0091732X025001099

17) Johnson, E. (2002). Chapter 4, Imaging God, embodying Christ: women as asign of the times. In Johnson,E. (Ed.) *The Church women want.* (pp.45-59). New York: Herder & Herder.

18) Lehman, E. C. (1993). Gender and ministry style: Things not what they seem. *Sociology of Religion, 54*(1). doi: 10.2307/3711838

19) Manning, C. J. Women in a divided Church: Liberal and conservative Catholic Women negotiate changing gender roles. *Sociology of Religion* 58.4 (1997): 375.

20) Moore, G., & Shackman, G. (1996). Gender and authority: A cross-national study. *Social Science Quarterly, 77*(2), 273-288.

21) Morris, R. C. (1995). All made up: Performance theory and the new anthropology of sex and gender. *Annual Review of Anthropology,24*(1), 567-592. doi: 10.1146/annurev.an.24.100195.003031

22) Ronan, M. (2007). Ethical challenges confronting the Roman Catholic women's ordination movement in the twenty-first century. *Journal of feminist studies in religion, 23*(2), 149-169. doi: 10.2979/FSR.2007.23.2.149

23) Simon, R. J., & Nadell, P. S. (1995). In the same voice or is it different?: Gender and the clergy. *Sociology of Religion, 56*(1), 63. doi: 10.2307/3712039

24) Sterringer, S. (2011) *And then God created her in God's own image.* (MA Thesis)

25) Sterringer, S. (2012) *Celebrating the gift of women in the life and mission of the Church.* (D.Min dissertation). ProQuest Dissertations Publishing, 3515545.

26) Zagano, P. *Women & Catholicism: Gender, communion, and authority.* New York: Palgrave Macmillan, 2011.

27) Zuckerman, P. (1997). Gender regulation as a source of religious schism. *Sociology of Religion, 58*(4), 353. doi: 10.2307/3711921

Hildegard of Bingen

28) Allen, P. (1985). *The concept of woman: The Aristotelian revolution, 750 B.C. – A.D. 1250.* Grand Rapids, Michigan: William B. Eerdmans Publishing Company, (pp. 252-337)

29) Baird, J.L. (2006). *The personal correspondence of Hildegard of Bingen.* New York: Oxford University Press.

30) Baird, J.L. & Ehrman, R. K. (1994). *The letters of Hildegard of Bingen.* Vol (1). New York: Oxford University Press.

31) _____. (1998). *The letters of Hildegard of Bingen.* Vol (11). New York: Oxford University Press

32) _____. (2004). *The letters of Hildegard of Bingen.* Vol. (111). New York: Oxford University Press.

33) Berger, M. (1999). *Hildegard of Bingen on natural philosophy and medicine.* New York: D.S. Brewer.

34) Bowie, F. & Davies, O. (1990). *Hildegard of Bingen: An anthology.* Great Britian: SPCK

35) Cameron, C. (2015). *Leadership as a call to service: the life and works of Hildegard of Bingen.* Connor Court Publishing: Australia.

36) Campbell, N.M. trans. (forthcoming). *Hildegard of Bingen. The Book of Divine Works.* Washington, D.C.: The Catholic University of America Press.

37) Clendenen, A. (2009). *Experiencing Hildegard: Jungian perspectives.* Wilmette, Illinois: Chiron Publications.

38) Craine, R. (1997). *Hildegard: Prophet of the cosmic Christ.* New York: Crossroad.

39) Davidson, A.E. (1992). *The Ordo Virtutum of Hildegard of Bingen.* Kalamazoo, Michigan: Medieval Institute Publications.

40) Emmerson, R.K. (2002). The representation of Antichrist in Hildegard of Bingen's *Scivias*: Image, word, commentary, and visionary experience. *Medieval Academy of America,* 41(2)

41) Feiss, H. (Trans.). (2000). *Explanation of the rule of Benedict: Hildegard of Bingen.* Eugene, OR: Wipf & Stock.

42) Flanagan, S. (1990) *Hildegard of Bingen: A Visionary Life.* New York: Routledge.

43) Fox, M. (1988). *The coming of the cosmic Christ: The healing of Mother Earth and the birth of a global renaissance.* San Francisco: Harper & Row.

44) Fox, M. & Sheldrake, R. (2014). *The physics of Angels: Exploring the realm where science and spirit meet.* Rhinebeck, N.Y.: Monkfish Book Publishing.

45) H., Bowie, F., & Davies, O. (1990). *Hildegard of Bingen: An anthology.* London: SPCK.

46) H., Evans, C. P., & Feiss, H. B. (2010). *Hildegard of Bingen: Two hagiographies.* Leuven: Peeters

47) H., & Fox, M. (1987). *Hildegard of Bingen's book of divine works with letters and songs.* Santa Fe, NM: Bear & Company.
48) Hart, C., & Bishop, J. (1990). *Hildegard of Bingen Scivias.* New York: Paulist Press.
49) Higley, S. L. (2007). *Hildegard of Bingen's unknown language: An edition, translation, and discussion.* New York: Palgrave Macmillan.
50) Hozeski, B.W. (1994). *Hildegard of Bingen's book of the rewards of life.* New York: Oxford University Press.
51) King-Lenzmeier, (2001). *Hildegard of Bingen: An integrated vision.* Collegeville, Minnesota: The Liturgical Press.
52) Lomer, B. (2009). *Hildegard of Bingen: Music, rhetoric and the sacred feminine.* Saarland: VDM Verl. Müller.
53) McInerney, M. B. ed. (1998). *Hildegard of Bingen: A book of essays.* New York: Garland Pub.
54) Newman, B. (1998) *Voice of the Living Light: Hildegard of Bingen and her world.* Los Angeles, CA: University of California Press.
55) _____. (1988). *Hildegard of Bingen: Symphonia.* New York: Cornell University Press.
56) _____. (1987) *Sister of Wisdom: St. Hildegard's Theology of the feminine.* Los Angeles, CA: University of California Press.
57) _____. "O FEMINEA FORMA: GOD AND WOMAN IN THE WORKS OF ST. HILDEGARD (1098-1179) Dissertation. Yale University. *ProQuest Dissertations and Theses* (1981): 387. *ProQuest Dissertations & Theses Full Text* **8211371**.
58) _____. (1992) Romancing the past: A critical look at Matthew Fox & the Medieval "Creation Mystics" *Touchstone: A Journal of Mere Christianity* summer http://www.touchstonemag.com/archives/article.php?id=05-03-005-f
59) Olive, C. J., & Swetnam, J. J. (2009). Self-actualization in the lives of medieval female mystics: An ethnohistorical approach. *ProQuest Dissertations and Theses,* 476. Retrieved September 21, 2014, from ProQuest Dissertations & Theses Full Text.
60) Pernoud, R. (1998). *Hildegard of Bingen: Inspired conscience of the twelfth century.* New York: Marlowe &.
61) Schipperges, H. (1997). *Hildegard of Bingen: Healing and the nature of the cosmos.* Princeton, NJ: M. Wiener.
62) _____ (1998). *The World of Hildegard of Bingen: Her life, times and visions.* (Cummings, J. translator). Collegeville, Minnesota: Liturgical Press.
63) Silvas, A. (1998). *Jutta & Hildegard: The biographical Sources.* University Park, Pennsylvania. Pennsylvania State University Press.
64) Sungenis, R. (2014). *The Geocentric Universe: According to the visions of St. Hildegard of Bingen.* State Line, PA: Catholic Apologetics International Publishing.

65) Sweet, V. (2006) *Rooted in the Earth, Rooted in the Sky: Hildegard of Bingen and Premodern Medicine.* New York: Routledge.
66) Throop, P. (1998). *Hildegard von Bingen's Physica: The complete English translation of her classical work on health and healing.*
67) Tillman, J. (2001). *The creative spirit: Harmonious living with Hildegard of Bingen.* Harrisburg, PA: Morehouse Pub.
68) Uhlein, G., & H. (1983). *Meditations with Hildegard of Bingen.* Santa Fe, NM: Bear & Comp.

Leadership Theory
69) Alvesson, M. & Spicer, A. (2011) *Metaphors we lead by: Understanding Leadership in the Real World.* New York: Routledge.
70) Hickman, G. R. ed. (2010). *Leading organizations: Perspectives for a new era.* Washington D.C.: Sage.
71) Houston, P. & Sokolow, S. (2013). *The Wise Leader: Doing the right things for the right reasons.* Bloomington, IN: Universe LLC.
72) _____ (2006). *The spiritual dimension of leadership.* Thousand Oaks, CA: Corwin Press.
73) Ladkin, D. (2010) *Rethinking Leadership: A New Look at Old Leadership Questions.* Northhampton, MA: MGP Books.
74) Manala, M. J. (2010). A triad of pastoral leadership for congregational health and well-being: Leader, manager and servant in a shared and equipping ministry. *HTS Teologiese Studies / Theological Studies, 66*(2). doi: 10.4102/hts.v66i2.875
75) Martin, J. (2012, May 10). Pope declares Hildegard of Bingen a saint. Retrieved from http://americamagazine.org/content/all-things/pope-declares-hildegard-bingen-saint
76) Nash, R. J. (2004) *Liberating scholarly writing: The power of personal narrative.* New York: Columbia University.
77) Northouse, P. G. (2013). *Leadership: Theory and practice.* Washington, D.C.: Sage.
78) Standish, N.G. (2007). *Humble leadership: Being radically open to God's guidance and grace.* New York: Rowman & Littlefield.
79) Vallier, I. The Roman Catholic Church: A Transnational Actor. *TransnationalRelations and World Politics.* 25.3 (1971): 479-502. www.jstor.org/stable/2706052
80) Wallace, R. A. The social construction of a new leadership role: Catholic women pastors. *Sociology of Religion* 54.1 (1993): 31. doi: 10.2307/3711840
81) _____. Women and religion: The transformation of leadership roles. *Journal for the Scientific Study of Religion* 39.4 (2000): 496-508.
82) _____. (1992). *They call her pastor: A new role for Catholic women.* New York: State University Press.

Methodology
83) Clark, I. L. (2007). *Writing the successful thesis and dissertation: Entering the conversation.* Upper Saddle River, NJ: Prentice Hall.
84) Matkovich, S. (2012). *APA made easy.* Place of publication not identified: YouVersusTheWorld.com.
85) Merrill, B., & West, L. (2009). *Using biographical methods in social research.* Los Angeles: SAGE.
86) Nash, R. J. (2004). *Liberating scholarly writing: The power of personal narrative.* New York: Teachers College Press.
87) Roberts, B. (2002). *Biographical research.* New York: Open University Press.
88) Starkey, D.(2009). *Creative writing: four genres in brief.* New York: Bedford/St. Martins

Other
89) Bourgeault, C. (2008). *The wisdom Jesus: Transforming heart and mind: A new perspective on Christ and his message.* Boston, MA: New Seeds Books.
90) Cary, P. (2000). *Augustine's invention of the inner self: The legacy of a Christian Platonist.* Oxford: Oxford University Press.
91) Cawthorne, N. (2004). *Witch Hunt: History of a persecution.* New York: Barnes & Noble.
92) Coakley, J. (2006). *Women, men, & spiritual power.* New York: Columbia University.
93) Dunnne, C. (2000). *Wounded healer of the soul.* New York: Watkins.
94) Fox, M. (1983). *Coming of the cosmic Christ,* San Francisco, CA: Harper Collins.
95) _____ (1983). *Original blessing.* Santa Fe, N.M.: Bear & Co.
96) _____ (1991). *Creation spirituality.* San Francisco, CA: Harper Collins.
97) _____ (2000). *One river, many wells.* New York: Penguin Putnam.
98) Golden, E. (2010). *Political and civic leadership: A reference handbook.* Los Angeles: SAGE Reference.
99) Henold, M. J. (2008). *Catholic and feminist: The surprising history of the American Catholic feminist movement.* Chapel Hill: University of North Carolina Press.
100) Houston, J. (1996). *A mythical life: Learning to live our greater story.* San Francisco: Harper Collins.
101) Kidd, S. M. (1995). *The dance of the dissident daughter.* New York: Harper One.
102) Lamott, A. (1994). *Bird by bird: Some instructions on writing and life.* New York: Anchor Books.
103) Logan, F. D. (2002). *A History of the Church in the Middle Ages.* New York: Routledge
104) Macy, G. (2008). *The Hidden History of Women's Ordination: Female Clergy in the Medieval West.* New York: Oxford University Press.

105) Meredith, M.E. (2005). *The secret garden: Temenos for individuation.* Toronto, Canada: Intercity Books.
106) Murdock, M. (1990) *The heroine's journey.* Boston: Shambala.
107) Ransome, H.M. (2004). *The sacred bee in ancient times and folklore.* New York: Dover Publications.
108) Rotelle, A., Paffenroth, & Ramsey, B. (2000). *Soliloquies: Augustine's inner dialogue.* Hyde Park, NY: New City Press.
109) Rush. J.A. ed. (2013). *Entheogens and the development of culture.* Berkeley, CA: North Atlantic Books, pp. 85-210.

110) Shamdasani, S., trans. (2009) *The Red Book: C.G. Jung.* New York: W.W. Norton & Company
111) Summers, M. trans. Kramer Sprenger *The Malleus Maleficarum* 1971 New York: Dover
112) Vaughan-Lee, L. (2015). *For love of the real: A story of life's mystical secret.* Point Reyes, CA: The Golden Sufi Center.
113) _____ (2013 2009). *The return of the feminine and the world soul.* Point Reyes, CA: The Golden Sufi Center.
114) _____ (2013 2007) *Alchemy of light: Working with the primal energies of life.* Point Reyes, CA: The Golden Sufi Center.
115) Zipes, J. (2012). *The irresistible fairy tale: The cultural and social history of a genre.* New Jersey: Princeton Press.

Encyclicals & Pastoral Statements

116) Benedict XVI. (n.d.). Apostolic Letter proclaiming Hildegard of Bingen as a Doctor of the Church (October 7, 2012) | BENEDICT XVI. Retrieved from https://w2.vatican.va/content/benedict-xvi/en/apost_letters/documents/hf_ben-xvi_apl_20121007_ildegarda-bingen.html
117) Mulieris Dignitatem (August 15, 1988) | John Paul II. (n.d.). Retrieved from http://w2.vatican.va/content/john-paul-ii/en/apost_letters/1988/documents/hf_jp-ii_apl_19880815_mulieris-dignitatem.html
118) Pope Francis, (2013) *Evangelii Gaudium.* Accessed at http://w2.vatican.va/content/francesco/en/apost_exhortations/documents/papa-francesco_esortazione-ap_20131124_evangelii-gaudium.html
119) _____, (2013) Press conference accessed at http://w2.vatican.va/content/francesco/en/speeches/2013/july/documents/papa-francesco_20130728_gmg-conferenza-stampa.htm
120) _____, (2015) *Laudato Si.* Accessed at http://w2.vatican.va/content/francesco/en/encyclicals/documents/papa-francesco_20150524_enciclica-laudato-si.html

Videos

121) Conti, M. *The Unruly Mystic.*
122) Maxwell, L. (2011) *Hildegard of Bingen and the Living Light.*
123) _____. (2015) *Trumpet of God.*

Made in the USA
Middletown, DE
14 July 2016